Understanding THE *Historical Books* OF THE *Old Testament*

VINCENT P. BRANICK

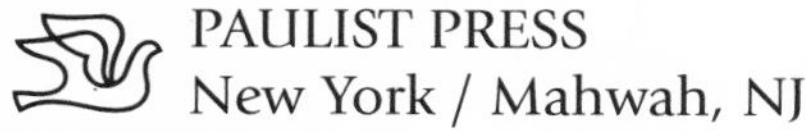
PAULIST PRESS
New York / Mahwah, NJ

Maps, artwork, diagrams by Vincent Branick

The scripture quotations contained herein are translations by the author.

Cover and book design by Lynn Else

Library of Congress Cataloging-in-Publication Data

Branick, Vincent P.
Understanding the historical books of the Old Testament / Vincent P. Branick.
p. cm.
Includes index.
ISBN 978-0-8091-4728-1 (alk. paper)
1. Bible. O.T. Historical Books—Criticism, interpretation, etc. 2. Bible. O.T. Apocrypha—Criticism, interpretation, etc. I. Title.

BS1205.52.B73 2011
222'.1061—dc22

2011008866

Published by Paulist Press
997 Macarthur Boulevard
Mahwah, New Jersey 07430

www.paulistpress.com

Printed and bound in the
United States of America

Contents

List of maps and illustrations

(Number indicates chapter; letter, sequence in chapter)

Dedicated to
Peter Ellis

Preface

This book began over ten years ago as a collaboration with Peter Ellis, who was interested in updating his monumental work, *The Men and Message of the Old Testament,* among the first in Catholic literature to introduce modern historical study of the Bible to students. The project with Peter did not succeed; however, my own teaching and study continually drew from this initial project in a development that moved further and further from Peter's work.

Peter died on December 21, 2009, as I was working intensely on the historical books and the prophets, so I do not know if he would at all approve of my work—some of which he had explicitly criticized as "abstruse." Shortly after his death, I contacted Judy Ellis, his widow, and asked for permission to publish these studies in my name alone, although I knew I was deeply indebted to Peter and that in fact these studies still contain some paragraphs that are clearly from the pen of Peter. I am not sure I could identify them all, nor do I want to strain them out of this study. Judy, then, gave me generous permission to proceed any way I wanted.

Hence, I dedicate this work to Peter. I also express deep-felt gratitude to Judy for her support in my studies. She had worked intensely typing and editing the earlier project. She had also been an essential line of communication between me and Peter as he more and more became an invalid. I sincerely hope that she and her sons, Mark and Eric, see in this book the legacy of her spouse and their father.

February 2010, Dayton, Ohio

Introduction

I. The Texts

As a category of the Bible, "the historical books" describe a sequence of books now found in the Greek Old Testament, or the Septuagint (LXX), beginning with Joshua and running through 4 Maccabees. The grouping seems to be based on the narrative character of all the books, some describing the major events in the history of Israel, others describing characters set in that history. This is the sequence more or less found in Protestant, Catholic, and Orthodox Bibles.

This grouping is different from the Hebrew Bible, where the books of Joshua, Judges, 1–2 Samuel, and 1–2 Kings are immediately followed by the fifteen books of the literary prophets, books named according to individual prophets from Isaiah to Malachi. Together in the Hebrew Bible, these books are known collectively as "the Prophets" (*ha-Nebi'im*), the second major part of the Hebrew Bible following "the Law" (*ha-Torah*). The books of Ezra-Nehemiah, 1–2 Chronicles, along with Ruth and Esther are placed in the third section of the Hebrew Bible, labeled generically as "the Writings" (*ha-K*[e]*tuvim*). The books of Judith, Tobit, and the books of Maccabees are not included in the Hebrew Bible. Nor are they found in the Protestant Bibles, which follow the Hebrew canon, or list of approved books.

Our study will follow basically the Catholic canon, taking some liberties, however, with the sequence of some books, as will be explained in the individual chapters.

The first part of this book (chapters 1–6) will study Joshua, Judges, 1 and 2 Samuel, 1 and 2 Kings. These books include large sections dedicated to the actions of the prophets Samuel, Elijah, and Elisha, as well as briefer descriptions of some twelve other named and unnamed prophets, starting with Deborah (Judg 4:4) and ending with Huldah (2 Kgs 22:14). Probably for this reason, these historical books were known also as "the Former Prophets." More recent scholars have pointed out the link of these books with that of Deuteronomy, especially through the theme of "a conditional covenant." Thus these books are often referred to as the Deuteronomist history.

The second part of this book (chapters 7–9) will explore the close parallels that 1 and 2 Chronicles have with the Deuteronomist history as well as the postexilic accounts in the books of Ezra and Nehemiah. This so-called "Chroniclers' history" provides essential background for understanding any writings after the Babylonian Exile of the sixth century BC.

The third part of this book (chapters 10–12) will turn to 1–2 Maccabees, narratives recounting the struggles of the Jews under the Hellenistic kings of the second century BC.

The fourth part (chapters 13–17) will treat the books of Ruth, Esther, Judith, and Tobit, which form a special group because of their overtly fictional character. The Protestant and Hebrew Bibles exclude Judith and Tobit, but the Catholic and Orthodox include them as part of "the historical books."

II. The Method

This study proposes both a historical and a theological understanding of these texts. The very nature of the books we will be studying warrants such a combination of approaches. None of these books is a historical account in the modern sense of history. Many recount historical events, but always as filtered through the intense religious faith of the authors and editors. These accounts are above all testimonies of faith.

For religious people of the Jewish or Christian faith today, these texts are supposed to nourish faith, to provide insight into God's ways, to mediate the word of God for the contemporary readers. Our attempt will be not only to search for the historical meaning of these texts, but also the way these texts speak of divine realities to people today.

Specifically, this presentation will attempt to bridge the gap between the historical faith of the authors and our faith today. This is not the same as simply allowing religious and inspiring thoughts to enter our minds while reading the Old Testament texts. Rather, it is a way to understand the authors—that collectivity of storytellers, writers, and editors—with their historical intentions and contexts as saying something to us today. Such a theological grasp of ancient documents is difficult. It involves letting the truth of the texts grasp us, yet the texts were not written for us. A huge cultural and historical gap separates us from the writers and editors of these texts, and we must respect that gap. As religious scholars, however, our expectation is to find a connection between the faith of these historical writers and our faith.

That continuity with the present appears especially in the historical faith that directed the writings and in the religious themes that often link the writings together. These themes—like the Temple, the importance of the Davidic monarchy, the link between sin and death, or the presence and absence of God in the life of the nation—arise from repeated clusters of stories and images and are meant to summon people to decisions. The faith expressed by these themes touch structures of life that reach beyond ancient historical contexts and embrace also our day, allowing the ancient text to speak to our day.

For all their linguistic and cultural limitations, the biblical authors were open to the divine mystery, which can address our modern concerns. With our own literary forms and our cultural perspectives, we attempt to touch and express that same mystery. Thus the biblical texts speak of God present with saving power in all times, yet at times withdrawing his obvious presence, leaving a frightful abyss of failure and collapse. These texts can thus address the modern anguish of life that at times appears as a gaping, apparently meaningless abyss—once the superficial illusions of wealth and power are removed. The biblical texts can address our fundamental questions, "Who is this God?" "Where is this God?"

For Christians reading the Old Testament, the power of the text flashes out especially in the New Testament's use of that Old Testament text. The New Testament usage is of course an indication of the faith of the New Testament authors, which often operated in disregard for the historical intention of the ancient Jewish writers. Yet the New Testament authors in fact often touched the faith presuppositions of the Old Testament. They saw connections and patterns that both give us insight into the theology of the New Testament writers and at the same time suggest an aspect of the mysterious reality envisioned by the Old Testament writers. As we probe the message of the Old Testament writers, we will briefly sketch the uses of their texts made by authors of the New Testament.

By no means is this study meant to substitute or even distract from reading the texts of Scripture. I have chosen certain passages from each of the books that have important significance for understanding our faith. The commentaries provided for each of these "significant passages" are meant to be read after a reading of the actual biblical text. I strongly suggest, therefore, that readers have two books open at once, the Bible and this book.

The English translations of the Hebrew, Aramaic, and Greek are mine. I would suggest reading the full biblical texts either with the New Revised Standard Version (NRSV) with the apocrypha or the New American Bible (NAB), two excellent translations. No translation can capture the artistic elegance of the original language, express the precise idea of the text, and read well in English. I chose to give priority to expressing the precise idea. The differences among the versions can dramatize the possibilities of the text.

PART I

The Deuteronomist History

1
Overview of the Deuteronomist History

I. The Collection of Stories

Despite some dissenting voices, many biblical scholars today continue for the most part to see the books of Joshua, Judges, 1–2 Samuel, and 1–2 Kings as a literary unit closely connected to the Book of Deuteronomy, which may have originally introduced these historical accounts. These scholars, therefore, refer to these accounts as "the Deuteronomist history." Working from the perspective of the Babylonian Exile of the sixth century BC, the historical authors—storytellers, writers, and editors—of the accounts apparently intended to compose a history extending from Moses in the desert down to the destruction of Jerusalem by the Babylonians in 587 BC, a history in which the faithful reader could see the hand of God forming and eventually destroying Israel.

To orchestrate Deuteronomy's theme of a conditional covenant, the authors, often referred to as the Deuteronomists, made selections from the narrative sources available to them, arranging and interpreting the sources by standard Old Testament literary techniques. The major sources edited by the Deuteronomists include the following:

a. The seventh-century version of Deuteronomy now found in parts of Deuteronomy 12—26
b. The legends of the judges in Judges 3—16

c. The Samuel, Saul, and David traditions in 1–2 Samuel with special dependence on the biographies of David and on the court history of Solomon (2 Sam 9—20; 1 Kgs 12)
d. The chronicles of the kings of Judah and Israel (1–2 Kgs)
e. A collection of legends about the prophets (1–2 Kgs)

In its completed form, this history is thus a compilation of popular narratives, royal chronicles, prophetic cycles, and even tax reports from the royal archives. Unlike modern authors, the Deuteronomists did not fuse their sources into an evenly flowing narrative. This unevenness is evident in 1 Samuel where fragments from different sources have been combined to narrate multiple accounts of the origin of the monarchy and the early history of David.

To emphasize the presence of God in Israel's history, the Deuteronomists added comments employing a variety of rhetorical techniques to make their theology more transparent. These techniques include the following:

a. Explanatory asides (for example, 1 Kgs 11 and 2 Kgs 17)
b. Explicit theological judgments (for example, the judgments made on each of the kings of Israel and Judah in the books of Kings)
c. Theological discourses, sometimes put into the mouth of God (for example, 1 Kgs 9:3–9), but more often put into the mouth of a prophet (for example, 1 Kgs 8:23–53; 11:11–13, 31–39; 14:7–16; 2 Kgs 20:16–19; 21:11–15; 22:15–19; 23:26–27)
d. Transitional additions and other interpretative discourses that give unity to the whole collection (Deut 1—4; Josh 1, 23; 1 Sam 12; 1 Kgs 8:14ff.; 1 Kgs 11; 2 Kgs 17)

The result of this work of editing or redaction is a history in which the Jewish exiles in Babylon could find not only the reasons for the catastrophe of 586 BC but could also hope for better things to come. If anything was clear from Israel's history, it was not only that she had failed her maker, but also that her maker had punished her for her failures. Now his hand was extended to raise her up after chastisement. It was the Deuteronomists' intention not only that Israel should understand why God had punished her, but also that she should remember that God's love far outran his punishing justice. Upon this love rested Israel's hope.

In this history, the Deuteronomists portray God saying to Israel:

> I Yahweh, your God, am a jealous God, inflicting punishments for their father's wickedness on the children of those who hate me, down to the third and fourth generation, but bestowing mercy down to the thousandth generation on the children of those who love me and keep my commandments. (Deut 5:9–10)

The Deuteronomist history, thus, is a history with a theological purpose. It would be a mistake, therefore, to look upon the Deuteronomist as a collector of facts intent on giving something like a modern documented history. Like the writers of the Pentateuch, the Deuteronomists believed that God operated in history and that history was the vehicle of his saving interventions. Their intention was to describe these interventions in Israel's history and Israel's response to them.

If a theological understanding of these texts involves finding the faith-filled intentions of the writers-editors, then we must constantly ask what these stories would have meant to exiles in Babylon. Why would the editors have gathered and modified these stories for this historical audience? We will pursue this question in the comments on the "significant passages." From that platform we can then pursue, in the "message" section of our study, the task of asking what divine mystery appears here that can speak to us. Reviewing the theological "themes" that reappear in the stories can aid in this task.

II. Dating the Events and the Writing

If we correlate the events described or implied in the text of the Deuteronomist history, we can develop the following chronology:

1250–1225:	Joshua's conquest of Canaan (Josh 1—12)
1225–1025:	The period of the judges (Judg 3—16; 1 Sam 1—7)
1025–1003:	The institution of the monarchy (1 Sam 8—12); reign of King Saul (chapters 13—31)
1003–970:	The reign of King David (2 Sam 1—1 Kgs 2)
932–722:	The divided kingdom up to the fall of Samaria and the deportation of the northern kingdom to Assyria (1 Kgs 12–2 Kgs 17)
700-621:	The composition of Deuteronomy and the finding of the book in the Temple (2 Kgs 22:8ff.)
587:	The fall of the southern kingdom to the Babylonians (2 Kgs 25)
587–539:	The Babylonian Exile

The last event narrated in 2 Kings is the "raising up" of Jehoiachin in 561 BC by Evil-merodach, the successor of Nebuchadnezzar (2 Kgs 25:27–30). The final form of the Deuteronomist history must therefore be dated no earlier than that date. Since nothing is said definitely about the end of the Exile (539 BC) and since the author shows no influence of Deutero-Isaiah (ca. 550–520 BC), it seems probable that the Deuteronomists themselves lived in exile sometime between 562 and 539 BC, probably close to 550 BC.

The individual books in the history show a complex stratification. At the earliest level are ancient folk stories and official documents. Judging from multiple introductions and other literary lumps, we can suppose that several early editions of the books arose before being compiled in the final historical sequence.

III. The Land Described

Since the land of Canaan is the scene of the majority of events narrated in the Old Testament, it will help to sketch the geography of Palestine. On the east the land was bounded by the desert and on the west by the Mediterranean Sea. On the southeast the country was bounded by the river Arnon east of the Dead Sea and on the south by a line that runs from the River of Egypt on the coast inland to the Arabah, the rift valley that extends south from the Dead Sea. In size the promised land covers an area of about 10,000 square miles, a bit larger than the state of Vermont. In length the distance is approximately 190 miles. In width it is about twenty-five miles in the north from the Sea of Galilee to Mount Carmel on the coast, and in the south it is about fifty-five miles from the Dead Sea to the Mediterranean.

The land can best be described as divided into four longitudinal sections running north-south: the coastal plain; the hill country; the Jordan river valley, from the source of the Jordan in the Lebanon mountains to the Dead Sea in the south; and the Transjordan plateau, from east of the Sea of Galilee in the north to the Zered River in the south.

The first of these longitudinal divisions, the coastal plain section, provided a poor coastline for seaports. As a result the inhabitants of Palestine, with the exception of the Phoenicians in the north, turned away from the sea to earn their living off the land by agriculture and husbandry. Connected with this coastal plain is a fertile area extending inland into the valley of Jezreel (known in Greek as Esdralon), a valley that begins near Carmel on the west and runs in a southeasterly direction. South along the coast, the Philistine plain between Carmel and the River of Egypt also provided some of the best arable land in Palestine. Between the coastal plains and the mountains lay the lowland district called the Shephelah, formed by the broken foothills leading up to the mountain region of Judah, but separated from it by longitudinal valleys. The Shephelah was the first line of defense for Judah on the west.

In the second of the longitudinal divisions, the hill country, the foothills of the Lebanon range roll down and join the mountain country of Samaria. This hill country rises to 1,700 feet above sea level at Mount Gilboa and to 3,000 feet at Mounts Gerizim and Ebal. This hill country then continues unbroken into Judea, reaching 2,500 feet at Jerusalem, 3,000 feet at Hebron, and declining to 1,000 feet at Beersheba.

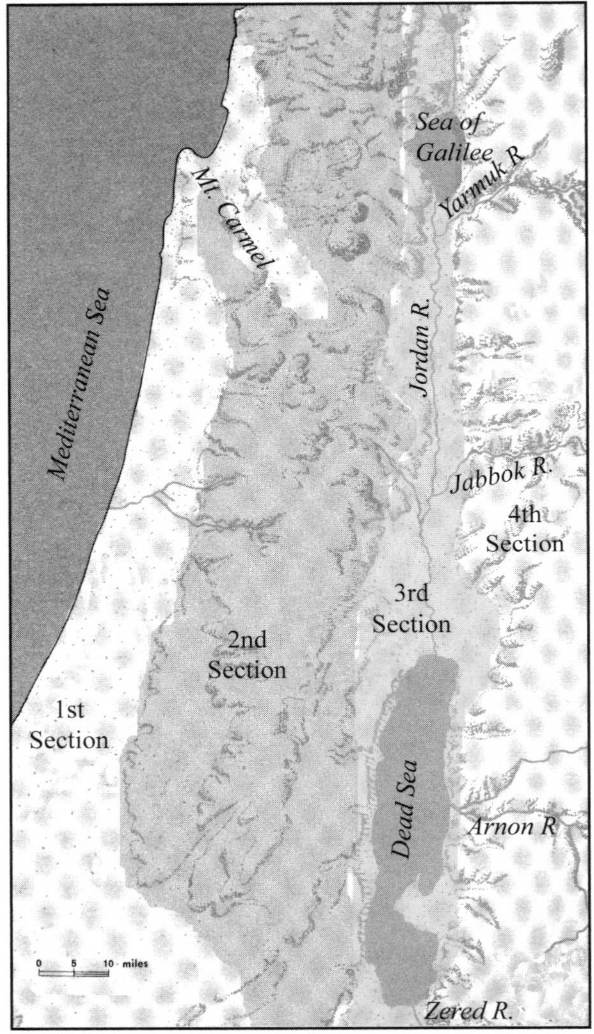

1A: Topographical Map

The third of the longitudinal sections, the Jordan Valley, is part of the great rift that begins in northern Syria, runs south between Lebanon and Anti-Lebanon down through the Gulf of Aqabah and on into Africa. The Jordan River, which flows through the valley, has its source at Banias near Caesarea-Philippi (ancient

Dan), descends rapidly, dropping from 1,000 feet at Banias to about sea level at Lake Huleh. Between the Lake of Huleh and the Sea of Galilee the river drops to 675 feet below sea level. Leaving the Sea of Galilee the river then winds down the valley (65 miles as the crow flies) to the Dead Sea, which is about ten miles wide, forty-five miles long, and thirteen hundred feet deep—1,292 feet below sea level.

The last of the four longitudinal divisions of Palestine, the plateau of Transjordan, is divided into five sections by four rivers. The rivers Yarmuk, Jabbok, Arnon, and Zered divide the plateau into the territories known, from north to south, as Bashan, Gilead, Ammon, Moab, and Edom, respectively. From Bashan in the north to Edom in the south, the plateau stays an average height of two to three thousand feet above sea level and is so level in sections that it was used as a natural highway, called from the earliest times the "King's Highway."

2
The Book of Joshua

I. Overview

A. The Peoples Conquered

The biblical authors generally speak of the early inhabitants of Palestine as "Amorites" and "Canaanites," sometimes applying Amorite to the people of the hill country and Canaanite to the people of the plains (see Num 13:29; Deut 1:7), more often using the terms synonymously. These people were Semitic and spoke a language differing only slightly from the language of the Israelites.

Although Canaan was in decline in the thirteenth century BC, its material culture was far above that of the seminomadic Hebrews. By modern standards their cities were tiny, rarely covering more than ten acres, but well built with fortifications and good drainage. In larger cities, such as Jerusalem and Megiddo, elaborate tunnels ensured a water supply in the event of a siege. Remains of fine houses surrounded by hovels indicate a society divided into rich and poor with no discernible middle class.

Politically the country was divided into small city-states, presided over by chieftains, called "kings" in Joshua (10:1–5). These "kings" were for the most part subject to the reigning pharaoh to whom they paid tribute in normal times. Fortunately for Israel, in the thirteenth century the city-states of Palestine were disorganized, due to an Egyptian foreign policy that kept them purposely disunited. When Israel entered Canaan, the only organized kingdoms she encountered were the Edomites and the Moabites in Transjordan. These she apparently avoided, directing her strength for the conquest of the hill country.

B. The Purpose of the Book

The Book of Joshua tells in part the story of that conquest. This book is named after its central character. It focuses on the Israelite wars in Canaan between the years 1250 and 1225 BC and the subsequent division of the conquered territory among the twelve tribes.

Joshua, the new leader, is already known from the Pentateuch. He appears there as leader in the war against the Amalekites (Exod 17), as aide to Moses at Sinai (Exod 24:13; 31:17), as one of the scouts appointed to reconnoiter the promised land (Num 13:1–16), and as the publicly appointed (Num 27:18) and officially commissioned successor of Moses (Deut 31:23).

The action in Joshua intimately links to the last events described in Deuteronomy. Thus Deuteronomy 34:1–9 records the death of Moses and the succession of Joshua. The Book of Joshua opens as Deuteronomy closes with the armies of Israel camped in the plains of Moab, completing the days of mourning for Moses before advancing to attack Canaan across the Jordan.

Like the book of Deuteronomy (see especially Deut 7), the Book of Joshua stresses the necessity of obedience to God's commands on the part of the people as a whole (Josh 1:6–9, 16–18; 23:16–26). Joshua is a model of that obedience (10:40; 11:15). The point of the stories, nevertheless, is to demonstrate that the conquest is the work of God. This point is demonstrated by the miracles wrought by God to enable his people to overcome the Canaanites (Josh 3; 6; 10) and by the failures of the Israelite armies at times of disobedience (see Josh 7:1–5). This rule for success and failure would ring true both for the followers of Joshua as well as the Jewish readers at the time of the Babylonian Exile.

C. The Literary Form and Date of the Book

While the stories in Joshua, especially the story of the fall of Jericho (Josh 6), are among the best known in the Bible, understanding these stories and their message depends upon understanding the kind of literature Joshua represents. Archeology gives us the

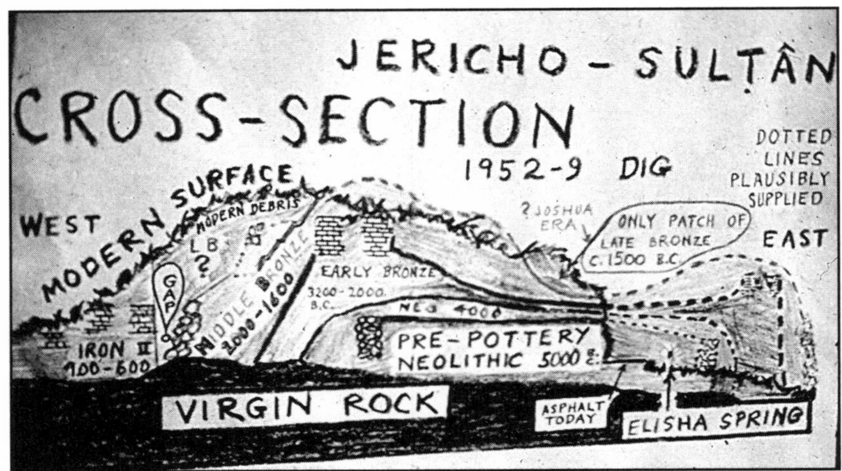

2A: Diagram of Tel es-Sultan (from Prof. Robert North's classroom)

first clues in determining the "literary form" of Joshua. The site of ancient Jericho, Tel es-Sultan, just outside of modern Jericho, has been intensely studied. Remains from that site point to a city that dates back to the Late Stone (Neolithic) Age and continues in the form of successive cities only up to the sixteenth century BC, the end of the Middle Bronze Age. The next city uncovered on the site dates from the ninth century BC, classified as Iron Age II. Thus the city of Jericho apparently did not exist at the time that we identify as that of the Israelite conquest of Canaan, the mid- to late-twelfth century, the Late Bronze Age. Likewise, according to archeology, the city of Ai, whose conquest by Israel is also a major story in Joshua, was also uninhabited at that time.

Another clue to the literary form of Joshua comes from the comparison of the descriptions in the book with those in Judges of similar events and with descriptions in other biblical books. The comparisons suggest that the writers of Joshua used the older stories of Judges to recount the conquest of Canaan. We even see some evidence to suggest that the stories in the books of Kings may also have influenced the stories in Joshua. Furthermore, the absence in the rest of the Bible of any mention of such events as the fall of Jericho or the covenant at Shechem also suggests a late origin of these stories as we have them in Joshua. When some of the latter refer back to the original leaders and the conflicts at the origins of the nation, reference is made to "the judges" (2 Sam 7:11; see 1 Chr 18:10), not to Joshua.

The Book of Joshua in its present form apparently arose in the attempt to bridge the gap between the well-known stories of the Hebrews in the desert and the experience of the Israelites occupying the land of Israel. Ancient popular stories about the conquest came to the aid of those trying to bridge the gap. These stories were then embellished with imaginative details that emphasized the thoroughness and ease of the conquest under God's power. All this strongly argues that the Book of Joshua is more a theological than a historical book, whose idealized and fictionalized accounts give far more information about Israel's faith of perhaps the sixth century rather than about the actual events of the thirteenth century.

It is difficult to date the book. The importance given to Shechem (Josh 24), a site close to the later city of Samaria, suggests either a time before the northern capital became a symbol of rebellion in the period of the divided kingdom (after 931 BC) or a time after Josiah again took control of Samaria in the seventh century BC (see 2 Kgs 23:19–20). Other material, especially the editorial bonding of stories together, suggests the work of the Deuteronomists of the sixth century. The "book of the Law" (*sefer ha-torah*) is presupposed and mentioned as a clear way of knowing the commands of God (1:7–8; 8:31–34; 23:6; 24:26). The theme of such a written code of conduct will not appear again until the second half of 2 Kings. The Law is not even mentioned in the books of Judges and Samuel—suggesting a late date for the stories of Joshua. The reference in 2 Kings 23:22–23 to the ancient celebration of the Passover—apparently referring to Joshua 5:10–11—argues for a composition of Joshua before the final editing of the Deuteronomistic history in the mid-sixth century. On the other hand, the description of the heavenly "commander of the Lord's armies" (5:13–15) is reminiscent of angels like Michael (Dan 10:13) and other anthropomorphic angels who appear in postexilic Jewish literature.

D. The Outline of the Book

The book is divided into three parts:

Joshua 1—12:	The conquest of Canaan
Joshua 13—21:	The division of the promised land among the tribes
Joshua 22—24:	The return of the Transjordan tribes, Joshua's farewell address and death

II. Significant Passages in Joshua

A. Joshua 1—12 / The Conquest of Canaan

1:1–11 ***The importance of observing the Law***

The book picks up from the last lines of Deuteronomy. Moses has died, ending one era. Joshua, filled with the spirit and ordained by Moses (Deut 34:7–9), ushers in the next. We are reminded of the divine promises of the land. But we are also alerted to the conditions for the fulfillment of those promises, the conditions already stressed in Deuteronomy 5:9–10, 26, obedience to the written Law of God.

2:1–24 ***The story of Rahab***

The key role of Rahab, the harlot of Jericho, runs counter to all the "patriotic" stories of the time, where heroes win the battle by means of their power. Here according to the biblical theme of an inappropriate character having a key function in God's plans (see 1 Sam 16:1–13; Jer 1), a woman of ill repute without clear motive becomes God's instrument for the initial conquest of Canaan. In the story Rahab confesses her faith in Yahweh (2:8–13). The stress given to the sparing of Rahab and her family along with the incorporation of her family into Israel (6:22–25) shows a conviction that non-Israelite peoples could become part of the life of Israel by reason of their faith despite their ethnic background.

Although conflicting with the later story of the miraculous fall of Jericho (Josh 6), the depiction of Joshua preparing for battle by sending spies into Canaan parallels the story of Moses acting similarly (Num 13; Deut 1:19–46). Several other parallels between Joshua and Moses in the course of the book point to a deliberate attempt to show how Joshua continues the leadership and traditions of Moses. God's guidance of Israel is not limited to the lifetime of any one hero. New leaders would guide Israel even in exile.

The Gospel of Matthew lists Rahab along with Salmon as the parents of Boaz, making her one of the progenitors of David and eventually of Christ (Matt 1:5, elaborating on Ruth 4:20–21 and 1 Chr 2:10–11). Hebrews 11:31 includes Rahab as a model of faith and James 2:25 makes her an example of good works.

3:1–17 *Crossing the Jordan*

The miraculous crossing of the Jordan, predicted in 3:5–13, is described as a stoppage of the river at Adamah (3:16), fifteen miles north of Sittim, while the Jordan was in flood stage (3:15; 4:18). As a matter of fact, much later history knows of several occasions when an overhanging bank collapsed into the Jordan and dammed it up for several hours, for sixteen hours in AD 1276 and for twenty-one hours in 1927.

More appropriate to the literary form of Joshua is a search for the descriptive parallels between this story and that in Exodus 12—15, where Moses led the people through a dangerous stretch of water under the guidance of God. Like Moses (Exod 17:8–13), Joshua will also assure a military victory by holding up a rod while the armies of Israel fight (Josh 8:18–26).

In Joshua the story of the crossing appears embellished by liturgical elements, the priestly procession with the ark of the covenant (3:3–13) and the erection of memorial stones by (or in) the Jordan (4:1–9). Perhaps the account as we now have it of the crossing developed in later liturgical ceremonies celebrating the fulfillment of God's promises against all odds. For God is the "living God in your midst" (3:10) and "Yahweh of the whole earth" (3:11).

Israel would never lose its orientation to the "promised" land. Its history even in exile would be seen as a desert experience, under the guidance of God, with the hope of again crossing the Jordan.

5:2–15 *The ceremonies at Gilgal*

Three episodes at or near Gilgal now function as transition stories, connecting the crossing of the Jordan to the conquest of the promised land: the circumcision of the Israelites (5:2–9), the celebration of the Passover (5:10–12), and the appearance of an angelic figure to Joshua (5:13–15). These episodes describe the end of one era and the beginning of another. The ceremony of mass circumcision takes place precisely in recognition of the end of the "desert generation" and the rise of the next (5:6–7).

The story of the Passover celebration parallels the story of Moses (Exod 12:1–28). Just as the Israelites celebrated Passover before leaving Egypt, so here they celebrate it before entering the promised land. The text in 5:12 specifically calls to mind the end of God's day-to-day care of the Israelites in the desert (see Exod 16). Now they must care for themselves with the "produce of the land." (The storyteller is not interested in showing how the Israelites at this stage of the conquest could possibly obtain the "produce of the land.") The absence of any mention of lamb meat suggests that the story of the celebration was developed when the feast was still just the "feast of unleavened bread."

Joshua's vision of "the captain of the hosts of Yahweh" clearly parallels the story of Moses and the burning bush (Exod 3). The

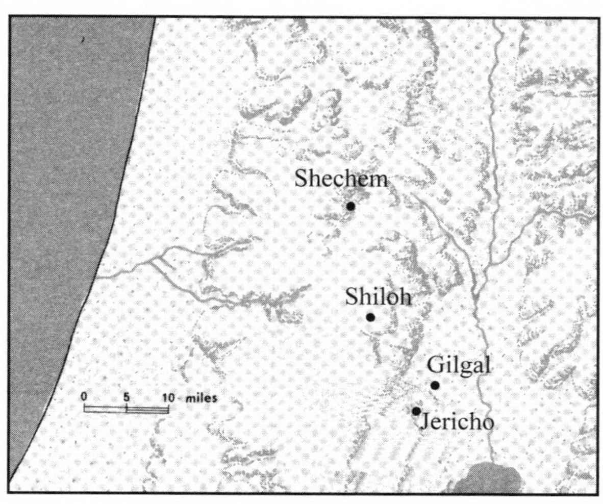

2B: Map of Gilgal, Jericho, Shiloh, Shechem

words about removing Joshua's sandals (5:15) are almost verbatim from Exodus 3:5. The image of God's "angel" fighting for the people of God becomes a prominent theme in the apocalyptic literature of a much later time (see Dan 10:20–21; Rev 12:7).

6:1–21 ***The siege and fall of Jericho***

As mentioned earlier, archeology suggests that the story of the fall of Jericho is basically fictional. This story and the other conquest stories in Joshua are idealized accounts. Again, the stress in this story on the sacred rituals (6:4–15) suggests a cultic setting for its origins. The ideal and sacred picture would give hope to exiles, when the actual world was so discouraging. The story here is told to show how the God of the Israelites is the one responsible for Israel taking possession of the land. The key line is the statement of Yahweh, "I have delivered Jericho and its king into your power" (6:2). Israel must acknowledge the work of God by considering the booty remaining in the fallen city as "sacred," as subject to the "ban" (*cherem*), under no condition to be used for human ends. To neglect the claim of God is to invite disaster.

6:17–19 ***The ban***

Perhaps one of the most disturbing aspects in all of the Old Testament is the instruction about the "ban" (see also Josh 10:28–40; 11:10–22; Deut 7:1–3; 20:16–19; 1 Sam 15:21). The prohibition in 6:18 "not to take anything that is under the ban," prepares the reader for the defeat of the Israelites at Ai (7:2–5) as a punishment for Achan's disobedience (7:10–26), and shows negatively that without obedience the conquest could not succeed.

The "ban" as defined in Deuteronomy 20:16–18 meant setting aside for destruction persons, places, or things deemed inimical to the kingdom of God. In Deuteronomy 7:1–4, the Israelites are warned to have nothing to do with the Canaanites lest they compromise their faith and turn to idolatry. The "ban" or "doom" was a way of preventing this compromise. The Moabite Stone, a ninth-century BC stele, describes King Mesha of Moab slaughtering the Hebrew population of Nebo as a way of "banning" or "devoting" this population to his god, Chemosh (see appendix 1). It was a brutal practice in a brutal time.

It may help to know that the instructions regarding "banning" the Canaanite populations were probably more "wishful thinking" on the part of the later biblical storytellers than an actual practice of the Israelites. As in Joshua 7, the references to "banning" often relate to it *not* being carried out (see 1 Sam 15). Many of the peoples "totally annihilated" in Joshua show up very much alive and well in Judges 1—2. The reference to "the treasury of Yahweh" (Josh 6:19) is one of the famous anachronisms of the Bible.

9:1–15 *The Gibeonites*

The Israelites are tricked into making a covenant with the Gibeonites (Canaanites of the hill country near Jerusalem). The story includes vocabulary typical of ancient covenant formulas and may in fact be an attempt to deal with a historical covenant made perhaps between the tribe of Benjamin and the Gibeonites in violation of prohibitions to make such treaties. The issue behind the discussion in the story appears to be based on Deuteronomy 20:10–18, where the Israelites are supposed to "ban" the local inhabitants but not those who are from afar. A note of reproach against the gullibility of the "Israelite princes" appears in the author's remark about their failure "to seek the advice of Yahweh" (9:14). On the whole, however, the sparing of the Gibeonites turns out to be good for both sides, and again like the story of Rahab, may be a way of understanding the incorporation of "outsiders" into the community of Israel.

B. Joshua 13—21 / The Division of the Land

13:1–7 *The divine command to apportion the land*

Although the second part of Joshua is dry reading, the names of cities and locations provide precious information for the historical geography of Israel. The section starts with a statement that stands in contrast to the preceding descriptions of comprehensive conquests: "A very large part of the land still remains to be conquered" (13:1). In fact large sections of Canaan, including the Philistine plain, the Canaanite cities along the Phoenician coast, Jerusalem, Megiddo, Beth-shan, and other large cities, held out against the Israelites until the time of David two hundred years later.

The mention of the Philistines in 13:2–3 is the only mention of these people in Joshua. They are the "Sea People" who settled in the southern coastal plain almost at the same time as the invasion of the Israelites under Joshua. Sailing from the islands of the Aegean or from Crete, the Philistines were an Indo-European people who attacked Egypt around 1190 BC, were thrown back by Rameses III, and settled down along the coast of Canaan. They then set up a confederation of city-states—Gath, Gaza, Ekron, Ashdod, and Ashkelon—in the fertile plain between Joppa and the River of Egypt. With their weapons of iron, they introduced the Iron Age into Canaan. In a short time they posed a mortal threat to the very existence of Israel (1 Sam 4—5) and led Israel to adopt a monarchic form of government (1 Sam 8). Except for a brief time under David, these cities were never fully subjugated by the Israelites. Much later the Romans will use the name of the Philistines to name the land "Palestine."

18:1 *Shiloh*

The ark and the meeting tent (*'ohel mo'ed*) are set up in Shiloh, about nineteen miles north of Jerusalem. No reason appears in the text for the choice of Shiloh. We read of no account of any journey from Gilgal. The ark and the meeting tent remain at Shiloh (see 1 Sam 1—3) until the destruction of the city apparently by the Philistines around 1060 BC (see 1 Sam 4—7).

C. JOSHUA 22—24 / JOSHUA'S FAREWELL AND DEATH

23:1–33 *Joshua's final plea to the Israelites*

Like other major leaders, Joshua gives a "farewell address" (see Jacob in Gen 49; Moses in Deut 1—33; David in 2 Sam 23:1–7 and 1 Kgs 2:1–9; and Jesus in John 13—17). As an old man, he addresses "all Israel" (23:2). Joshua's speech repeats the sentiments voiced in Deuteronomy 7:1–26 and 32:30–39, showing here the influence of the Deuteronomist editors. The fulfillment of Yahweh's promises depends on the observance of his Law. An allusion to the Babylonian Exile seems to appear with the repeated warning of "perishing from the good land which Yahweh your God has given to you" (23:13, 16). The ideas expressed in this chapter form an elegant inclusion with chapter 1:1–9 and may have been the original ending of the Book of Joshua.

The exiles would have read this story as an explanation of how they "perished from the good land." Observance of the Law of Yahweh, however, arises here as a key to identity and prosperity far more important than having such identity structures as temple or king. At the time of Joshua there was neither.

24:1–33 ***The covenant at Shechem***

Another and apparently much older account of Joshua's final address to all of Israel appears in the last chapter of the book. This time the solemn ceremony is at Shechem. This account appears to be echoed in 8:30–35 with its mention of Gerizim and Ebal, mountains that flank Shechem. There too the issue is commitment to the Law, a challenge given to the "whole assembly" (*qahal*) of Israel as they listen to the reading of "the book of the Law" (8:35; see Neh 8:1).

Shechem was a major center in the hills of Ephraim about thirty miles north of Jerusalem. The Yahwist tradition describes Shechem as a sacred place already at the time of Abram, the place where Yahweh appeared to the patriarch and first promised him that land, and a place where Abram built an altar to Yahweh (Gen 12:6–7). In the postexilic period on into the New Testament period, it was the religious center of the Samaritans.

Nothing is said in the Book of Joshua about the conquest of Shechem. If, as many scholars believe, there dwelt in the region around Shechem relatives of the Israelites who remained in Canaan (see Gen 34) when their brethren under Jacob went down to Egypt, then it is not unlikely that these people welcomed the invading Israelites. If this hypothesis is sound, the Shechem renewal ceremony suggests the story originally described a peaceful amalgamation of friendly Canaanites into the covenant federation, as the Israelites extended the covenant to new tribesmen. In the present text, however, the renewal ceremony involves all of Israel.

As the ceremony begins, Joshua recites in the words of God a historical summary that evidences a remarkably ancient character (24:2–13). Like the briefer creedal statement of Deuteronomy 26:5–9, the summary provides the sequence on which the pentateuchal authors appear to have developed their saga. The absence of the Sinai events again suggests a more complicated synthesis of Exodus and covenant traditions than the simple sequence given in the later canonical form of the Pentateuch. Other details in the historical summary of Joshua are distinctly different from those in the pentateuchal saga, suggesting the independence of Joshua 24 from the later accounts of the same events. We see, for instance, mention of a "darkness" or "thick fog" (*ma'aphel*) that protected the Israelites from the Egyptians (24:7), of Jericho putting up a battle and being subdued by "hornets" (24:11–12; see also Exod 23:28; Deut 7:20), and of the ancestors worshiping other gods both in Mesopotamia and in Egypt (24:14).

Shifting from God's words to those of Joshua, the book closes with an appeal to make a decision either to serve God or to worship the foreign gods: "If you will not serve Yahweh, choose today whom you wish to serve" (24:15). By insisting on the real possibility of Israel not choosing Yahweh, Israel's choice is laid out in way unparalleled in the Bible.

Joshua rallies the people: "As for me and my house, we will serve Yahweh" (24:15). In the end Israel decides, "We too will serve Yahweh, for he is our God" (24:18). The people take responsibility for the covenant. This is the core decision of the confederation. It is the decision every generation of Israelites will have to make.

III. The Message of Joshua

A. Review of Themes

The stories of Joshua appear to revolve around the following themes:

- Correct conduct and sin as determined by the written Law of God (1:7–8; 23:6; 24:26)

- The land as a gift of God and the divine fulfillment of promises (passim)
- Crossing a definable threshold and border from one place to another, from one epoch to another (3:1–17; 5:2–15)
- An inappropriate character functioning in a saving role (2:1–24)
- Some openness to non-Israelites (2:1–24; 9:1–15; possibly 24:1–33)
- The importance of deliberate commitment to God (24:15–24)

B. The Theology of Joshua

1. The God Who Fulfills Promises

Crossing the Jordan into the promised land enters powerfully into religious imagery. It is the great liminal—or more properly "fluminal"—event. The image suggests the movement of an oppressed or suffering people of God with a sense of a destination at hand, a conviction that oppression and suffering are not the last word in God's plan for his people, a hope that God will soon save his people. God had promised a land "flowing with milk and honey" (Deut 6:3; 11:9). In this book God fulfills that promise.

Crossing the Jordan is also the image of a people following a divinely empowered leader like Moses. Like Joshua, both Elijah and Elisha dry up the waters of the Jordan (2 Kgs 2:7–16). The parallels between Joshua and Moses dramatize the permanence of God's care beyond the limits of one human life. The death of Moses does not change things. The death of the first generation, including Moses, along with the crossing of the Jordan describes a clear discontinuity with the past. Yet as the new Moses, Joshua keeps the inaugural graces of the desert present in the succeeding generation.

Jesus is baptized in the Jordan marking the beginning of the gospel (Mark 1:9–11 and parallel passages), and brief mention is made of John and Jesus "across the Jordan" (John 1:28). Crossing over into the promised land becomes an image in Christian imagination of eschatological fulfillment.

2. The God of Death

However, the Book of Joshua with its description of the wars of extermination or "ban" poses a huge challenge for Christian understanding. The description of these wars appears to be the authors' way of lamenting the tragedy of the loss of faith in fact suffered by most of Israel during the monarchy due to the assimilation of Canaanite religions.

The biblical authors most likely would have answered the challenge by insisting that the life and death of every creature is in the hands of God. When, however, the people killed are those we know and love, we are forced to picture God as savage. This is the God of the Book of Joshua. In the stories of the "ban" we clearly have a picture of a God who clearly is dangerous and even wild. How can this picture be reconciled with that of a kinder, gentler God, a father figure loving and caring for his people, a picture also drawn by the Old Testament?

An extraordinary parallel arises from nature. Modern news accounts depict natural disasters: tsunamis drowning a hundred thousand people in a matter of hours, hurricanes turning cities into piles of trash, wildfires devastating forests and towns—bringing about death on a massive scale. These are scenes of violent nature, the same nature that is also portrayed as benevolent and life-giving, something with which we need to be in harmony. The modern naturalist movement has taught us about the need to accept "the wilderness"—the wild and even savage side of nature—or we deny something of our own selves. Ecologists have pointed out how some of the worst natural disasters are the result of our attempts to thoroughly domesticate nature, to turn it into a tool for our purposes, to destroy the wilderness—at our own peril.

Yet for all its savagery, nature continues to elicit wonder and even love. Individuals have found personal energy and healing in its contemplation. People are drawn to its beauty all the while aware how easily they can be killed by not respecting its power. The lesson in all this, I believe, seems to be the need for a delicate balance of love and fear, a sense of reverence and awe for a reality that is larger than ourselves, from which we also draw energy and life. We need to domesticate nature in limited ways, to turn some wilderness into gardens and farms. This seems to be a God-given task (Gen 1:26; 2:15) as well as a modern social necessity. Yet this human-centered project must operate in the wider sense of a beautiful yet dangerous whole that we call nature, accepted for what it is, not just for what we want it to be.

The authors of the Book of Joshua seem to have had a similar sense of God. They bring out the awesome and dangerous power of Yahweh by portraying him as the God of death. This is the God who cannot be domesticated—even by elaborate religion. This is the God whom Isaiah would see and immediately sense, "I am doomed" (Isa 6:5), the God whose ark Uzzah would inadvertently touch and be struck dead (2 Sam 6:6–7). This is the God who is much greater than ourselves and our conceptions of divinity. This is the God we do not understand. In these stories we need to focus on theology, not ethics.

Of course, with the description of God bringing about massive death through the conscious and willful act of human beings, we have a major clash with the commandment not to murder (Exod 20:13) and to care for the defenseless (Exod 22:20–23) as well as the New Testament exhortation, "Love your enemies" (Matt 5:44; Luke 6:27). There is no clear resolution to this clash. We can only say that the wars in Joshua reflect a brutal and evil time. In the description of the wars of extermination, the concern to preserve the faith against foreign contagion is clouded with such brutality that we end up with these grotesque descriptions of merciless slaughter—whether these killings actually happened or not. It is the context of the whole Bible that allows us to see the grotesque for what it is and dismiss it.

Using the context of the whole Bible we can exercise a kind of benevolent interpretation. In these descriptions we can limit our vision to a proclamation of God fulfilling his promises—against all odds. In the figure of Joshua and the Israelite armies, we see dramatized the power of God's repeated promise to Abraham, "It is to your descendants that I will give this land" (see Gen 12:7; 13:15; 15:18; 17:8; 24:7), a promise renewed to Isaac

(Gen 26:4). With the ark of the covenant, God leads the way. The "living God" of Israel is in fact "Yahweh of all the earth" (3:10–11) disposing of all the land as he wishes and delivering his people from all enemies. In this way Joshua can be a book celebrating the obvious presence of God.

3. The God Who Demands Commitment

Human sinfulness continues to spoil the picture. Other stories in Joshua of disobedience and military defeat remind us of the need for faithful responsibility to the covenant. God and his promises are not some magical power by which human beings can manipulate the future. Although the land is central in this book, simple presence in the land does not guarantee God's protection.

The people must choose God. This choice becomes the real basis for the identity of Israel. Moreover, this choice is codified by "the book of the Law," a written document whose permanence long survives the temporary spoken word, a writing that can bind together future generations to that of Joshua. The last actions of Joshua depicted challenge the people and all future generations to join him and his "household" to serve Yahweh (24:15). We have here the formation of Israel.

3
The Book of Judges

I. Overview

As we move on to the Book of Judges, we are actually backing up. This book contains some of the most ancient stories of the Bible, even if the events they describe are supposed to have occurred after Joshua. These stories appear with a certain crudeness and realism that allow us to glimpse realities much earlier than the idealized pictures in Joshua. The stories of Judges are stories of struggle and violence. They are stories of an intermediate time without the end-time idealism symbolized by the crossing of the Jordan. These stories in the Book of Judges range from exemplary stories about heroes, Othniel (3:7–11), Ehud (3:12–30), and Deborah (4:1—5:31), to gruesome stories of brutality, like that of Abimelech's slaughter of Migdal-shechem (9:46–49) or the mutilation of the Levite's concubine (19:1–30)—all of them describing violence.

Few books in the Bible give as much prominence to women as does the Book of Judges. We meet first Deborah, judge and prophet in Israel (4:4), in an exemplary story of leadership. The description of a woman in these roles apparently did not need any explanation. The story also includes Jael, the woman assassin of Sisera and rescuer of Israel (4:17–22). Jael disappears without comment as does the unnamed woman assassin of Abimelech (9:53–54). The unnamed wife of Manoah and mother of Samson dominates the "birth annunciation" story of Samson and appears to comprehend the situation better than her husband (13:2–25). Micah's mother, not father, appears as the custodian of the money used to create a puzzling image of Yahweh (17:1–5). On the other hand, the descriptions of Delilah and the other Philistine lovers of Samson (14:1–20; 16:1–21) develop the theme of seductive feminine beauty. The stories about Jephthah's daughter (11:29–40), the Levite's concubine (19:1–30), as well as the story of the women seized for the tribe of Benjamin (21:1–23) say little about these women as individuals but leave the reader riveted on them and the abuse they suffered.

A. The Role of the Judges

The book is named for its twelve protagonists. Our English translation calls them "judges" from the Greek translation, *kritai,* "discerners" or "judges." The judges, however, are not judicial magistrates. They are military leaders sent by God at critical moments in Israel's history to save the nation from destruction. The Hebrew term, *shophtim,* is better translated simply as "leaders" or "chieftains." The verb from which the title comes, *shaphat,* refers to a broad range of leadership actions, ranging from giving precise administrative decisions (4:4–5) to leading an army in battle (3:10–11).

Common to these leaders—with the exception of Abimelech—is the absence of office or institution that gives them power like the office of king. Instead, they are "raised up" individually by God for extraordinary feats during a time of political crisis. The storyteller expresses this character of their leadership by referring to the divine spirit "coming on" them (3:10), "clothing" them (6:34), or "moving" them (13:25). We today would call them "charismatic" leaders, having power not by office but by a personal "charisma."

Traditionally, the judges are divided into six major and six minor judges according to the space they receive in the book. To these twelve judges should be added Eli and Samuel, mentioned in 1 Samuel 1—7, as well as Bedan, the "lost judge" listed in 1 Samuel 12:11 (Hebrew text). Abimelech, whose story is told with obvious disapproval in the middle of the book, does not function as a judge, but as a usurper who tries to initiate a royal house before its time (9:1–57).

As presented in the central section of the book, we have the following twelve judges:

Judge	Text	Tribe/Origin	Oppressor
1. Othniel	3:7–11	Kenaz	Aram-Naharaim
2. Ehud	3:12–30	Benjamin	Moab, Ammon, and Amelek
3. Shamgar	3:31	Philistines	
4. Deborah and Barak	4:1—5:31	Ephraim & Naphtali	Canaanites at Hazor
5. Gideon	6:1—8:35	Manasseh & others	Midian
[Abimelech	9:1-57	Shechem]	
6. Tola	10:1–2	Issachar	
7. Jair	10:3–5	Gilead	
8. Jephthah	10:6—12:7	Gilead	Ammon and Philistines
9. Ibzan	12:8–10	Judah	
10. Elon	12:11–12	Zebulun	
11. Abdon	12:13–15	Ephraim	
12. Samson	13:1—16:31	Dan	Philistines

B. Israel at the Time of the Judges

Unlike the centralized nation described by the Pentateuch, Israel in the Book of Judges exists as a loose confederation of tribes, without central authority, whose bond was some form of ethnic kinship, some geographical proximity, but above all a common religious faith in Yahweh. For the most part, the judges led a tribe or a group of tribes. If the chronologies given for each of the judges are to be taken seriously, we must understand that several of the stories were taking place at the same time in different parts of Israel. The cumulative time of four hundred or so years for all the judges would otherwise not fit in the 175 years generally identified as the period of the judges, the years between Joshua and Samuel.

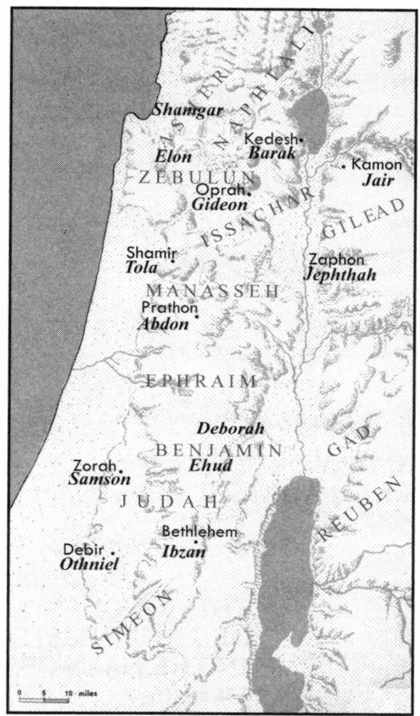

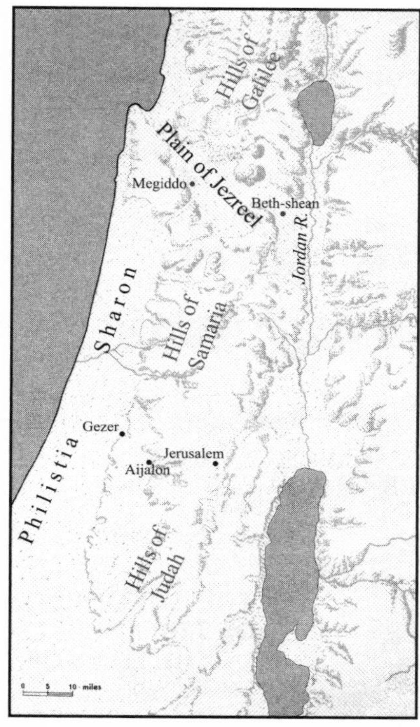

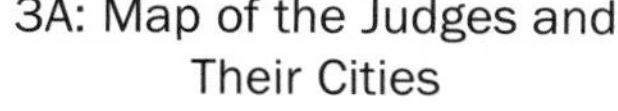
3A: Map of the Judges and Their Cities

3B: Map of Canaanite Cities at Time of the Judges

To understand the wars narrated in Judges, we must again step back from the idealized pictures in Joshua and understand the limited scope of the original conquest of Canaan, restricted to the hill country of northern Galilee, Samaria, and Judah. Judges 2—3 as well as Joshua 13:1–7 and 17:11–13 describe the plains of Sharon and Philistia as well as cities like Jerusalem, Megiddo, and Beth-shean as not conquered. The plain of Jezreel remained in the hands of the Canaanites and divided the northern from the central tribes; while Jerusalem, Aijalon, and Gezer in the central hill country continued to be held by the Canaanites and thus divided the central tribes from those in the south.

C. The Intention of the Editors

Interpreting the stories means first trying to understand how the storytellers and writers would have wanted the earliest listeners and readers to understand the stories. It also means trying to understand why the stories are recounted and now placed in this epic of Israelite history from Joshua to the fall of Jerusalem. In chapter 2, we see a summary narration, where we can gain an insight into the final editors' intention:

> And when that generation [around Joshua] too had been gathered to its fathers, another generation followed it which knew neither Yahweh nor the deeds that he had done for the sake of Israel. Then the sons of Israel did what displeased Yahweh and served the Ba'als....Then Yahweh's anger flamed out against Israel. He handed them over to pillagers who plundered them; he delivered them to the enemies surrounding them....Then Yahweh appointed judges for them, and rescued them from the hands of their plunderers....It was thus that Yahweh took pity on their groaning....But once the judge was dead, they relapsed and behaved even worse than their ancestors. (2:10–19)

In the subsequent stories of oppression and rescue an element of repentance is stressed: "The Israelites cried to Yahweh" (3:9; 3:15; 4:3; 6:6; 10:10). Thus the Deuteronomist editors use a four-part schema, by which they introduce many, but not all of the stories:

a. *sin,* "doing wrong in the eyes of Yahweh," often specified as serving Ba'al
b. *punishment,* usually invasion by the surrounding nations
c. *repentance,* usually expressed by the words, "They cried out to Yahweh"
d. *liberation,* always by God sending one of the judges

This schema points to the intentions of the final editors to depict national suffering as punishment for sin and to stress the importance of repentance.

Critics see several levels of composition in Judges as a compilation of ancient stories. An early composition may date from sometime after the fall of Samaria. Then around 621 BC after the finding of "the book of the Law" in the Temple, Judges along with Joshua underwent the Deuteronomists' revision, visible especially in the moralizing reflections in 2:6–23 and 10:6–16, the formula for the stories of the judges, and especially in the introduction to the book (1:1—2:5).

D. Glimpses into the Ancient Traditions

Outside of the later editorial additions, we see no reference to the ark of the covenant, to the meeting tent or sanctuary of the Lord, or to the Law—all of which supposedly came from the desert experience of the Exodus. Within the stories themselves we see no evidence of any written elements of what would be part of our Bible. The setting of these stories would most likely be a time only of oral tradition.

However, apparently imbedded in this oral tradition is the story of the Exodus from Egypt. This tradition is particularly clear in the story of Gideon, set in the north, when an anonymous prophet utters the message from Yahweh, "It was I who brought you out of Egypt and led you out of a house of slavery" (Judg 6:8). Gideon himself cites the tradition with the complaint, "Where are all the wonders our ancestors tell us of when they say, 'Did not Yahweh bring us out of Egypt?'" (6:13). The tradition appears again in the story of Jephthah, a story from Gilead (11:13, 16; see also 19:30).

E. The Parts of the Book of Judges

In its present form the book is divided into three parts:

Judges 1:1—3:6:	Context and theological objectives
Judges 3:7—16:31:	Stories about the judges
Judges 17—21:	Appendices: the tribes of Dan and Benjamin

II. Significant Passages in Judges

A. Judges 1:1—3:6 / Context and Theological Objectives

1:1–8 ***The first introduction to the book***

Just as the Book of Joshua began with the words, "After the death of Moses" (Josh 1:1), the Book of Judges begins, "After the death of Joshua" (Judg 1:1). Judges actually has a second introduction at chapter 2:6–9, which repeats almost verbatim the last lines of the Book of Joshua (see Josh 24:28–31). Both introductions stress the issue of continuity and transition.

The setting is a land in which the Canaanites are not yet completely conquered (see Josh 13:1–7; Judg 1:18–36 and passim). Judah and Simeon, the southern tribes, are given prominence, reflecting the perspective of the editor. Adoni-Bezek (1:4–7) is probably the Adoni-Zedek, king of Jerusalem, supposedly defeated at the battle of Gibeon, in Joshua 10:1–15.

B. Judges 3:7—16:31 / The Heroic Stories of the Judges

1. The Story of Deborah and Barak

4:1—5:31 ***Deborah and Barak***

The story of Deborah and Barak is interesting in many ways. It is the only story of the judges involving a couple, a woman and a man. Deborah is in charge. She is introduced as a "prophetess" (*nebi'ah*) who in that role "was judging Israel" (4:4). As the first with a prophetic role in the whole Deuteronomist history, she is part of an inclusion or "bookends" structure with Huldah, the prophetess, the last with a prophetic role mentioned in this historical saga. The exiles in Babylon reading this story would be reminded of the importance of listening to the prophets.

A crisis is caused by the oppression of Jabin, the Canaanite king of Hazor, the largest city in northern Canaan, located near the modern Lake Huleh. (According to Joshua 11:1–15, Jabin and the whole city of Hazor were already wiped out in the wars of conquest.) Deborah from Ephraim commands Barak from Naphtali with an oracle of Yahweh to march against Jabin's forces led by Sisera. Barak insists on Deborah's personal support and together they defeat Sisera. Whatever the cause and severity of the oppressive situation, Yahweh can turn things around. This is a message of hope to be repeated throughout this book, a message that would not be lost on the later readers in exile.

According to the prose account of the battle (4:1–24), Barak follows Deborah's prophetic instructions and attacks from a higher ground with a large army. The battle takes place on the western edge of the plain of Jezreel near Megiddo. The story contains the prophecy of Deborah, "Yahweh will deliver Sisera into the hands of a woman" (4:9), an example of biblical irony. In the mouth of Deborah, it rings as if she would be the woman. In reality, it is Jael (4:21–22) into whose hands Yahweh delivers Sisera. The lethal hospitality of Jael (along with Judith's treatment of Holofernes) has been a favorite theme of many artists.

The second account is in poetic form, the Canticle of Deborah (5:1–31), one of the oldest examples of Israelite poetry, very difficult to translate because of its obscure vocabulary and grammar. Again celebrating Deborah and Barak, it ends with Jael piercing the head of Sisera. The battle against the Canaanite army,

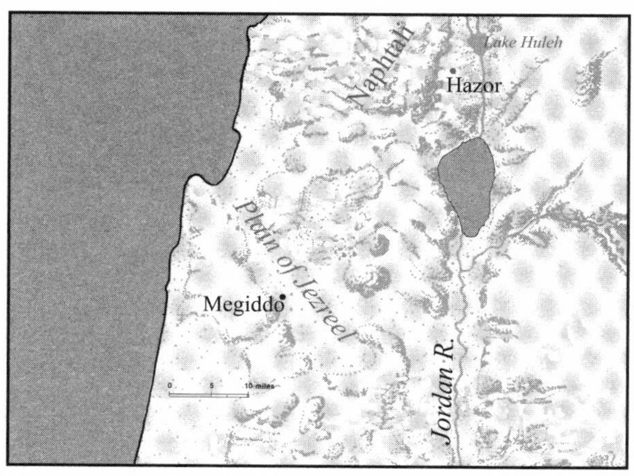

3C: Map of Cities in the Story of Deborah

however, is described more in terms of God using the waters of heaven to wash them away (5:20–21; see 5:4). The list of the northern tribes—Ephraim, Benjamin, Zebulun, Issachar, Naphtali (5:14–15)—describes one of the largest armies led by a judge. On the other hand, Reuben, Gilead, Dan, and Asher appear to be blamed for not joining in the fight (5:15–17).

2. The Story of Gideon

The story of Gideon (6:1—8:32) begins with a description of the oppression by the Midianites, a people from Arabia, nomads who raided as far as Moab (Gen 36:35) and were involved in the Sinai wars (Num 22:7; 31:1–9). This story in Judges is the last one about the Midianites, who disappear from history, although Trito-Isaiah predicts their reappearance as friendly worshipers of Yahweh in the end-times (Isa 60:6).

6:7–40 *The call of Gideon*

After a self-standing oracle by an anonymous prophet, including a clear reference to the Exodus tradition (6:7–10), we read about the call of Gideon. In this scene, Gideon's interlocutor is called alternately "the angel of Yahweh" and "Yahweh," much like the angel in the story of Hagar (Gen 16:1–14) or the angel in the call of Moses (Exod 3:1–6). Gideon expresses intense reluctance to trust the angel, expressing another reference to the Exodus tradition (Judg 6:13). Gideon is probably best known for the sign of the fleece, where God without any indication of impatience gives a sign and then reverses the sign at the request of Gideon (6:36–40).

7:1–25 *Defeat of the Midianites and Amalekites*

After destroying the Ba'alist altar of his own father (6:25–32), Gideon is now armed with the spirit of God (6:34) and calls into force a coalition of Manasseh, Asher, Zebulun, and Naphtali (6:35). In the ensuing battle with the Midianites and Amalekites, a major theme of Judges appears. The Israelites must not think of their military successes as due to themselves. They must understand that these successes are from God. Therefore, under the direction of God, Gideon reduces his army to a fraction of its original number. Then using the ruse of a night attack with horns and torches, he succeeds in routing the enemy forces.

8:1–32 ***The revenge of Gideon***

The episodes that now continue the story of Gideon take on a sinister tone. We hear of the jealousy of the Ephraimites against Gideon (8:1–3) and of the noncooperation of the leaders of Succoth and Penuel (8:4–9), leaders that Gideon then tortures, killing the inhabitants of these towns along with the prisoner kings of Midian (8:10–21). These are not stories of rescue from oppression. No mention is made of Yahweh directing the fight. The silence on these two matters suggests that the storyteller was not trying to elicit approval. Gideon's reaction to the Israelites who wish to make him king echoes stories of later storytellers who insist that only Yahweh can be king of Israel (Judg 8:22–23; see 1 Sam 8:4–9).

3. The Story of Jephthah

10:6—11:11 ***Jephthah***

Oppressed by the Ammonites, the people of Gilead, a Transjordan clan of Manasseh located south of Bashan, call upon Jephthah to lead their forces against the oppressors. At the time, Jephthah is a bandit chief because of the brutal exclusion he suffered from his brothers (11:2–3). The story begins with the now familiar schema: sin, oppression, repentance. However, the saving action of God is delayed: "I shall rescue you no more" (10:13). In the end, however, God does come to the rescue of Israel—with a note of divine pathos: "Yahweh…was grieved by the trouble of Israel" (10:16).

11:12–28 ***Negotiation with the Ammonites***

The account of Jephthah's negotiations with the Ammonites is striking for a number of reasons. First of all, it includes a description of the conquest from the point of view of Ammon, who in effect refers to the Exodus tradition without a reference to Yahweh: "When Israel came up from Egypt they seized my land" (11:13; see also 11:16). Secondly, it includes a description of the deity of the Ammonites, "Chemosh, your God," who is placed in parallel with "Yahweh, our God" (11:24). Chemosh is actually known from archaeology as the god of the Moabites (see appendix 1: the Moabite stone). The flexibility of perspective is remarkable. The straightforward description of Chemosh suggests an Israelite belief that Yahweh may not be the only God, although he is the only God for Israel. We call this type of faith "monolatria" in distinction from "monotheism."

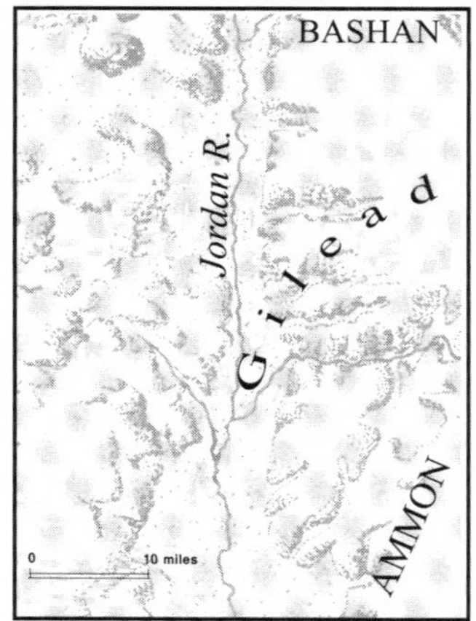

3D: Map of Gilead in the Story of Jephthah

11:29–40 ***Jephthah's vow***

The negotiations are fruitless. "The spirit of Yahweh came on Jephthah" and he moves out to war (11:29). This part of the story includes the infamous vow of Jephthah to kill and sacrifice whoever would fit the meaningless criterion, "the first person to meet me from the door of my house when I return in triumph" (11:31). The person turns out to be his daughter. The ensuing story accents the suffering of Jephthah and his daughter, whose sorrow is highlighted by a contrast with the description of her premature joy as well as by lamentations according to the "custom in Israel" (11:39–40). The story includes no criticism of the sacrifice of the girl, except to insist on the grief of Jephthah, who must now pay the price of his violence. Perhaps we have a remnant of the practice of human sacrifice in ancient Israel (see also 2 Kgs 16:3; Jer 7:31) and a mourning ritual connected with such sacrifices.

12:1–6 ***The shibboleth incident***

There follows another example of tribal jealousy. Echoing the hostility in an earlier story (8:1–3) between the army of Gideon from Manasseh and the tribe of Ephraim, a senseless slaughter of brothers breaks out.

4. *The Story of Samson*

The stories of Samson, the Danite, now follow (13:1—16:3). These stories are certainly the best known in the Book of Judges. The background is the threat of the Philistines (13:1). Samson is called to be a Nazirite, that is, one dedicated to lead a simple and ascetic life, abstaining from alcoholic liquors and refraining from cutting his hair, considered a sign of vitality and, therefore, of a life that belonged to God (see Num 6:1–21). Other famous Nazirites include Samuel (1 Sam 1:1), John the Baptist (Luke 1:15), and perhaps Paul as portrayed by Luke (Acts 18:18; 21:23).

13:2–25 ***The birth of Samson***

In this annunciation scene, the "angel of Yahweh" alternates with "Yahweh" himself much as we saw in the call of Gideon (6:11–24). Because the angel addresses his parents, Samson joins the list of God's people called from the womb, like Ishmael (Gen 16:7–14), Isaac (Gen 17:15–21; 18:9–15), Samuel (1 Sam 1:12–18), Jeremiah (Jer 1:4–10), John the Baptist (Luke 1:5–22), Jesus (Luke 1:26–38), and Paul (Gal 1:15). For many of these vocations, the sterility of the mother or some other obstacle to conception accents the importance of the person to be born.

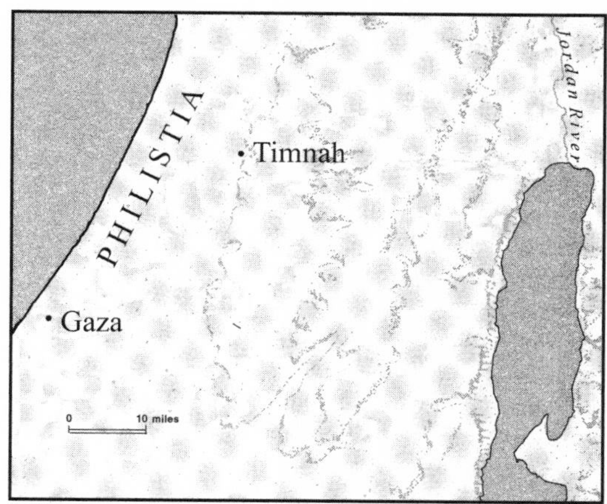

3E: Cities in the Story of Samson

The ensuing stories of Samson appear to be organized around the Philistine women in his life. The stories about the first wife from Timnah (14:1—15:20) describe an escalating violence between Samson, whom "the spirit of Yahweh seized" (14:19; 15:14), and the Philistines. The brief story of the harlot of Gaza (16:1–3) describes the mortal enmity between Samson and the Philistines.

16:4–31 ***Samson and Delilah***

The stories about Delilah of Sorek portray Samson as particularly stupid and susceptible to the betrayal of the woman he loved. The tables are turned, however, as the Philistines assemble in their temple to mock Samson, who had been blinded and deprived of his strength. The Philistines attribute their domination over Samson to their god, Dagon. Samson, the wounded savior, however, prays to Yahweh for strength. Thus the real conflict is between Dagon and Yahweh. As a result, Samson inflicts mortal harm on the enemy, but he must die in the effort.

C. Judges 17—21 / Additions about Dan and Benjamin

Additions to the stories of the individual judges form the third section of Judges. The additions are framed by the repeated comment, "In those days there was no king in Israel, and every man did as he pleased" (17:6 and 21:25; 18:1; 19:1). The inclusions suggest that the editor presents the stories as examples of anarchy. The stories are different from the earlier stories of the judges. No "spirit of Yahweh" raises up the military leader. No foreign oppressor is the object of war. Instead, we have the slaughter of the peaceful people of Laish (17—18) and the fratricidal war against Benjamin (19—21).

17:1–6 ***The household shrine of Micah***

We begin the additions with a story of an Ephraimite, Micayehu, later called Micah (17:5). The story begins in midcourse with a remark about a past theft and an oath. An earlier form of the story may have included the full account of these incidences. Micah confesses to the "theft," returns the large sum of silver (1,100 weights), which the mother has turned into an image or idol of Yahweh, later described as a god (*'eloha,* 18:24; perhaps also 18:27). Apart from the editors' comments about the anarchy present in the premonarchical period (17:6), nothing in this story or in the succeeding episodes involving this idol suggests disapproval. We have a glimpse here into the murky beginnings of Israelite faith.

Chapters 19—21 form a unified story of intense violence, but this time in the form of Israelite against Israelite. This is a story of fratricidal slaughter. It begins with the deadly rape of a Levite's concubine (19:1–28). This crime of the city of Gibeah becomes above all a crime of inhospitality, strikingly parallel to the crime of Sodom (Gen 19:1–11). Here, however, no angels save the intended victim. In order to publicize the outrage committed by the people of Gibeah, the Levite slices up the body of the victim concubine—whom we hope is already dead—and sends the pieces throughout the land (19:29–30).

20:1–11 *The assembly at Mizpah*

Like Shiloh, Mizpah is a place of assembly before Yahweh for all Israel. Gibeah in Benjamin is the future home of King Saul (1 Sam 10:26), located between Jerusalem and Ramah.

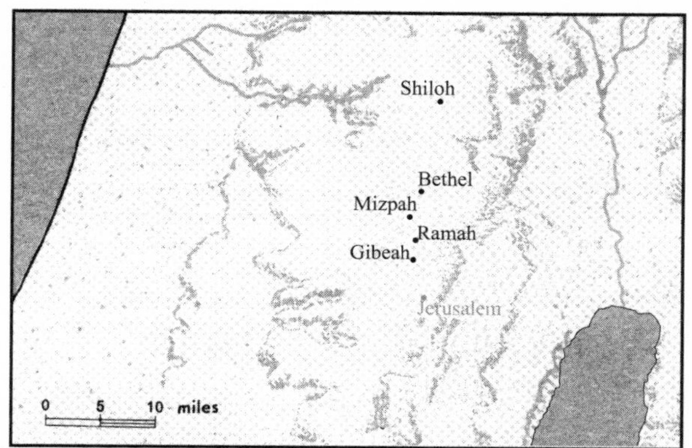

3F: Map of Mizpah, Gibeah, Ramah, Bethel

21:1–25 ***The slaughter of Benjamin***

In the ensuing attack, the storyteller emphasizes the fierceness of the fighting, deadly for both sides (20:14–28). Eventually the Benjaminite army is slaughtered (20:36–46), and the other towns of Benjamin are wiped out (20:48). The remorse of Israel for the destruction of Benjamin (21:1–7) leads to further violence against Jabesh in Gilead in order to capture women for the remnant of Benjamin (21:8–14). The Benjaminites who did not receive women from Jabesh are then encouraged to seize the daughters of Shiloh (21:15–23). The last lines describe Israelites "in that time each going to his own tribe and clan...each to his own inheritance...each did what was right in their own eyes" (21:24–25). The violence of the time left Israel as dismembered as the Levite's concubine.

III. The Message of Judges

A. Review of Themes

The following themes seem to dominate the passages we selected from the Book of Judges:

- Sin as "doing wrong in the eyes of God," often as worshiping Ba'al (4:1; 6:1; 10:6; 13:1)
- The role of women (4:4, 17–22; 9:53–54; 11:29–40; 13:2–25; 14:1–20; 16:1–21; 17:1–5; 19:1–30; 21:1–23)
- The role of violence against oppression (passim)
- God's unpredictable rescue through charismatic leaders (passim)
- The human weakness that remains with divinely inspired leaders (8:1–32; 10:6—11:7; 16:4–31)
- The way violence moves to senseless slaughter (8:10–21; 11:29–40; 21:1–25)

B. The Theology of Judges

1. Sin and Punishment

As edited by the Deuteronomists, the stories of foreign oppression are carefully presented as not random vicissitudes of history but as following a divine rationale. They are the result of the sins of the people. Most of the time in the introduction of the stories, these sins are described vaguely as "doing evil in the eyes of God" (4:1; 6:1; 13:1). Twice they are specified as forms of Ba'alist worship (3:7; 10; 6; see also 2:10–19). Even in these later editorial additions, no mention is made of the Law or the book of the Law. Rather, the basis of good and bad is simply God and how he sees things ("his eyes").

The immoral anarchy of the period is summed up with the description of "each doing what was right in his own eyes" (21:25). Such an insistence on individual judgment sounds great to us with our insistence on individual autonomy. Most likely the authors and editors of Judges intended this to express a dire situation, devoid of divine guidance. The Book of Judges is describing the need for Yahweh's measure of right and wrong, one that would bind individuals together into a nation, one that would assure divine blessing on that nation.

2. The God of Violence

The Book of Judges is a book about violence and a violent people. The episodes generally begin with scenes of oppression, attributed to the sins of the people. The book ends with the slaughter of Benjamin and its aftermath. Except for the Canticle of Deborah (chapter 5), very little joy and optimism appear in this book. The authors in effect ask us to gaze into the abyss of war caused by the people forgetting God.

But God is not completely absent. He answers prayers and raises up a "savior-warrior," often a weak and unlikely savior. For all their violence, the judges act under God. They are gifted by God with a special spirit, a gift that could be called a charism of violence. This gift from God, however, does not transform their lives into "holy" persons—at least as we today picture a holy person. Gideon engages in torture and murder. Jephthah sacrifices his daughter. Samson has problems with women. The spirit of God leaves most wounded. It leaves Samson dead.

Yet we still sense some admiration for these leaders, especially for the tragic hero, Samson. They act for the benefit of the people. Their charism of violence does not help them, but it saves the people from oppression. Some accept that responsibility without hesitation (Othniel, Ehud); some, with conditions or hesitations (Barak, Gideon); others show no sense of responsibility but just seem willy-nilly to be God's instrument (Samson). The stories of the judges are stories of God's action through imperfect agents, who remain imperfect even under the action of God.

In the Book of Judges, violence is often necessary. Violence—or counterviolence—even springs from the spirit of God. Violence is the means of "saving" the people. However, once out of the bag, violence escalates beyond what is necessary. The last section of the book (chapters 17—22) along with descriptions of strife within Ephraim (8:1–3; 9:22–49; 12:1–6) appear to be placed here to describe how violence can be turned back on the people into fratricidal slaughter. The charism of violence thus appears here as an extremely dangerous charism. God raises up the military leader, but God's salvation is perverted when the human element takes over and turns the military power toward the attainment of human ends. If God is present in these scenes, his presence is muted.

3. *The God of an Intermediate Time*

Perhaps the best way to understand the message of Judges is to see it in its historical perspective and in the "age" of the stories. We read here some of the oldest accounts in the Bible. We must therefore be ready for crudeness as we probe the origins of God's people. We read here also accounts of evil times. The judges arise in a time of oppression. The charism of violence appears necessary for that time. Any disapproving judgment therefore should be directed first to the situation of the judges that requires a violent response. The Deuteronomist editor sees that situation to be rooted in the infidelity of the people.

We are reading stories of an intermediate time in salvation. The nonviolent ethic with which Christians are familiar from the Gospels is an "eschatological" ethic, an ethic of the end kingdom. The violent ethic of Judges is not eschatological but rather "mesological," an ethic of an intermediate time. Violence appears necessary to the degree that humanity lives in a world not yet transformed by the eschatological fulfillment of God.

4
1 and 2 Samuel

I. Overview

The books of Samuel continue from Judges the story of Israel. These books open with Israel as a loose confederation of tribes governed still by charismatic leaders, starting with Eli and then Samuel. As the story progresses, however, all this changes. The people demand a king, a dynastic ruler whose political power would rest more on human office than on being touched individually by God ("being raised up"). The first king is Saul; the next, David. Under Saul and David the tribes of Israel fuse into a highly structured and unified kingdom.

Samuel appears as both the last of the judges and also as a prophet. As a prophet he is instrumental in appointing first Saul and then David to kingship. He is the pivot around whom the transformation of Israel takes place. Thus his name is given to these books.

A. The Story Line

The story begins in the eleventh century BC. The last judges of Israel, Eli and Samuel, attempt in vain to liberate their people from the domination of the Philistines. Toward the middle of the century, the ark of the covenant is captured by the Philistines (1 Sam 4). Shiloh is apparently destroyed at this time. Although returned after seven months, the ark is placed in storage in a backwoods town (1 Sam 5).

Sick of oppression, envious of the Moabites and the Edomites with their hereditary kings and standing armies, the Israelites clamor for a king (1 Sam 8). An interesting controversy appears here. Would the change of Israel into a kingdom change the very essence of Israel? We hear two voices struggling with the question, "Whose kingdom is it?" Convinced that Israel's destiny lies in fidelity and obedience to God as her only king and that human kings will only serve to entice the people away from God by making them put their trust in "horses and chariots," Samuel nevertheless is constrained to accede to the people's wishes and choose a king, Saul the Benjaminite (1 Sam 9—10). Saul, however, fails to subject himself to God's demands and is rejected (1 Sam 15).

David, Saul's successor, on the contrary, is a man after God's own heart. Through the prophet Nathan, God promises that David's dynasty will be perpetual and its kings will be adopted by God as sons. The covenant will now be bound up with David's family (2 Sam 7). Thus, the figure of David dominates the theology of Israel. He is to be the representative of God, the true king. The human king is to be the instrument, at times weak and ineffective, through whom God works out the ultimate destiny of Israel. As succeeding kings failed to live up to God's standards, the prophets returned to the figure of David to express their assurance that God will not abandon his people (Isa 11:1–3; Jer 30:9; Ezek 34:23). The figure of David becomes welded to the image of the savior—despite the fact that David in the books of Samuel ends up a sinner punished by God, a tragic figure suffering the loss of his sons.

The story in Samuel thus wanders through joy and bitterness, victory and defeat, as this ambiguous "kingdom" appears on earth. God's presence is sensed behind the scenes. His intervention appears mostly through prophets, who have critical roles in this book.

B. The Composition

Sections of the books of Samuel seem to stand by themselves and may have been composed before being incorporated into the whole. These sections are marked often by distinctive styles, images, and themes, which then disappear in texts outside the section. For instance, the story of the ark of the covenant in 1 Samuel 4—6 and 2 Samuel 6 may once have been an independent narrative. The story of David's rise to power in 1 Samuel 16 to 2 Samuel 5 stands out by the way it shows the skill of one of Israel's greatest storytellers. Nathan's prophecy and David's prayer in 2 Samuel 7 might have developed in religious circles. For many years, scholars noted the particular style of 2 Samuel 9—20 along with 1 Kings 1—2, which coheres as a remarkable story of the struggle to succeed David on the throne. This account is extraordinary in ancient literature for the historical detailing of the intrigues and failings in the house of a revered king.

Thus again we may have a work composed of many strata stemming from many historical periods. The actual sources of the books of Samuel may well have been put into written form in the reign of Solomon to prove the legitimacy of the dynasty of David and the legitimacy of the succession of Solomon. They were probably reedited during the reign of Hezekiah (715–687 BC) and finally revised and retouched by the Deuteronomists in the sixth century BC. The relatively minor appearances of typically Deuteronomist additions suggest the books of Samuel were largely intact by this time. Apparently the Deuteronomists retained the books as a defense of the Davidic dynasty's legitimacy and perpetuity—beliefs of no small importance for the hopes of the disillusioned exiles of the Babylonian Exile.

C. Glimpses into Ancient Traditions

With 1 Samuel we see the early traditions of the ark of the covenant (4:1—7:1). This is a tradition that may stem from the desert wanderings of the Hebrews. Some of the oldest texts now found in the Torah speak of the ark much as it is presented in 1 Samuel, namely, as a war palladium (Num 10:33–36; 14:44). The tradition reappears in the story of David making Jerusalem his political and religious capital (2 Sam 6).

The Exodus tradition itself occurs frequently in the ark narrative (4:8; 6:6) and the Samuel stories of 1 Samuel (8:8; 10:18; 12:6, 8; 15:2, 6–7). It appears also briefly in 2 Samuel in the story of David's concern for the Temple (7:6, 23).

On the other hand, neither the story line nor the later editing give any indication of the existence of any book of the Law during this period of the eleventh and tenth centuries BC. Rather, it is the prophets in the story with their oral pronouncements that evaluate the actions and lives of the kings. This period of political turmoil and war would not be conducive to the rise of other literature.

D. The Divisions of the Books of Samuel

Originally one work, Samuel was later divided into two books. Together, the books can be subdivided by topics as follows:

1 Samuel 1—7:	The last judges, Eli and Samuel, and the Philistine oppression
1 Samuel 8—15:	Samuel and Saul, the institution of the monarchy, and Saul's rejection
1 Samuel 16—31:	Saul and David; David befriended by Saul, later persecuted
2 Samuel 1—4:	David, king over Judah after the death of Saul
2 Samuel 5—12:	David, king over all Israel
2 Samuel 13—20:	Rebellion against David
2 Samuel 21—24:	Appendices

II. Significant Passages in 1 and 2 Samuel

A. 1 Samuel 1—7 / Eli and Samuel

1:1–28 ***The family of Elkanah***

The account begins with the first of many stories of divine election of one person over a more likely rival. Hannah, one of Elkanah's two wives is barren, but it is she who will be mother of Israel's greatest judge, Samuel.

The scene opens in Shiloh, now the religious center of Israel. It had been that center apparently from the time when Joshua moved the tent there from Gilgal (Josh 18:1; also Judg 18:31; 21:19). Centuries later, Jeremiah will point to the ruins of Shiloh as an example of God's withdrawal of his favor from his chosen city (Jer 7:12; 26:6, 9; also Ps 78:60). We have no description of Shiloh's destruction, but we can assume that the Philistines destroyed it in the war about to be described.

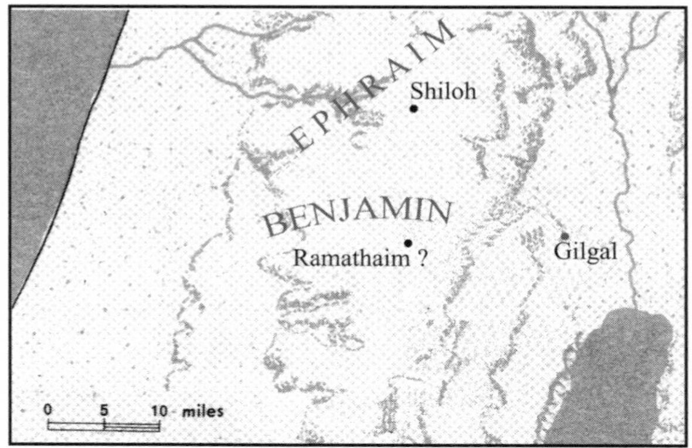

4A: Map of Shiloh, Gilgal

God's blessing of Hannah comes after much bitterness suffered at the hands of her rival, Peninnah. It comes also as an answer to a prayer "before Yahweh" (1:3), a prayer considered unusual at that time because it was not pronounced out loud. God's answer comes through Eli the priest. Her son Samuel is conceived and born. Like Samson (Judges 13), Samuel is to be dedicated to God by what appears to be a Nazirite vow (1:11; see Num 6). Some ancient manuscripts found at Qumran explicitly describe the child as dedicated to become a *nazir* (1:22).

2:1–10 *Hannah's song*

Hannah's prayer celebrates a powerful God and his readiness to reverse the fortunes of human beings, even to the point of casting the living down to the realm of death and raising them up again (2:6). This unhesitating affirmation of the unconditional power of God becomes in fact the theological starting point for a much later explicit faith in the resurrection of the dead. For the exiles in Babylon reading this song, this affirmation of God's power was a call to hope. The "mighty" and "well-fed" rulers of Babylon could be dispossessed by God, while the "hungry" and "needy in the dust and ash heaps" could be "raised" and "seated with nobles" (2:4–8). Reference to God's "anointed" (*mashiach,* 2:10) as well as the warrior imagery (2:1, 4, 9) reminds us of how this song is really geared toward the future king of Israel.

In writing his story about the mother of Jesus, Luke took inspiration from this song of Hannah to compose Mary's Magnificat (Luke 1:46–55). This song also fits well Luke's deep concern for the poor.

3:1—4:1 *The call of Samuel*

The story continues with the captivating account of Samuel's call. The picture of Samuel sleeping before the ark of the covenant in the sanctuary of God suggests a priestly office, involving an intimacy with God absent in later traditions when the inaccessibility of God was stressed (see Lev 16). God, through Eli the priest, leads Samuel to the response, "Speak, Yahweh, your servant is listening" (3:9). Yahweh then "came and revealed his presence" (3:10), though we are not told how. A revelation of divine judgment follows.

This call narrative establishes Samuel's authority. With Samuel we have one of the major named prophets in Israel, whose work is to allow the "word of God" to manifest its powerful effect (see 3:19), even when that effect is disaster, as it is here for the house of Eli. Samuel thus here unites the roles of priest and prophet. He will soon be identified also as judge in Israel (7:15). The exiles in Babylon are reminded how true and just authority is rooted in prophecy.

Luke's description of the development of the boy Jesus (Luke 2:42) appears as a deliberate echo of Samuel (1 Sam 2:26).

4:1–11 *Defeat at the hands of the Philistines*

In the next few chapters, attention focuses on the ark of the covenant. Samuel recedes from the stage until 7:3. These shifts might indicate the boundaries of a distinct tradition or document inserted here. Clearly the ark appears here as a war palladium, or symbol of divine military protection. This military aspect appears in the earliest traditions found now in the Book of Numbers that link the ark to battles in the Sinai desert (see Num 10:33–36; 14:44). Other stories of the ark, like those in Joshua 3—6 as well as the editorial comment about the ark in Judges 20:27, appear to be written much later.

The story of the capture of the ark and the defeat of the Israelites emphasizes the domination by the Philistines, the state of affairs that led to the demand for a king, described in the next section (1 Sam 8—12). The story is also a striking one of disillusionment concerning the presence of God and his readiness to help. "The glory [*kabod*]" of God symbolized by the ark is not welded to Israel (see 4:21–22), a theme that the prophet Ezekiel orchestrates in his visions (Ezek 10:1–19; 11:22–23). The capture of the ark is the setting for the downfall of the house of Eli.

6:1—7:1 *The return of the ark*

As the story is told, God is in control. He allows his ark to be captured. Once in the hands of the Philistines, however, the Philistine god, Dagon, falls prostrate before it; the Philistines are afflicted with "hemorrhoids" (chapter 5). Finally against all natural instincts, the two nursing cows leave their calves and return the ark to Israelite territory. God remains in charge even with the loss of the religious symbols of his presence.

The message would not be lost on the readers in exile some five hundred years later. The foreign gods are no match for Yahweh, even when his people face abject defeat.

The ark is not returned to Shiloh or to Nob, the new religious center (see 1 Sam 21:2–10). It is stored in a backwoods village, Kiriath-jearim, about eleven miles northwest of Jerusalem where it remains until David decides to move it to Jerusalem (see 2 Sam 6). This geography is significant. The ark is in storage and in some way so is the history of Israel. When Psalm 78 retells the history of Israel, it skips from the Philistine war described here in Samuel (Ps 78:59–64) to the divine choice of David and Mount Zion, the Temple mount in Jerusalem (Ps 78:65–72), as if the intervening story of Saul in the absence of the ark had no theological significance.

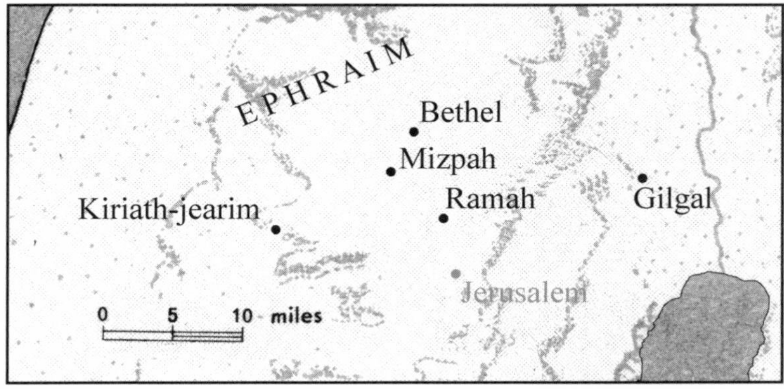

4B: Map of Kiriath-jearim, Ephraim, Bethel, Gilgal, Mizpah, Ramah

7:15–17 ***Samuel as judge***

The Deuteronomists' summary of Samuel's function as judge describes a circuit through three major sanctuaries in southern Ephraim, Bethel, Gilgal, and Mizpah, along with his home base at Ramah, another religious and political center for Israel. Located about two miles northwest of Ramah and about eight miles north of Jerusalem, Mizpah is also the site of the first two of three great assemblies during the judgeship of Samuel (7:7; 10:17 and 11:14).

B. 1 Samuel 8—15 / Samuel and Saul

In the history of the institution of the monarchy, the Deuteronomists seem to fuse two different versions: the antimonarchist version (8; 10:17–24; 12) and the promonarchist version (9:1–10, 16; 11). The monarchy thus arises from a basic ambiguity. How important is it to have a king? If the king were taken away, could Israel survive? The editors here explicitly include the view that the people's demand for a king showed their lack of trust in God, manifested by their demand for a king (8:7). This was displeasing to God, even though he acceded to their wish. By expressing the faith of the antimonarchists that God alone is Israel's true king, the writers of 1 Samuel also prepare the way for the rejection of Saul (chapter 15) as well as for the election of David, who will rule, not like the surrounding Gentile kings, but as God's obedient vicar and instrument (see Deut 17:14–20).

8:1–22 *The request for a king*

The story of Saul begins with an antimonarchist account of the people's demand for a king "as other nations have" (8:4, 20). The request is interpreted by God as a rejection of him "as their king" (8:7). The tradition of Yahweh as the king of Israel is celebrated in psalms 93 and 95—99 and appears as well in the Torah (Exod 15:18) and the prophets (Isa 33:22). The real issue is thus the relationship between the people and Yahweh, their God.

Samuel announces good news and bad news. The good news is that God will grant their request. The bad news is that the king will be an oppressor. In any case, the period of the judges is over and a new institution arises.

9:1—10:16 *Saul*

The introduction of Saul, son of Kish, begins with a long list of ancestors and a stress on his handsome appearance (9:1–2). The ensuing story of this peasant in search of his father's lost asses may originally have come in two forms with different details. One form seems to describe a long journey with an encounter with an anonymous "man of God." The other form seems to describe a short journey with an encounter with the now well-known Samuel. The two stories are here meshed into a delightful account, bearing some signs of minor inconsistencies yet filled with suspenseful delays—all about how God selected Saul, the first king of Israel.

Through a revelation of God, Samuel is instructed to anoint (*mashach*) Saul as "commander" (*nagid*) of Israel. At first, Samuel does this privately (10:1). Thus, Saul becomes the first kingly "anointed one" or "messiah" (*mashiach*) of the Old Testament. The anointing is permanent, qualifying Saul even after he is later rejected by God (see 24:7). All this is God's work, who in effect gives Saul "another heart" (10:9). At the end of the story we hear of a secrecy that enshrouds the new "kingship" (*malukah*, 10:16).

In this story we are also given a glimpse of the earliest forms of prophecy in Israel. "The sons of prophets" appear here in a sort of ecstatic or mindless dance to the accompaniment of music, called here a "prophetic state" (10:5–6). We see also a concerted effort to identify the role of "seer" (*ro'eh*), one privy to special knowledge, with that of "prophet" (*nabi'*), one who speaks for God (9:9), two roles that perhaps were originally distinct. In the final form of the story, likewise, we see the title "man of God" clearly designating Samuel, earlier called "prophet" (see 3:20).

11:1–15 *Victory over the Ammonites*

The narrator now relates the military ability of Saul in the Ammonite war at Jabesh-gilead, a city to the north in Transjordan. Gibeah, the city that was totally destroyed in Judges (Judg 20:34–48), is described here as Saul's city (1 Sam 11:4; see 10:26). The brutal terms offered by Nahash the Ammonite indicate the desperate situation of Israel at this time (11:2). Saul, still working as a peasant farmer, is seized by the spirit of God in the manner of the judges to save Israel. The action of Saul cutting a pair of oxen into pieces that are then sent throughout Israel as a call to war (11:7) echoes the butchering of the Levite's concubine (Judg 19:29–30).

Because of his success against Nahash the Ammonite, the Israelite people in the presence of Yahweh "made Saul king" (*melek*). This takes place at the third great assembly under Samuel, this time at Gilgal. This acclamation repeats that of 1 Samuel 10:17–24, the second great assembly that was at Mizpah. These cities may actually mark how identical stories were handed down with variations at different population centers.

13:2—14:22 *The Philistine war and the battle of Michmash*

In the next war story, we are introduced to Jonathan, the son of Saul, by a description of his victory over the Philistine garrison at Michmash in Benjamin. This battle opens the war again with the Philistines. The Philistine garrisons at Gibeah (13:3) and Bethel (10:5) plus the Philistine corner on the iron market (13:19-21) explain the oppression that led the Israelites to demand a king. Practically single-handed, however, Jonathan sends the Philistine army into panic (14:1–15). Eventually, Saul and his forces join the battle, but with an explicit refusal to consult Yahweh (14:19).

In the middle of the narrative and somewhat interrupting it, the editor places the first account of God's rejection of Saul. It is connected with Saul's sacrifice at Gilgal. Although Saul waits the

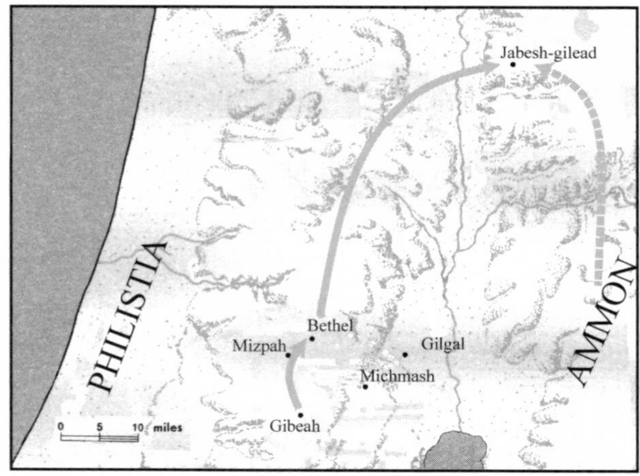

4C: Map of Saul's Battles

seven days demanded by Samuel (10:8) and although Samuel gave Saul the authorization, "Do whatever you judge feasible, because God is with you" (10:7), Saul's holocaust is interpreted in 13:13–14 as disobedience, leading to the collapse of his kingship and his replacement by David. As presented, the divine reason for such an extreme outcome is not clear. Saul did what Samuel told him to do, and later we will see David offering sacrifices like a priest (2 Sam 6:17; 24:25). Perhaps by taking matters into his own hands and not waiting a few more hours, Saul failed to understand God's timing, which seems like an intolerable delay in human understanding. What he "judged feasible" was wrong. However difficult it is to understand the sin of Saul, its placement here at the beginning of his reign reflects the editor's way of warning the reader at the beginning of so many successive reigns; this king was not one of the good kings of Israel.

15:10–35 ***Another version of Saul's disobedience and rejection***

In a parallel account of Saul's rejection, the king apparently disobeys the command of God given through Samuel to slaughter the Amalekites (15:3), a people of the Judean desert in the south. Saul counters with a defense that he has not disobeyed God but simply wanted to offer God sacrifices from the booty.

The result again is a perplexity for the reader as to why Saul is rejected. The reason is not clear. But clearly Yahweh is a God who exalts the humble and deposes the mighty as he wills (2:4–8).

Samuel then declares the principle upon which alone human kingship in Israel can survive: "Does Yahweh delight in burnt offerings and sacrifices as much as in obedience to the voice of Yahweh? Behold, to obey is better than sacrifices and to hearken, than the fat of rams" (15:22). This principle reflects the stress common in the prophets that sacrifices and other religious ceremony are worthless in the sight of God when detached from a heartfelt commitment to moral life (Isa 1:10–20; Hos 6:6; Amos 5:22–25; Mic 6:6–8). This stress finds its way into the Gospel of Mark, where Jesus approves of the understanding that love is more important than "all burnt offerings and sacrifices" (Mark 12:33).

The prophetic gesture of tearing cloth (15:27–28) will appear again to describe the tearing away of the northern kingdom from Rehoboam, Solomon's successor in Judah (1 Kgs 11:30; see also John 19:23–24).

God's rejection of his own personally chosen messiah, conveys a sense of divine danger. God's promises and actions in the past are no bases for complacency. God cannot be manipulated on the basis of the past, as the exiles in Babylon well knew. He can and will reject and destroy those who do not live up to their calling—even those most central to his plan.

C. 1 Samuel 16—31 / Saul and David

The next section of Samuel introduces David. Again by making use of sources, the editors end up with several conflicting accounts of David's entry into Saul's court. From then on, we watch the demise of Saul and the rise of David. In these narratives, the editors take great pains to show that God chose David, that David obtains the throne of Israel reluctantly, and that he held the person of Saul, the anointed of God, in utmost respect.

16:1–13 *The anointing of David*

Samuel's last gesture is to anoint Saul's replacement. The story is clear about God directing the event: "You are to anoint for me the one I point out to you" (16:3). The youngest son, the one not even present at the first interview, is selected. This story, along with the Goliath story that follows, illustrates God's choice of improbable saviors. This is a message of great hope at times of national distress.

David is anointed and thus becomes the second great kingly "messiah" of the Old Testament. At this time, "the spirit of Yahweh rushed (*tsalach*) on him" (16:13) as it did for Saul (see 11:6; also 10:6, 10), stressing the continuity between judges and kings. For David, however, the action of the spirit is linked with his anointing. The handsome character of David is stressed, as it was for Saul (16:12).

16:14–23 ***The introduction of David to the court***

David's first introduction to the royal court is based on his musical ability. At the same time, we are introduced to Saul's mental instability. In contrast, David, described as a skillful harpist, a stalwart soldier, an able speaker, and handsome in looks, makes his first steps to the throne.

17:1–58 ***David and Goliath***

The second and independent introduction to the royal court involves one of the best-known stories in the Bible. It begins with David as a courier bringing supplies to his brothers in the army of Saul (17:12–23). It continues with David resisting the hostility of older brothers (17:27–3), a theme that reaches back to the story of Jacob and Esau (Gen 25:19–34).

While the sling was indeed a deadly weapon in the hand of David, the storyteller draws a contrast between the giant Goliath with his armor, sword, spear, and scimitar and David, who could not fit into Saul's armor. The contrast is between human might and "the name of Yahweh Sabaoth, the God of the armies of Israel" (17:45). David's attitude is that of both trust in God, who protected him in fights with savage animals, as well as zeal for God's honor (17:36–37, 45–47). The theological purpose of this story is clear. David destroys the giant and is presented to Saul by Abner (17:57). David is beginning to look very kingly. But all this is under God's control.

In 2 Samuel 21:19, one of David's men, Elhanan, is named as the slayer of Goliath, the Gittite, which means a person from Gath. Somewhere in the developing traditions regarding David, names were transferred, either David for Elhanan or Goliath for some unknown formidable enemy.

18:1–5 *David and Jonathan*

After the story of Goliath, the beginning of David's rise to military power, the editors add the story of a "covenant" (*berit*) of love between David and Jonathan (18:1–5), the person who in the normal course of events would inherit the throne of Saul. Jonathan was in no way opposed to David's rise (see also 23:14–18).

18:6–30 *Saul's attempts to kill David*

In an amalgam of independent and somewhat disjointed stories, the editors of the book portray Saul's self-destruction, in the grip of "an evil spirit from God" (18:10). Saul's jealousy of David includes attacks on David's life. But David only becomes stronger. Even the plot involving Saul's daughter Michal ends with David becoming Saul's son-in-law. All this adds to the legitimacy of David's claim to the throne.

21:1—22:23 *David the fugitive*

After David's life is spared through Jonathan's intercession (18:18—19:6) and by Michal's stratagem (19:11–17), David has no choice but to become a fugitive, which he will remain until Saul is killed. The exiles in Babylon would take special note of this story of David the refugee. The same image will reappear later in David's exile from Jerusalem in flight from his son, Absalom (2 Sam 15:13—16:14). David first flees with a band of loyal fighters to Nob, a sanctuary that appears to have replaced Shiloh. Here Ahimelech the priest allows David and his men to eat the sacred breads of the sanctuary. Ahimelech also gives David the sword of Goliath (21:2–10).

Mark the evangelist will recount a story of Jesus appealing to this incident as evidence of the flexibility of divine regulations. In

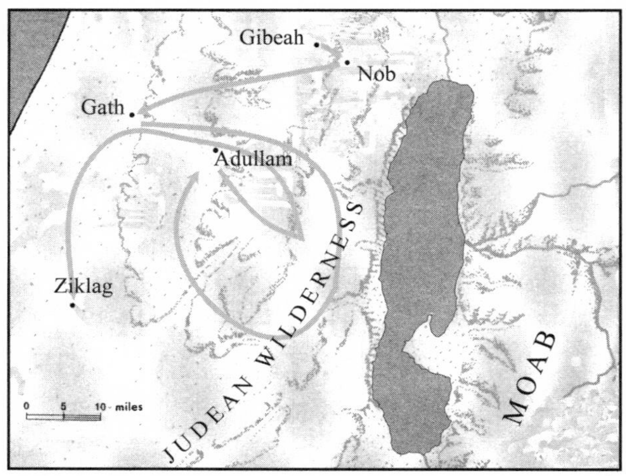

4D: Map of David's Flight from Saul

Mark's account, Ahimelech's son, Abiathar, is the priest of Nob (Mark 2:25–26).

From Nob, David goes to the Philistines, the archenemies of Israel. At Gath, David pretends to be mad, which the Philistine king, Achish, takes as a reason to spare David (21:11–16). A parallel story describes David returning to Achish in Gath, where be becomes a vassal (*'ebed*) and is given control of the Philistine city of Ziklag (27:1–12; see also chapter 29). The association of David and his militia with the enemies of Israel must have been an embarrassment for the later supporters of David as king. Details in the various accounts reflect efforts at damage control.

In the subsequent escapes that take him to Adullam and Moab, the homeland of Ruth, David's great-grandmother, David is aided by the prophet Gad, who advises him to leave for the land of Judah (22:5). This prophet will reappear in 2 Samuel 24.

Meanwhile, David is betrayed to Saul by Doeg, the Edomite, who reports the help Ahimelech the priest gave David. Under Saul's command, Doeg puts to death the priests of Nob along with their families and animals (22:6–19). By attacking Yahweh's priests in office, Saul has declared his enmity with God. Only Abiathar, Ahimelech's son, escapes, reports the crime to David (22:20–23), and, as we learn later, brings David the "ephod" (see

23:9). David, not Saul, now has the backing of both prophet and priest. The friendship between David and Abiathar lasted the rest of David's life.

24:1–23 ***David spares Saul***

David's flight from Saul takes him into the Judean wilderness between Gath and the Dead Sea. At one point, Saul unknowingly falls into David's grasp. David refuses to lay a hand on "Yahweh's anointed." The death of the messiah must remain in God's hands. Instead, David secretly cuts off the end of Saul's mantle and then later calls to Saul to show him how he could have killed him (24:1–16). David will obtain the throne not by seizing human opportunities, but by aligning himself with God's ways.

Saul momentarily repents of his persecution of David and proclaims David's future right to the throne: "I know that you shall surely be king and that sovereignty over Israel shall come into your possession" (24:21). The reader could not ask for a clearer statement of David's legitimacy as future king. Saul asks in return only that David spare his family, to which David gives his oath (24:23). Chapter 26 gives another version of this story.

25:1 ***Samuel's death***

The brief notice of Samuel's death, repeated in 28:3, includes the description of "all Israel gathering" to mourn. At a time when civil warfare could have easily destroyed Israel as a unity, the funeral of Samuel provides us with a glimmer of God's plans. The notice prepares for the story in chapter 28 of Saul's sinful consultation of dead Samuel.

25:2–43 ***David and Abigail***

One of the great capable women of the Bible, Abigail, now appears. She is described as "intelligent and attractive" (25:3) but married to a churlish boor. When Nabal, her husband (whose name means "senseless" or "foolish"), rudely refuses to give any aid to David and his men, Abigail, his wife, jumps into the breach and on her own provides the needed support. David was ready to take matters into his own hands and slaughter the house of

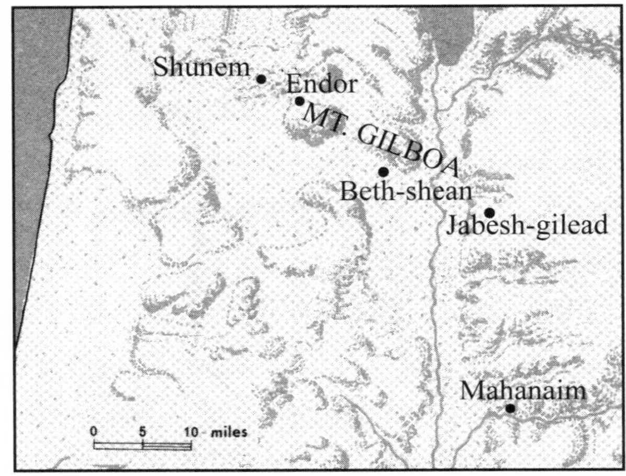

4E: Map of Mt. Gilboa, Endor, Shunem, Mahanaim

Nabal, but Abigail skillfully intercedes and prevents David from the bloodshed and personal vengeance, which apparently was considered evil here (25:26, 33). Like a prophet, she announces to David and all the readers, "Yahweh will certainly establish a lasting dynasty for my lord, because your lordship is fighting the battles of Yahweh" (25:28). David in return proclaims her blessed (25:33). On hearing of his wife's action, Nabal drops dead, and David marries the attractive widow.

28:1–25 *Saul's final battle against the Philistines*

The story begins with the Philistines mustering their forces and advancing to Shunem in the plain of Jezreel to the north. Saul assembles his army across the valley on Mount Gilboa (28:4). Dismayed by the silence of God, Saul turns to the woman of nearby Endor as a medium through whom Saul could consult the dead Samuel, who predicts the defeat and death of Saul and the rise of David: "Yahweh has done to you what he foretold through me: he has torn the kingdom from your grasp and has given it to your neighbor David" (28:17). Saul's consultation with the woman of Endor seems to be a deliberate contrasting parallel with David's listening to the advice of Abigail.

31:1–13 ***The death of Saul***

Defeated by the Philistines on Mount Gilboa, Saul's sons, Jonathan, Abinadab, and Malchishua, die in battle and Saul himself runs on his sword (31:1–6). The people of Jabesh-gilead (see 1 Sam 11) risk their lives to give the king and his sons a decent burial (31:11).

Thus the first book of Samuel closes as it began—with the Philistines in control. Israel's first king is disastrously defeated, his armies dispersed.

D. 2 Samuel 1—4 / David, King of Judah

The next section in Samuel describes the aftermath of the battle of Gilboa. In the north, the forces of Saul retreat to the Transjordan city of Mahanaim, where Ishboshet, a fourth son of Saul, is made king by Abner, the general of the Israelite army. In the south, David is acclaimed king of Judah.

1:19–27 ***David's elegy for Saul and Jonathan***

One of the most expressive laments in the Bible, David's elegy mourns the deaths of Saul and Jonathan. The poem has a special depth where David thinks of his friendship with Jonathan. Yet Saul too is included in the lament, where an intensely positive picture of this king emerges.

2:1–7 ***David anointed king***

Following divine directives, David makes his headquarters at Hebron in Judah. The Judahites then secede from Saul's unified kingdom and anoint David king of Judah at Hebron, the principal city of their territory. David's communication with the men of Jabesh-gilead, a city in Transjordan, indicates David's effort to make political capital in favor of a kingdom extending beyond Judah.

2:8–16 ***Ishboshet king of Israel***

Abner, commander of Saul's army, supports Ishboshet (Ishba'al), Saul's son, as king of the remaining tribes. In the Hebrew text his name is Ishboshet, where *boshet* means "shame," probably a slam by the Deuteronomist editors. Many English translations here use his name from 1 Chronicles 8:33, "Ishba'al," where *ba'al* means "lord," but is also the proper name of the Canaanite god. Mahanaim, a city east of the Jordan, apparently becomes the capital for Ishboshet.

For seven years, internecine warfare between the adherents of David and Ishboshet (2:17–32) leads to the progressive eclipse of the house of Saul (3:1). One result of this war is the hatred of Joab, David's general, for Abner, Saul's commander (see 3:22–30).

3:6–21 *Abner and David*

Abner breaks with Ishboshet when the new king interprets Abner's espousal of one of Saul's concubines as an attempt to usurp the kingdom (see 2 Sam 12:8; 16:20–22: 1 Kgs 2:17, 21, 22). Abner then sends secret messengers to David (2 Sam 3:12). To test Abner's intentions, David demands the return of his wife, Michal (3:13–16). Abner rallies the elders to support David (3:17–19), meets with David at Hebron, and agrees to bring over to him the northern tribes (3:20–21).

3:22–39 *The murder of Abner*

The peaceful agreement is destroyed by Joab's hatred for Abner, whom he assassinates as blood vengeance for the death of

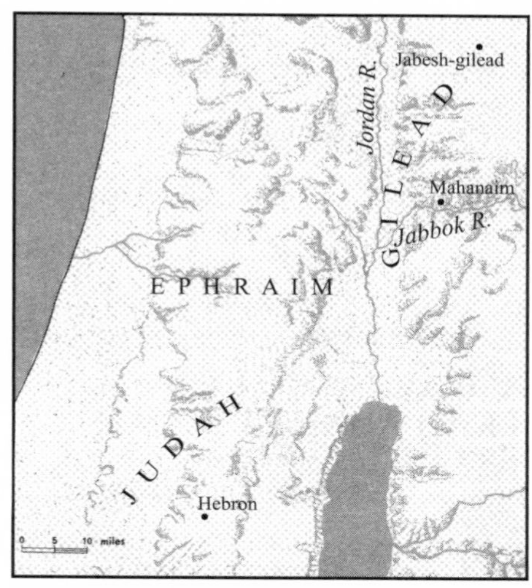

4F: Map of Hebron, Jabesh-gilead, Mahanaim

his brother, Asahel (2:22). The chance of union between the tribes is almost ruined, but David's genuine sorrow and honorable obsequies for Abner effectively absolve him of the murder in the eyes of the northern tribes (3:31–39).

David here appears weak and dejected. In his deep depression, he fails to take any action against Joab. This complexity of character will continue through the story.

4:1–12 *The murder of Ishboshet*

Ishboshet is assassinated by Rechab and Baanah, his two company leaders, who are subsequently executed by David. The writers of Samuel are at great pains to show David innocent of the blood that destroyed the house of Saul. With Abner and Ishboshet dead, opposition to David disappears, and the way is open for the house of David to succeed the house of Saul.

One remaining member, Mephiboshet, the son of Jonathan and grandson of Saul, is described here as crippled as a child at the time of the deaths of Jonathan and Saul and therefore apparently out of consideration for succession to the throne. (Many English translations here use his name from 1 Chronicles 8:34, Meriba'al.) According to later stories, David takes great pains to care for Mephiboshet (2 Sam 9; see also 19:25–31) and spares him from the gruesome vengeance of the Gibeonites (21:7).

E. 2 Samuel 5—12 / David, King of All Israel

The next major section of 2 Samuel describes David as king of all Israel. Many stories are brought together here to portray a king chosen by God who basically rules as God's representative, yet who is weak and sinful. Unlike those of Saul, his sins do not result in rejection by God. Under his leadership Israel is united, the surrounding enemies vanquished, and Jerusalem is made the religious and political center of the land. The ark reappears as the symbol of God's presence among his people. Except for the brief interruptions caused by the rebellion of Absalom and Sheba, David will reign from 1010 to 970 BC, when he is succeeded by Solomon.

5:1–5 *David king of all Israel*

The assembly at Hebron results in David becoming king of all Israel. The selection is made on three bases: (a) ethnic relationship ("We are your bone and your flesh."), (b) David's military abilities ("You led the Israelites out and brought them back"), and (c) a divine promise to David ("You shall shepherd my people Israel and be commander [*nagid*] of Israel"). What promise could the assembly be referring to? Earlier, Abner cites a divine promise to David as military savior from the Philistines (3:17), and the prophetic words of Abigail quote a divine promise to David with wording similar to that of the assembly (1 Sam 25:30), but the "official" form of the promise will appear only in the mouth of Nathan in a later story after David is on the throne (2 Sam 7:7–8). The appointment of David here is described as a "covenant" (*berit*) between him and the elders of Israel and as the elders "anointing him king of Israel" (5:3).

The summary description of the years of David's reign follows the pattern we find throughout the books of Kings. David *rules* only 33 years over the united kingdoms of Israel and Judah (probably 1003/02 to 970 BC), but the length of his *reign* is 40 years because it includes all the years he was king in any sense (5:4–5).

5:6–10 *The capture of Jerusalem*

David makes the ancient Canaanite city of Jerusalem his new capital, combining strategic reasons with political reasons. Its position was that of a natural fortress. At the same time, its location outside of Judah could dispel the jealousy of the sensitive northern tribes. Its location inside Benjamin could placate the remaining supporters of the Saul dynasty.

The reference to "the lame and the blind" and their exclusion from "the house" is a puzzle for interpreters (5:8). It might be some later addition trying to associate a well-known saying with David and his attack on Jerusalem. It does not make much sense in this context. The Gospel of Matthew seems to refer to this line as it describes Jesus by contrast in the Temple approached by "the blind and the lame," whom he cured (Matt 21:14).

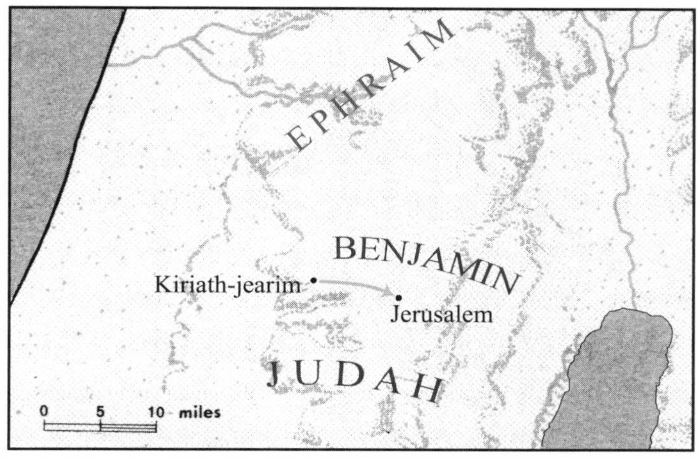

4G: Map of Jerusalem, Kiriath-jearim

The "Millo" (5:9) appears to be a fortification perhaps on the vulnerable north side of the city. It is mentioned again among Solomon's construction projects (1 Kgs 9:15, 24; 11:27).

6:1–23 *The ark brought to Jerusalem*

The ark narratives of 1 Samuel 4—6 are now picked up in a story about David. The new king consolidates his position by bringing the ark of the covenant to Jerusalem, making the city the religious as well as the national capital. Kiriath-jearim, the town where the ark had been in storage (1 Sam 7:1), is here called Ba'ale-jehudah (6:2; see Josh 15:9).

The story of Uzzah (6:6–9) disturbs the modern reader out of considerations of fairness. The ancient readers were probably concerned less by issues of fairness and subjective guilt than by the objective danger of the ark. Again we have a portrayal of the high-voltage danger of God's holiness (see Exod 19 and 33; Isa 6). The story is balanced here by that of Obededom (6:10–12), where the nearness of this holy object brings blessings. As a result, David resumes his project to bring the ark to Jerusalem.

The musical instruments, the dancing, and the procession described here reflect later Temple processions and liturgies (see Ps 132). David functions as priest offering "holocausts and peace offerings before Yahweh" (6:17). Unlike the holocausts and peace offerings of Saul (1 Sam 13:9–14), David's offerings incur no blame.

The barrenness of Michal appears to be part of the theme of how the house of Saul dies out (6:23).

7:1–29 ***The prophecy of Nathan***

At this point, we meet Nathan the prophet, whose prophecy of an eternal dynasty is the climax of the books of Samuel. Worried about the discrepancy between his "house of cedar" (see 5:11) and God's tent, David decides to build a temple or house (*bayit*) for God. To show that the prophet's message is not his own, the account describes the initial encouragement by Nathan, which is then followed by a complete reversal once the "Word of Yahweh (came) to Nathan" (7:4). Returning to David, Nathan tells him not to build a temple and does so in language that argues against building *any* temple at *any* time (7:5–7). Read by the exiles in Babylon, this prophecy would remind the faithful of how they could be very good Israelites without a temple.

In the middle of verse 11, the direct address of Yahweh is interrupted: "Yahweh reveals to you...." Here the oracle of Nathan shifts its focus to the "dynasty" or "house" (*bayit*) of David and how a descendant of David will build a "house" or temple to Yahweh. Most important, God promises to make the dynasty of David endure forever (*'ad 'olam*; 7:12–16). Unlike the Sinai covenant described in Deuteronomy (Deut 11:10–31), the promises here are unconditional. Even if the king fails and does wrong, the covenant with David will stand. This unconditional covenant is the theme of Psalm 89. The theme contrasts with the Deuteronomist insistence of a conditional covenant, holding only so long as the people obey God (Deut 28).

The kings following in David's line will be "sons" of God, and God will be a "father" to them (7:14). The Davidic kings were never considered divine, as were the pharaohs, but they were considered "sons of God" (Ps 2:7; 110:3), using a Hebrew idiom, "son of..." to express a special relationship or characterization. David expresses his amazement in prayer (7:1–29), ending with a stress on the "eternal" character of God's blessing on Israel and David's house (7:25–29).

The hope generated by Nathan's oracle about the "house" of David carried Israel beyond the tragedies that were to follow, beyond the failures of the vast majority of the Davidic kings as recorded in the books of Kings. With the birth of each new Davidic prince, the people and the prophets were filled with expectation. Two centuries later, Isaiah expressed the feelings of the people at the birth of a new crown prince:

> For a child is born to us, a son is given us;...
> From David's throne, and over his kingdom
> Which he confirms and sustains by judgment and justice,
> Both now and forever. (Isa 9:5–6)

Five centuries later, Ezekiel in exile would promise in the name of God:

> I will appoint one shepherd over them
> and he will pasture them, my servant David;
> he will pasture them and be their shepherd.
> I, Yahweh, will be their God,
> my servant David shall be their prince among them....
> (Ezek 34:23–24)

11:1—12:25 *David and Bathsheba*

The war with Ammon and the Arameans (10:1–19) sets the stage for David's crimes of adultery and murder. While Uriah is in the field with Joab besieging the capital of Ammon, David commits adultery with his wife, Bathsheba (11:1–5). Unable to conceal the adultery (11:6–13), David writes to Joab instructing him to arrange Uriah's death in battle (11:14–25). David then marries Bathsheba (11:26–27).

The prophet Nathan returns to accuse the king, whom earlier he had so profusely blessed. This role of the prophet, demanding that the king obey a higher law, is unparalleled in the ancient world. Nathan does this by way of a parable (12:1–4), which brings David to repentance and personal pardon (12:13). Later tradition identified Psalm 51 as expression of David's repentance.

The crimes of adultery and murder, however, bring a sentence of punishment. From Nathan, David hears: "The sword shall never depart from your house" (12:10). This foreshadowing text sets the tone for the remainder of the court history that describes David's tragic family life. These chapters thus become a type of hinge to the next section of 2 Samuel. The child conceived in adultery dies, the innocent son of David in the place of the sinner. In some way the sin of David is expiated. In some way the matter is over, as David's sudden shift of behavior suggests (12:20–23). Bathsheba conceives and bears another son, Solomon (12:24), who will succeed David (1 Kgs 1).

F. 2 Samuel 13—20 / Rebellion against David

Actually the effects of David's sin remain. A large section now tells the story of the "sword" that will plague the house of David because of his sin (12:10–11). David's sins of sensuality and murder are repeated in his sons. In the end, the enemies of David are no longer the neighboring nations. They are within his house. This unflattering depiction of David and his family gives this narration an extraordinary historical character. This appears to be a narration of how things actually happened.

13:1–39 *The rape of Tamar*

The story of the "sword" begins with Amnon's incestuous rape of Tamar (13:1–20). Fratricide then follows rape. Tamar's brother Absalom murders Amnon and flees to Geshur (13:21–37), north of Gilead and east of the Sea of Galilee, the land of his mother (3:3). Tamar is the tragic figure here. While her personal suffering is detailed, her fate does not seem important to the author.

The focus remains on David, who mourns over the death of Amnon. With the exile of Absalom, David loses two sons (13:37–39). In this portrayal David appears indecisive, even weak. An indecisive refusal to discipline his son, Amnon, for the rape of his sister, appears in a LXX variant—supported by Qumran fragments—of 13:21, which adds the words, "but he did not rebuke his son Amnon for he favored him as his firstborn."

David's weakness appears here also with the insistence that he "pined away for Absalom" (13:39; see also 19:1–4).

14:1–33 *The return and revolt of Absalom*

The story of Absalom's return is interesting for the parable it contains. Coached by Joab and following the method of Nathan, the "wise woman" of Tekoa (14:2) creates a story taken from everyday life that elicits a response from the listener, which in turn is applied to the real life situation of the listener. Thus Absalom is allowed to return to Jerusalem and eventually be pardoned by the king (14:33). Joab who arranged this return will later kill Absalom (18:14).

The story of Absalom's revolt against his father follows (chapters 15—18). In their description of Absalom, the authors of the court history carefully portray him as cold and calculating (13:23–28), thoroughly unscrupulous (14:30), ruthlessly resourceful (15:1–6), a patient plotter (15:7), and utterly amoral (16:21–22).

15:13—16:14 *David's flight from Jerusalem*

By quick action, David escapes with some loyal troops from Absalom's rebel army, passing out to "the desert" through the Kidron Valley, east of Jerusalem, over the Mount of Olives, where he weeps over Jerusalem (15:23, 30). He hears that Mephiboshet (Meriba'al), Jonathan's son, has turned against him (16:1–4), and he is cursed by Shimei, a Benjaminite (16:5–14).

David, however, manages to plant spies in the court of Absalom. The priests Zadok and Abiathar, with their sons, remain with the ark in Jerusalem to send information back to David (15:24–29). More important, Hushai is planted in Absalom's court (15:32–37).

What happens next is completely in God's hands, a situation that reflects the whole history of David. The storyteller captures the attitude of David, not in control of the events, not knowing what is to happen. "If (*'im*) I find favor in the eyes of God, he will bring me back (15:25). "Perhaps (*'ulay*) God will look on my affliction and restore good to me" (16:12). The words indicate that David does not know what God intends to do in this bad situation, but David can stare into this abyss believing that God is in control. The message would not be lost on the exiles in Babylon five hundred years later.

17:1–24 *Absalom's mistake*

Back in Jerusalem, Ahitophel's counsel is rejected by Absalom, who listens to Hushai, David's planted agent. This decision by Absalom is the fatal mistake that allows David to regroup across the Jordan at Mahanaim, the old capital of Saul's son, Ishboshet (2 Sam 2:8). Ahitophel the traitor hangs himself. These are stories of human plots and counterplots. However, the reader is alerted to God's script (17:14b).

18:1—19:9 *The death of Absalom*

As his army leaves Mahanaim, David gives orders to spare Absalom, but Joab (18:9–15) deliberately disobeys and kills him in the course of the battle, fought east of the Jordan. When David receives the news, he forgets the victory in his grief over Absalom (19:1–4 [18:33—19:3]) until Joab rebukes him and compels him to go out and see the people (19:5–9). David is severely punished through the death of his son, but he is not rejected by God.

As the beloved crown prince, Absalom would have been the designated heir to the throne. Instead he becomes another "messiah" or "anointed one" (see 19:11) who must die, this time on a tree. By this death a younger son, Solomon (12:24), moves closer to the throne.

19:9–44 *The reconciliation*

The Judahites are won over again to David with the help of the priests Zadok and Abiathar and that of Amasa, Absalom's general (17:25), who is promised to replace Joab (19:11–16). Later, Joab will treacherously assassinate Amasa with impunity (20:9–10, 23) just as he had assassinated Abner (3:27) and Absalom (18:14). David pardons Shimei and the Benjaminites (19:17–23) along with Mephiboshet (19:24–31). After rewarding friends like old Barzillai (19:32–40), David crosses the Jordan at Gilgal, like Joshua of old (19:41). Despite a growing rift with the Judahites, the northern tribes are reconciled to the rule of David (19:10–11, 41–44).

G. 2 Samuel 21—24 / Appendices

In the last four chapters of 2 Samuel, an editor collected several independent accounts about David, all without clear historical context: the Gibeonite revenge killing of seven descendants of Saul (21:1–14), four battles with the Philistines (21:15–22), a copy of Psalm 18 (22:1–51) along with a short psalm presented as the "last words of David" (23:1–7), a list of David's warriors (23:8–39), and the story of the census (chapter 24).

24:1–25 ***The census***

One last sin of David closes the books of Samuel. The sin is the census of the people (24:10). No explanation clarifies why this census is sinful. Perhaps the promise to Abraham of descendants as uncountable as the stars (Gen 15:5; see also 1 Kgs 3:8) lay behind seeing any census of Israel as a sin (yet see Num 1).

The prophet Gad, introduced in the story of David's flight from Saul (1 Sam 22:5), conveys God's judgment and gives David a choice of punishment (24:11–14). David chooses an epidemic of three days to afflict all the people. If the king sins, all the people suffer. The epidemic begins but is halted before it can destroy Jerusalem.

Again under the instructions of Gad, the prophet, an altar is set up on the "threshing floor of Araunah" on the hill north of Jerusalem for holocausts and peace offerings that David himself offers (24:18–25). According to Chronicles, this is the hill upon which the Temple of Jerusalem was built in the reign of Solomon (2 Chr 3:1; see 1 Chr 21). Although this connection is not made in the Deuteronomist history, the identification of this holy place may be the main reason for this story, concluding the books of Samuel and connecting to the books of Kings.

III. The Message of 1 and 2 Samuel

A. Review of Themes

Several prominent themes involving many people and situations seem to govern the stories of 1 and 2 Samuel:

- Suffering as punishment for sin but also a part of salvation (1 Sam 2:1–10; 3:11–14; 4:18; 18:6–30; 31:1–13; 2 Sam 13—20)
- Divine rejection of chosen persons (1 Sam 2:4–8; 13:10–14; 15:10–35; 28:8–15; 31:1–13)
- Divine choice of improbable persons (1 Sam 2:4–8; 16:1–13; 17:12–51)
- The key role of prophecy in Israel (1 Sam 3:1–4:1; 9:26–10:13; 2 Sam 7:1–17; 12:1–25; 24:11–14)
- The ark of the covenant, an important but dispensable symbol (1 Sam 4:4–11; 6:1–7:1; 2 Sam 6:1–19)
- The kingdom as an ambivalent form of God's people (1 Sam 8:1–18; 10:17–24)
- The importance of divine anointing (1 Sam 9:26–10:1; 16:1–13; 24:1–23; 2 Sam 2:1–4)
- Warfare for the good of the people (1 Sam 11:1–15; 13:2—14:22; 17:1–54; 2 Sam 6—8; 10; 21:15–22)
- The messiah king as weak and fallible (1 Sam 13:10–14; 15:10–35; 22:11–19; 2 Sam 11:1—12:25; 24:1–25)
- David as image of God's salvation on earth (1 Sam 16—2 Sam 10)
- The important role of Jerusalem (2 Sam 5:6–12; 6:1–19; 24:16–25)
- The key role of the dynasty of David (2 Sam 7:8–17)

B. The Theology of 1 and 2 Samuel

If we are to find a theological message in the books of Samuel through the historical faith and intentions of the authors, we must remember that they are writing in retrospect. They know the ending of the stories. They must deal with the religious issue: Where is the God in whom they believed as these stories unfolded? How can his saving plan be found in these events? The books of Samuel are supposed to be a description of how Yahweh guided his people from a tribal confederation into a kingdom, as a protection against the oppression of Israel's enemies. The guidance, however, is very strange.

1. Sin and Punishment

Moral failings dog the story in the books of Samuel from the early tales of priestly corruption (1 Sam 2:12–17) to the unexplained sin of David's census (2 Sam 24). The books focus mostly on the sins of the kings, Saul and David, not those of the people. From these sins arise military defeats, political upheaval, and even pestilence for the nation. Saul's career changing sins seem to be trivial, mostly failure to observe some details of the instructions given through the prophet regarding war (1 Sam 13:2–14; 15:4–23). As a result, Saul is rejected. David's sin against Uriah is major, interpreted by the prophet as an abuse of power against a weaker person (2 Sam 11—12). But David is forgiven. All of these failings take center stage in these national epics, whose purpose is to express the identity of Israel.

In these stories no mention is made of the Law or of any written expressions of divine covenantal ordinances; rather, it is the prophetic word that comes as the basis of accusation and judgment (see also 2 Sam 24:11–14), clarifying what is evil from what is right. The stories of priestly corruption or royal abuse of power would seem to presuppose the readers' or listeners' disapproval at the point of telling the story. The prophet's word dispels any doubts as he speaks of divine disapproval in these matters. The prophetic word proclaiming God and the divine sense of right and wrong serves to limit sacred and royal power and authority.

Other sins of Saul are not accompanied by prophetic judgment but seem to elicit the disapproval of the readers. Saul's attempt to kill David is described as the influence of "an evil spirit" (1 Sam 18:10–11). The story of Saul's slaughter of the priests of Nob includes the refusal of the king's servants to be part of such a deed (22:11–19). Saul's consultation of the medium of Endor appears as the king's efforts to circumvent God's refusal to communicate (28:5–19), a point then made by the dead prophet consulted (28:16).

The sins of the Davidic princes are described without mention either of the Law or of prophetic denunciation. Amnon's rape of his sister is interpreted by Tamar herself as something "that is not done in Israel" (*lo' ye'aseh ken beyisra'el*; 2 Sam 13:12).

Absalom's murder of his brother, Amnon, along with his attacks on his father, David, cause grief to David but remain without moral commentary by the storyteller or the characters in the story, except for attempts to downplay the evil (see 14:1–11). The same is true of Joab's murder of Absalom (18:14; 19:2–9).

2. The God of Failure and Disaster

The kingdom arises only after two failed attempts. First, the family of Eli calls on "Yahweh of hosts" to accompany Israel as it tries to defend itself against the attack of the Philistines. The result is defeat, the capture of the ark, and the death of Eli and his family (1 Sam 4).

The faith of the authors moves them to see God present in this disaster. They express that faith by connecting that disaster to the sins of Eli's family and the terrifying words of condemnation through the prophet Samuel issued before the events (1 Sam 3:11–14). They also express that faith by the story of God having the ark returned in a wondrous manner and without any help from the Israelites (chapters 5—6). God is still in charge, but the lesson is learned. God's protective presence cannot be manipulated by any earthly thing, even by a sacred object like the ark. God chooses to let historical events play out. He can work with historical contingency. But he is not capricious.

In a second misstep, God calls Saul to the kingship through his prophet Samuel, a leadership that starts with military success (1 Sam 10—14). Yet God then rejects Saul, who is stricken with an "evil spirit" and eventually killed in battle. Saul becomes the tragic figure in which election and destruction seem ever more closely bound.

The authors of Samuel are willing to gaze also into this disaster and still find God, the God who raises up the humble and deposes the mighty. Although the authors link the disaster to sins of Saul, these sins are not at all clear, as the demise of Saul is woven into the rise of David.

David finally becomes king through a series of events guided by divine providence (2 Sam 2—5). This occurs only after David is protected from the lethal attacks of God's other anointed messiah (1 Sam 19—30). Retrospect gives us a perspective to see the hand of God guiding events. David is an unlikely candidate. He comes forth despite many mistakes. Just as God picked the wrong king to start, Jesse picked the wrong sons to show Samuel. David failed to find support in the royal palace, and Saul had sons to succeed him. The author of the story seems to delight in the portrayal of these obstacles, because they all show the hand of God moving David to the throne. For a while David does it all right, and Saul does it all wrong. Human decisions, of course, are made, but God must be there on the sidelines calling the plays. We see, therefore, in the rise of David a combination of historical events and divine providence—divine providence inexorably moving history according to God's plan yet bouncing around in the contingency of human decisions.

The saving presence of God seems finally institutionalized as we read of David's military victories (2 Sam 6—8 and10) and of God's promise to his dynasty through the prophet Nathan (2 Sam 7). Once on the throne, however, David sins (2 Sam 11—12). The peace of his kingdom collapses. We then read of incest, murder, and rebellion. In the Davidic monarchy, what appeared to be a clear sacrament of God's saving presence becomes a screen behind which God seems to withdraw.

All this was predicted by Samuel, who warned the people of an overbearing kingship (1 Sam 8:4–18). All this conforms to the Deuteronomist theology of a conditional covenant. God can be present as a blessing or a curse (Deut 11:26–31; 30:15–20). God is not absent. But his presence takes on an ominous and destructive quality. Yahweh is not the God of the domesticated garden but rather the God of the dangerous wilderness. The tone is set for the Book of Kings. The cracks have emerged, but the gaping abyss will appear only at the end of the next books.

The authors of Samuel were willing to gaze into this ugly picture to see the presence of God. This picture formed the heart of the stories that Israel would tell its posterity about itself, about its identity and its relationship with God. Other nations would tell stories of unmitigated heroism and nobility. Israel tells stories of sin, failures, and disasters. God is present through the prophetic words of Samuel, Nathan, and Gad, but God operates in historical contingency, in a flow of ups and downs. The final editors of Samuel clearly saw these stories as speaking to the exiles in Babylon. Later readers could see these stories as speaking for all times.

3. The God of David

In the meantime, for all his sinfulness, for all his tragic weaknesses, the person of David becomes a symbol of God's presence. The portrayal of the early David is for sure idealized by the storytellers. As God's anointed, David takes on impressive theological significance. He is God's representative, the messiah. He is a "son of God." In his reign divine justice should be experienced. Down the road, theological hope will be expressed in terms of a future anointed king, a future messiah, a future David.

The authors of Samuel present us with a hero who is very human, allowing us to view God's presence through David's eyes. He is introduced as "a skillful musician, a valiant soldier, an intelligent speaker, a handsome man" (1 Sam 16:18). As a man of honor, David is a loyal friend of Jonathan and maintains his profound respect for Saul as God's messiah as well as for Saul's family, despite the mortal rivalry which that family posed for David. Very appealing to the modern reader is the depth of feeling David exhibits at the death of Saul and Jonathan. With magnanimity he pardons former adversaries. As a deeply religious man, David accepts the word of the prophets with reverence and humility and basically seeks the will of God in his political decisions.

At the same time, David's life is full of struggle. Recruited into the service of Saul, David quickly suffers the effects of Saul's "evil spirit," reducing David to a fugitive powerless to attack his adversary. Although the story of the defeat of Goliath stresses David's courage and calm, the storyteller does not miss the chance to highlight the danger to the young David. David's rise to the throne of all Israel is marred by the hostility of the northern tribes and the brutality of his own general. He begs in vain for God to spare the life of his illegitimate son and then has to face the lethal hostility of his favorite son—only to find him dead. The portrayal of David grieving over Absalom is one of utter desolation. It is only in this desolation that David finds God—who also according to later prophets grieves over his children (Hos 11:1–4; Isa 1:2; Mal 1:6). The "charism of kingship," like that of judgeship, takes a heavy toll on the recipient of the gift.

Yet David is faithful. The last scene is one of David worshiping Yahweh. He is bound to God, who strengthens him in war and chastises him in life. He listens to the prophets. He repents. He keeps going. The figure of David thus becomes the figure of a faithful servant facing personal darkness with the trust that God must be there.

Focused on all that was great in David, Matthew the evangelist understood how the hope of Israel was looking for a son of David. In telling the story of "Jesus Christ, the son of David" (Matt 1:1), Matthew insists on seeing God's salvation in the form of a "king of the Jews" (2:2). This title is also the inscription on the cross (27:37). The blind and the weak call out to Jesus, "son of David" (9:27; 15:22; 20:30). For Matthew the promise to David of an everlasting throne and kingdom (2 Sam 7:13, 16) would be fulfilled in Jesus, the anointed of God, who would be with his disciples, "always, until the end of the age" (Matt 28:20).

5
1 and 2 Kings

I. Overview

At the origins of the monarchy in Israel and especially at the foundation of the Davidic dynasty, the hopes of Israel ran high. These were hopes in a dynasty blessed by God and guaranteed by a promise of perpetuity.

With the passage of four centuries, however, history appeared to contradict these hopes. The first disaster occurred in 932 BC when the northern tribes seceded from the tribal union established under Saul and David, setting up a new dynasty and a new kingdom to rival that of Judah. In 722 BC, Samaria, the capital of the new northern kingdom, was besieged and captured by Shalmaneser V, and the ten northern tribes are carried off to Assyria never to return (2 Kgs 17). The southern kingdom of Judah did not fare much better. In 587 BC, the southern kingdom fell to the Babylonians led by the great Nebuchadnezzar. The Temple was burned to the ground. Jerusalem was destroyed. The independent rule of the Davidic kings came to a jarring halt (2 Kgs 25). Was the faith of Israel and its hopes in divine promises all one massive illusion? How could a good and faithful God allow this?

A. The story line

Writing in Babylon for the disillusioned exiles, the authors of Kings examine the history of the kingdoms without glossing over the disasters. The authors in fact seem to go out of their way to emphasize the ugliness of the story. The books of Kings open with David, an old, cold, and impotent man (1 Kgs 1:1–4). Through a palace intrigue, Solomon is named successor over his older and ambitious brother, Adonijah (1 Kgs 1:5–53). The story of Solomon ends on the sour note of his sins (1 Kgs 2—11). An unfavorable judgment is leveled on the vast majority of the kings. Even more emphatically, a general condemnation of the kings appear in the comments given at the major divisions of the history, at the end of Solomon's reign (1 Kgs 11), at the destruction of the northern kingdom (2 Kgs 17:7–23), and at the downfall of the southern kingdom (2 Kgs 24:1–4). By no means is this story like the obsequious court annals of ancient Egypt and Mesopotamia.

The Book of Kings is really a prophetic indictment of Israel and Judah. It is a theological history of the kingdoms. As is clear from editorial comments, the authors' purpose was to point out the causes of the fall of the kingdoms. They were, first, the failure of the kings to observe the monotheism demanded by God in the Sinai covenant and, secondly, the nonobservance, especially for the northern kingdom, of the unity of sanctuary in Jerusalem. This institutional sin along with Ba'alist contamination of Israel's faith led to the death of the northern kingdom. The catastrophe of 586 BC then followed inexorably as a punishment for the failures of the southern kings.

The appearance of the prophets reminds us of God's presence in this discouraging history. Nathan dominates the palace intrigues that lead David to select Solomon, whom Nathan then anoints as king (1 Kgs 1). The prophet Ahijah is instrumental in the designation of the northern kingdom's first king, Jeroboam (1 Kgs 11:29–38). With the evil reign of Ahab and Jezebel in the north, the authors of Kings introduce the stories of Elijah (1 Kgs 17—19; 2 Kgs 1). Succeeding Elijah, Elisha then enters the scene (2 Kgs 2—9; 13:14–21). Meanwhile, the prophet Micaiah son of Imlah appears before both Ahab and Jehoshaphat to announce God's intention to let Israel march to destruction (1 Kgs 22). Isaiah counsels King Hezekiah (2 Kgs 19—20), and Huldah, the last prophet to appear in this narrative, counsels King Josiah (2 Kgs 22:14–20).

B. The Composition of the Books of Kings

The authors of Kings clearly refer to three pre-exilic written sources for their lengthy account: "the book of the chronicles of Solomon" (1 Kgs 11:41), "the book of the chronicles of the kings of Israel" (1 Kgs 14:18 and passim), and "the book of the chronicles of the kings of Judah" (1 Kgs 14:29 and passim). We can assume that the stories of the prophets, especially those which could stand alone without a reference to kings, were passed down independently in prophetic circles.

While critics are undecided on the provenance of the Book of Kings as a whole, a number of texts (1 Kgs 4:24; 8:46–53; 9:1–9; 2 Kgs 17:19–20; 21:10–15; 22:16–20; 23:26–27; 24:2–4; 25:27–30) indicate that Kings was written late in the Exile in Babylon. Other texts seem to point to a pre-exilic origin, roughly the time of Josiah (1 Kgs 8:8; 2 Kgs 8:22; 17:24–34). This diversity most likely reflects the different sources used by the compilers.

This collection of stories probably underwent several editions. Some indications suggest a first collection at the time of Josiah (640–609 BC), triggered perhaps by the discovery of the "the book of the Law" around 622 BC. From its concluding statements concerning King Jehoiachin (2 Kgs 25:27–30) and its silence about the release from exile under Cyrus, the final edition took place after 561 BC, the thirty-seventh year of exile, but before 538, the liberating edict of Cyrus.

Clearly written as one continuous work, the account was later divided into two books or scrolls. The work as a whole falls into three major parts:

1 Kings 1—11:	The history of Solomon's reign
1 Kings 12—2 Kings 17:	The synoptic history of the northern and southern parts of Solomon's divided kingdom
2 Kings 18—25:	The history of the surviving southern kingdom until its downfall in 586 BC

C. Chronology of Events Described

The events described in 1 and 2 Kings span the period from roughly 970 BC, the last year of King David, to 561 BC, the release of Jehoiachin in Babylon. This is the period of the Etruscans and the founding of Rome in Italy, the founding of Carthage in Africa, the rise of the Assyrian Empire and its conquest by the Babylonian Empire in Mesopotamia, as well as the succession from the twenty-first to the twenty-sixth dynasties in Egypt. It was a period of repeated invasions and conquests. Carved stones or stele throughout the Middle East along with baked clay tablets from Mesopotamian archives describing these military activities allow us to identify and date many of the wars and other political events mentioned in Kings.

970	The death of David and the succession of Solomon
932	The secession of the northern tribes under Jeroboam I
927	The attack of Pharaoh Shishak (Shoshenq I) of Egypt
882–871	Omri's founding of Samaria, the new capital of the northern kingdom
874–852	The mission of Elijah
854	The battle of Qarqar, temporarily halting the Assyrian westward advance
852–793	The mission of Elisha
734–732	The Syro-Ephraimite war and the attack by Tiglath-pileser III of Assyria
724–722	The Assyrian siege and destruction of Samaria under Shalmaneser V and Sargon II
715–686	The twenty-nine year reign of Hezekiah, designated coregent/heir apparent in 728
701	The attack and siege of Jerusalem by the Assyrian Sennacherib
640–609	The thirty-one year reign of Josiah
622	Religious reforms and the discovery of "the book of the Law" in the Temple

612	The fall of Nineveh to the Babylonian king, Nabopolassar
609–598	The eleven-year reign of Jehoiakim
605	The battle of Carchemish, a victory of the Babylonians over the Egyptian-Assyrian alliance
598	The capture of Jerusalem by the Babylonian Nebuchadnezzar and the first deportation
598–587	The eleven-year reign of Zedekiah
587	The capture and destruction of Jerusalem by Nebuchadnezzar, the destruction of Solomon's Temple, the exile of the people of Judah, and the end of the Davidic kingdom
561	The release of exiled Jehoiachin from prison

D. Glimpses into the Beginnings of Biblical Literature

The late editorial additions with their comments and evaluations refer to the existence of "the Law of Moses" or "the book of the Law of Moses" (1 Kgs 2:3; 2 Kgs 10:31; 14:6) at the time of the final editing of the books of Kings in the mid-sixth century. However, the older sources giving the story line events show no such existence before the discovery of "the book of the Law" during the reign of King Josiah, around 622 BC (2 Kgs 22:8–13). Until that time divine guidance took place through the oral instructions of the prophets. This seventh-century event may well mark the beginning of "the Bible" as we know it.

If not an editorial addition, the emphasized linking in 2 Kings 23:21–23 of the feast of Passover with the reign of Josiah (640–609 BC) evidences a major development in the Exodus traditions at this time (see also 1 Kgs 6:1; 8:51, 53; 12:28; 2 Kgs 21:15). Whatever is behind this "discovery," some text of the Law—perhaps something close to the Book of Deuteronomy—must have existed before the Exile. Otherwise it would be difficult to explain the intense postexilic interest in the Law as a means of reconstructing the identity of the Jews (see Neh 8—9).

The story of Solomon stresses his wisdom and his composition of proverbs (1 Kgs 5:9–12). The courtly setting with its new "leisure" class could very likely have prompted the early development of what we know as the Book of Proverbs—an appropriation of even earlier Egyptian literature. The social setting, beginning with Solomon and extending through the period of the divided monarchy, also could likely have led to the written composition of oral traditions about the patriarchs and the Exodus, developing the strands (J and E) that scholars now identify as woven into our books of Genesis, Exodus, and Numbers. Likewise, the religious setting of the Temple liturgy that developed during these centuries would have led to the eventual composition of many of the psalms.

It is also during this period that we should see the origins of the prophetic books of our Bible. From the eighth century on, prophets arose in both the northern and southern kingdoms whose preachings were somehow recorded. Most likely disciples of these prophets captured their oral preaching into notes, which were then collected and edited into longer "books." These collections were likely preserved in special prophetic circles prior to the Exile and became highly regarded after events showed the validity of the prophecies—often long after the death of the prophets.

If we look carefully at the editorial editions and therefore at the theology of the sixth century, we find frequent reference to the Exodus traditions with a clear effort to unite those traditions to the covenant or Horeb [Sinai] traditions. As evidenced by its vocabulary and Deuteronomist themes, 1 Kings 8 appears as an editorial clarification from the hand of the Deuteronomist. Here we have reference to "the ark" and "the two stone tablets which Moses had put there at Horeb when Yahweh made a covenant with the Israelites at their departure from the land of Egypt" (8:9; see 8:21, 51, 53; 2 Kgs 17:36). The story of the Exodus as we know it from the Torah (Pentateuch)—or at least from Deuteronomy—is taking form.

The reference to God's "covenant with Abraham, Isaac, and Jacob" (2 Kgs 13:23) is probably a Deuteronomistic comment, a judgment based on the similarity with Deuteronomy 4:31. But the reference to "the God of Abraham, Isaac, and Israel" found in the ancient Elijah stories (1 Kgs 18:36) suggests at least the oral traditions of the patriarchs were circulating at the time of Elijah (see also 1 Kgs 18:31), traditions that we now have in the Book of Genesis. Other subtle details in the Elijah stories parallel elements from the story of Moses (see 1 Kgs 18:21—19:18), but it is difficult to know whether these elements originated in the Elijah circles or the Moses circles. In any case, the time of the kings from Solomon on is the most likely period for the development of the early traditions (J, E, and D) now woven together with postexilic priestly traditions (P) in our Torah or Pentateuch.

II. Significant Passages in the Books of Kings

A. 1 Kings 1—11 / Solomon

The story of Solomon is centered on the building of the Temple (5:15—9:25). Before that account, Solomon is introduced as the one endowed with wisdom, riches, and glory, carrying the great hope that charged his early reign (3:1—5:14). After the account about the building of the Temple, things change. Solomon's fame, wealth, and wisdom appear more in the king's personal service. His sins invite God's anger (9:26—11:13). Just as the earlier part stressed the security of Solomon's power (2:12–46), so the later part emphasizes threats and attacks (11:14–25). Framing the entire account are stories of prophetic interventions: Nathan's maneuvers to bring Solomon to power over the twelve tribes (1:1—2:11) and Ahijah's gesture foretelling the loss of the northern tribes (11:26–43). These chapters on Solomon thus form a chiastic structure, a structure of inverted symmetry like the Greek letter *chi* (X):

A: prophetic intervention (1:1—2:11)
 B: security (2:12–46)
  C: promise (3:1—5:14)
   D: the Temple (5:15—9:25)
  C′: disappointment (9:26—11:13)
 B′: insecurity (11:14–25)
A′: prophetic intervention (11:26–43)

1:1–53 ***The succession of Solomon***

First Kings 1—2 contains the finale of the court history of David (2 Sam 9—20; 1 Kgs 1—2) and covers the story of Solomon's succession to the throne. With the help of Joab, David's military commander, and Abiathar, the priest, Adonijah, David's oldest son, attempts to have himself declared David's successor (1:5–10). Nathan the prophet, however, intervenes. With the help of Bathsheba he apparently concocts a ruse about a fictitious promise (1:13), and the two persuade David to nominate Solomon as king. Zadok the priest sides with this faction and anoints Solomon (1:11–40). The narrator says nothing about any divine intervention in his choice, although this succession of Solomon is accompanied by prayer (1:36–37, 48).

2:1–46 ***The death of David***

The hand of the Deuteronomistic editors can be seen in opening lines (2:3–4) of David's "farewell address," with its reference to the statutes, commands, and ordinances written in the Law of Moses and the need to be faithful to God with one's whole heart and whole soul. This is the first mention of the written Law of God since the Book of Joshua. The books of Kings will make repeated references to the "statutes and commands" of Yahweh, many in sections that reflect the Deuteronomists' thought and style, usually an indication of an editorial insertion. Here also is the Deuteronomistic insistence on the conditional character of God's promise of dynastic indefectibility ("If your sons so conduct themselves..."; 2:4), in contrast to the unconditional promise in Samuel 7:14–15.

After narrating David's death and farewell address, the story describes the destruction of the Adonijah faction. Interpreting Adonijah's request to marry Abishag, David's last wife, as pretension to the throne, Solomon proceeds to kill him (2:25). There follow then neutralization of Abiathar (2:26–27), the death of Joab (2:28–35), and that of Shimei, the pardoned Benjaminite who had cursed David (2:36–46). The section ends with the description of Solomon "with royal power firmly in his grasp" (2:46). What did the writer-editors think of all this? They describe David as apparently advising the killing of Joab and Shimei (2:5–9). Yet the contrast with David's accession to the throne is striking.

3:1–28 ***Solomon's wisdom***

The authors now portray the promising start of Solomon's reign. "Solomon loved Yahweh and obeyed the statutes of his father David" (3:3). At Gibeon, about seven miles northwest of Jerusalem, Solomon's dream revelation functions to incorporate his reign into Yahweh's covenant with Israel and David in particular (3:5–14). Along with the gift of wisdom, God bestows on Solomon the gifts of riches, fame, and long life. Yet these endowments rest on the condition expressed by God, "If you follow me by keeping my statutes and commandments" (3:14).

The first gift requested by Solomon is a "listening heart" needed to govern the people and to distinguish good from evil (3:9). God responds by giving an unparalleled wise and understanding heart (3:12), so that the people see that the king has "the wisdom of God (*hochmat 'elohim*) in him" (3:28). This wisdom appears as a type of encyclopedic knowledge and skill in formulating proverbs (5:9–14). Included in this gift, however, is also that of clever administrative prudence, dramatized by the well-known story of the rival mothers claiming the same child (3:16–28). Wisdom here appears as far superior to long life, riches, and victory over enemies (3:11), an affirmation of the

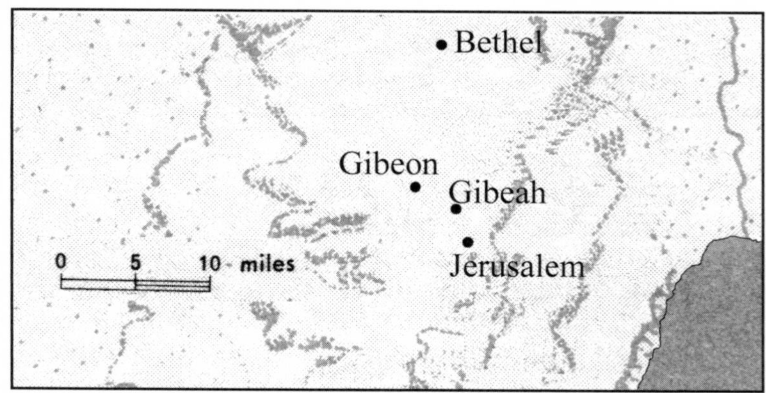

5A: Map of Gibeon, Gibeah, Jerusalem

importance of the understanding heart or mind for a good life. Such wisdom remains a gift of God and is in effect an initiation into the life of God (3:28).

Later biblical editors will ascribe the body of biblical Wisdom literature to Solomon, much like the Law is ascribed to Moses and the Psalms to David. Biblical Wisdom literature may in fact stem from the time of Solomon when the wealthy court population, appearing now for the first time in Israel, was faced with the need for education in such matters. The option to seek human transformation and refinement in the mind or heart rather than in riches or military might is thus traced to Solomon.

6:1–38 *Solomon's Temple*

One of the wonders of the ancient world and the first elaborate edifice dedicated to Yahweh was the Solomonic Temple of Jerusalem, in Hebrew named simply "the house" (*ha-bayit*). As modern archaeology indicates, the building was erected on the hill just north of the city of David where at present the Muslim Dome of the Rock is located—which according to 1 Chronicles 22:1 would be Ornan's (Araunah's) threshing floor (2 Sam 24:15–25). The construction work was done by Phoenicians (5:20) and forced Israelite labor (5:27).

Although the account in chapter 6 is detailed, we get only a general sketch of the shape of the edifice. We can distinguish a type of outer porch (*ha-'ulam*), ten by twenty cubits (fifteen by thirty feet) in size, and behind it a rectangular building (*ha-hekal*) about thirty cubits (forty-five feet) high with a floor plan of about sixty by twenty cubits (ninety by thirty feet). This building was reserved for the cultic personnel and the sacred furnishings. In the back third of the building, a sanctuary (*ha-debir*), twenty by twenty cubits (thirty by thirty feet), sheltered the ark of the covenant along with cherubim statues, functioning like winged guardians of the ark, and other treasure (see Gen 3:24; Ezek 28:14–16). This inner sanctuary was also called "the holy of holies" (8:6), a Semitic way of forming the superlative adjective, "the holiest." Around the building was an annex (*yazia'*) and a series of large courts where the people gathered. The general architecture of the Temple clearly reflects Phoenician influence, as

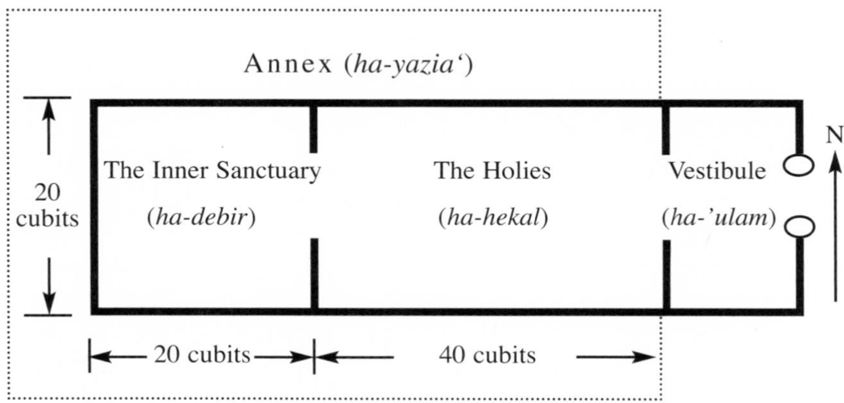

5B: Floor Plan of Temple

1 Kings 5:15–32 admits. The Solomonic Temple was clearly not renowned for its size but apparently for its beauty—constructed of white limestone, cedar woodwork, gold, silver, and precious fabrics—and for the "mysterious presence" of God (later called the *shekinah*) above the ark in the holy of holies.

For the Deuteronomist editors of this history, the Temple had great significance. It was to be the only place chosen by God where sacrifice was to be offered to Yahweh (Deut 12:4–6). The symbolic dating of this construction, 480 years (12 x 40) after the Exodus (6:1), suggests that this Temple was the end term of Yahweh's rescue of his people. Yet the oracle given to Solomon stressing obedience to God (6:11–13) implies that continued existence of the Temple was conditional (see also 3:14; 9:4–9). Obedience was more important than sacrificial worship. God was greater than the Temple.

8:1–13 ***The dedication of the Temple***

The leaders of all the tribes gather for a great celebration. The month is Tishri (September/October), here called Ethanim (8:2). The seven-day festival would therefore be Succoth, the feast of Booths (or Tabernacles), one of the three great annual feast days in Israel. The priests place the ark of Yahweh along with the sacred vessels in the holy of holies, establishing continuity between the Temple worship and Israel's ancient religious traditions.

According to the later editorial addition, the ark contained "the stone tablets that Moses had put there at Horeb when Yahweh made a covenant with the Israelites" (8:9). Again we see a Deuteronomistic allusion to the Law of God (see 2:3). After this story of the dedication of the Temple, the Deuteronomist history never speaks of the ark again.

God responds as he responded in the desert (Exod 40:34–35; see also Ezek 43:5), filling the inner sanctuary with a sign of his presence, the "dark cloud" (1 Kgs 8:10–12). The Temple is intended to be a place where God "may abide forever" (8:13).

It is clear how important the Temple is for the Deuteronomist historians. Yet this importance will not prevent God from allowing the Temple to be destroyed because of the sins of the kings and people. The editors know this and will state this in no uncertain terms.

9:1–9 *A promise and a warning*

A theophany like that at Gibeon (3:5–14) concludes the dedication of the Temple. The appearance of God provides the theology that dominates the books of Kings. God blesses the Temple, placing there his "name," "eyes," and "heart" (9:3), promising Solomon to confirm his throne "forever" (9:5). This promise, however, depends on a condition, keeping God's "statutes and decrees" (see 3:14; 6:12–13). If the king and Israel fail to keep the commandments and statutes and worship strange gods, then "this Temple shall become a heap of ruins" (9:8). Infidelity at this point will entail not just the fall of a dynasty or the defeat of an army, but total destruction of the Temple and wholesale deportation of the people (9:7). The exilic theology of the Deuteronomist historian clearly appears here.

11:1–13 *Solomon's sins*

Before mentioning the appearance of enemies who would expose cracks in the glorious Solomonic façade (11:14–23), the writers speak explicitly of Solomon's sins. The critique starts with the foreign marriages, many no doubt political marriages of convenience, which led Solomon to build temples for the foreign gods of his foreign wives, as Deuteronomy 7:3–4 warned against (see also Exod 34:11–16).

For the third time God speaks directly to Solomon (see also 3:5 and 9:2). This time we hear a word of judgment in language reflecting a similar judgment of Saul (1 Sam 15:28). The first disaster is decreed, the kingdom will be divided—the first step toward the final catastrophe of 587 BC.

11:26–43 ***The beginning of the secession of Israel***

Jeroboam, an Ephraimite labor foreman, is abetted by Ahijah, a prophet from Shiloh (also in Ephraim) to rebel against Solomon, just as Bathsheba and Solomon were encouraged by Nathan (1:11–45). The prophecy of the divided kingdom comes first in the form of a prophetic gesture, the tearing of the prophet's cloak (see 1 Sam 15:27–28; see also John 19:23–24). Jeroboam is offered a promise like the promise to David (2 Sam 7), but only on condition that he follow God's ways, statutes, and commandments (11:38). At first thwarted in his apparent rebellion, Jeroboam flees to Egypt (11:40). After Solomon's death he returns (12:2) and becomes the first king of the northern kingdom upon its secession in 932 BC.

This section of Kings then ends with the standard summary regarding the reign of the kings of both Judah and Israel. The number forty for the number of years in the reign of Solomon might be the typical approximation found in ancient Semitic stories.

B. 1 Kings 12—2 Kings 17 / The Synoptic History of the Kings

Provoked by the obstinacy of Rehoboam, the split in 932 BC was in fact more of a return to the original disunity of the twelve-tribe confederation. In extent, wealth, and manpower the northern kingdom far surpassed the southern, but its wealth invited attack, and its tribal rivalries left it continually prone to political upheavals.

In this part of Kings the writers juxtapose excerpts from the respective chronicles of Israel and Judah to present a synoptic view of both kingdoms. Their procedure is to complete the narrative of each reign once begun then deal with the concurrent reigns in the other kingdom. For each reign the writers follow a formula: the synchronization of the beginning of the reign under consideration with that of the other kingdom, the length of the reign, the judgment on how the king observed the covenant and the unity of sanctuary, the citation of the writers' sources, something about the death of the king, and the name of his successor. For the southern kings the writers add a note about the age of the king and the name of his mother.

The attempt to coordinate the kings of Judah and Israel in a synoptic history has long baffled many biblical scholars. The biblical data for the most part can be followed, however, if we allow for two important factors. First and most important, a coregency allowed the reign of a father and son to overlap. We in fact read about the coregency of Uzziah and Jotham (2 Kgs 15:5). I would suggest this system of father and son ruling together also for Jehoash and Jeroboam II in the north as well as for Asa and Jehoshaphat, Amaziah and Uzziah, Ahaz and Hezekiah in the south. In Kings *the length of the rule of a king* usually, but not always, extends into his coregency, while *the date when he "became king,"* indicated in terms of the year of reign of the rival king, is linked in general to the year when the king became sole ruler.

The second factor that allows us to use the biblical data in the synchronization of the kings is the way the southern kingdom tended to "postdate" the accession of the king, counting the number of years in a reign only from the first New Year's enthronement ceremony, not counting the first partial year of the reign. The northern kingdom, on the other hand, seemed to count the first even partial year of a reign. Furthermore, the unit of the year was measured at times from fall to fall; at other times, from spring to spring. Many difficulties remain; however, by using these factors we can employ almost all the chronological indications in Kings (see appendix 2) to make the synoptic history of the kings shown below.

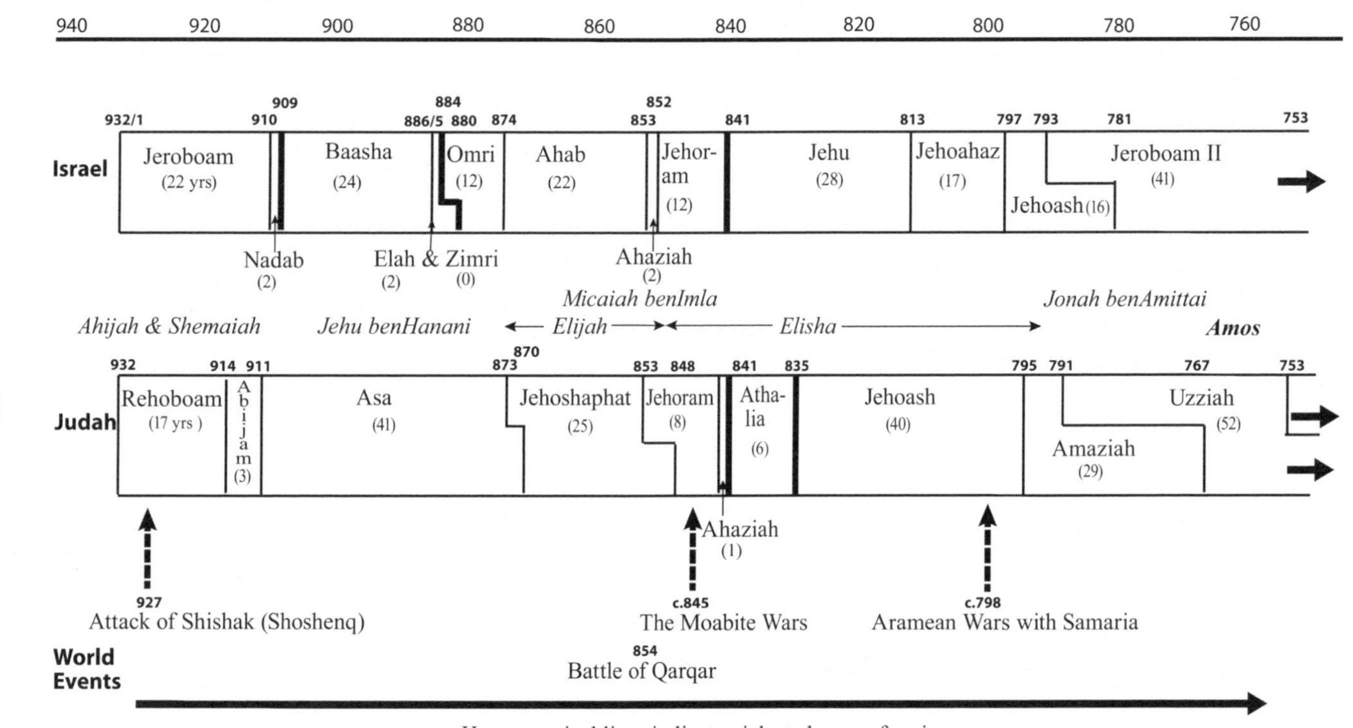

5Ca: Synoptic History of the Kings

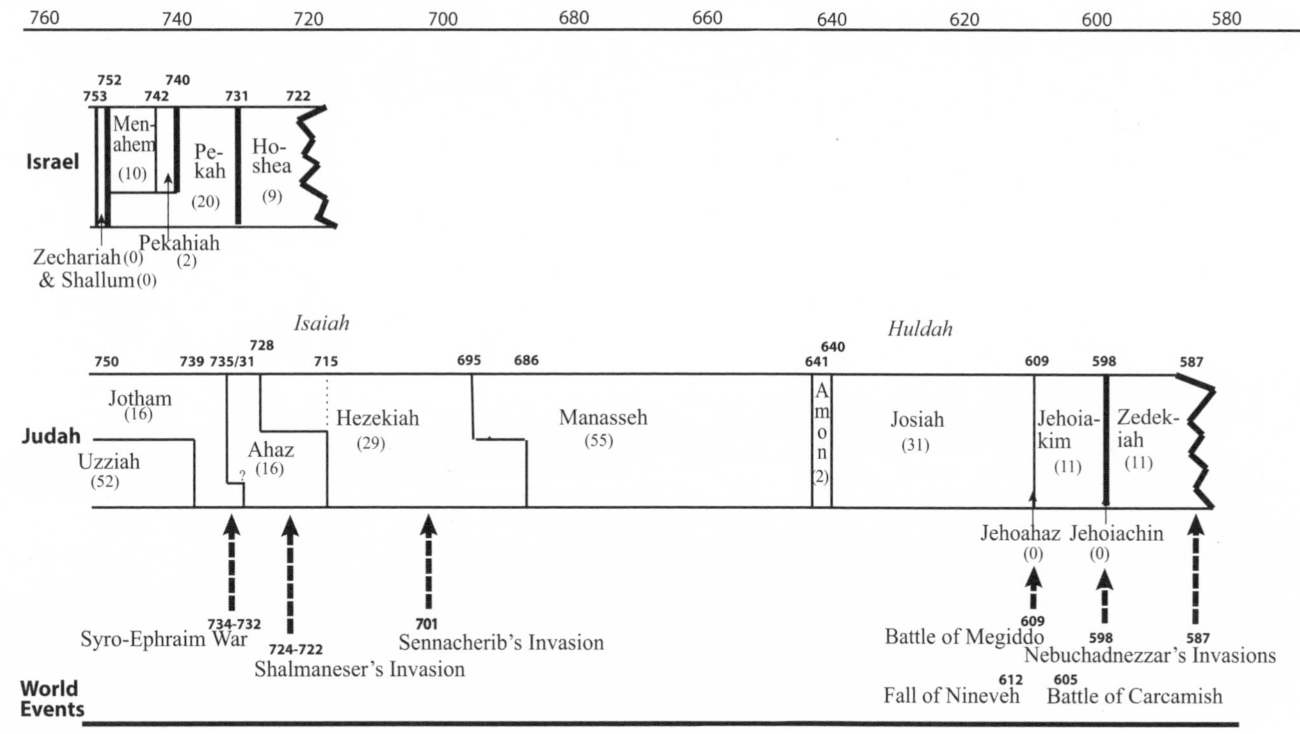

5Cb: Synoptic History of the Kings

12:1–25 ***The secession***

Rehoboam, Solomon's son, inherits the discontent of his father's subjects. Arrogantly threatening the northern tribes assembled at Shechem with more oppression than his father (12:11), he loses them forever to the dynasty of David. The intervention of Shemaiah, a "man of God" or prophet, prevents warfare (12:21–24). Rather sympathetic to the northern cause (possibly indicating a northern tradition incorporated here), the authors are clear about the theological cause underlying the catastrophe. The sins of Solomon have lead God to rip apart the kingdom of David as Ahijah ripped his cloak (11:1–35).

12:26–32 ***The shrines of Israel***

For political reasons, Jeroboam I, son of Nebat, builds temples at Dan and Bethel, at the northern and southern extremities of the northern kingdom. This is the great "sin of Jeroboam" that infects all the later northern kings in the eyes of the southern authors and leads to the blanket condemnation of all the northern kings. It disobeys the order in Deuteronomy to perform all sacrifices and offerings in "the place Yahweh, your God, chooses out of all your tribes and picks as his dwelling" (Deut 12:5). This ordinance along with the Book of Deuteronomy is much later than the time of Jeroboam, and therefore the condemnation is anachronistic. However, the Deuteronomistic editors are trying to understand the utter destruction of the northern kingdom in 722 BC and searching for an underlying sin that would have provoked God to allow this disaster to occur.

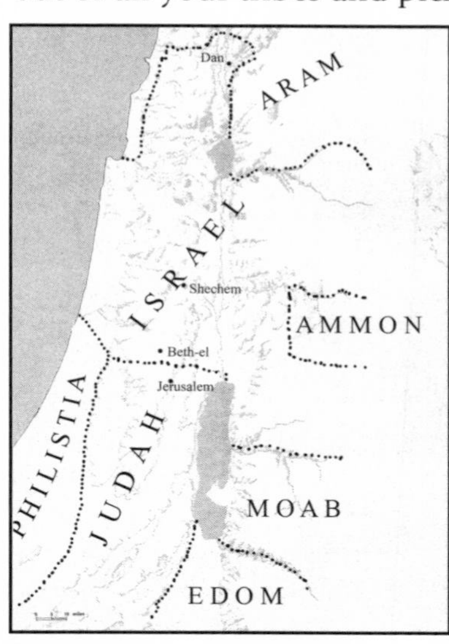

5D: Map of the Divided Kingdom

Jeroboam also ordains his own priests outside of the Levitical order and institutes feast days to rival the festivals at the Temple in Jerusalem (12:31–32). The "calves" of Jeroboam (12:28, 32) may in fact have been a sarcastic reference to statues of bulls—an incorporation of Ba'alist themes—to replace the cherubim on the ark for the throne of God.

13:1–34 ***Two unnamed prophets***

Several stories from prophetic traditions appear in connection with Jeroboam. One is about an unnamed prophet ("man of God") from Judah who denounces the king (13:1–10). Connected with that story is a legend about "an old prophet" who tricks the "man of God" from Judah into breaking a command of God and thus getting killed, convincing the "old prophet" that the "man of God from Judah" was speaking the truth (13:11–32).

The themes of these stories include the quasi-magical power of God's word, the courage of true prophets, God's protection of prophets from secular power (see 2 Kgs 1:1–16), the testing of prophets by opposing prophets, and eventually the destruction of the altar of Bethel.

The hand of the seventh-century editors can be found in the "prediction" of King Josiah's reform, described in 2 Kings 23:1–25, where we find an interlocking reference (23:16–19) back to the story of the man of God from Judah. The promise, "a child shall be born to the house of David," reflects the optimistic celebrations at the birth of Davidic princes. The vocabulary reminds us of the promise of Isaiah (Isa 9:5).

14:1–20 ***Ahijah the prophet***

Another story of the prophet Ahijah follows, also rooted in the prophetic traditions that are woven so prominently into this Book of Kings. Here Ahijah pronounces the coming death not only of the royal prince, Abijah (14:12–13), but also of the whole house of Jeroboam (14:10–11), and the entire kingdom of Israel (14:15–16). The Deuteronomist editor makes sure we see these evils as punishment for the sins of the king (14:8–9, 16).

After a twenty–two year reign (932/1–910 BC), Jeroboam is succeeded by his son, Nadab (910–909), who is assassinated by Baasha (15:25–31). The scene (14:21–31) then switches to the south and the seventeen-year reign of Rehoboam (932–914 BC). Rehoboam is also condemned for cultic acts, probably the Ba'alist fertility cults of Canaan (14:23–24). The attack and pillaging in 927 BC by Shishak, known in Egyptian texts as Shoshenq, thus appear as divine punishment. Rehoboam is followed by his son Abijam (15:1–8, called Abijah in 2 Chr 12:16). He rules three years (914–911 BC) and is succeeded by his reforming son Asa (15:9–24), whose reign extends forty-one years (911–870 BC).

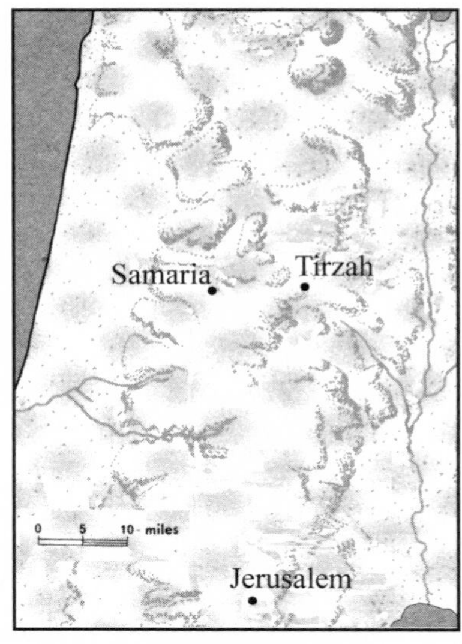

5E: Map of Tirzah, Samaria

Meanwhile up north, Baasha assassinates Nadab (15:27), takes over, and rules twenty-four years (909–886/5 BC). His son Elah succeeds him but is assassinated along with his whole family by Zimri around 884 BC (16:8–11). Zimri, Tibni, and Omri (all generals in the Israelite army) wage internecine war (16:15–22).

16:23–28 *The reign of Omri*

Omri is finally successful and leaves the city of Tirzah, where the northern kings from Jeroboam had ruled. He founds the new capital of Samaria, which will be the seat of the northern kingdom until it is destroyed in 722 BC. Judged unfaithful by the authors, nothing more is said about Omri, who ruled twelve years (884–873 BC). From secular historical records we suspect that he was one of Israel's greatest kings.

16:29–33 *The reign of Ahab*

Ahab (874–853 BC) succeeds his father Omri and marries Jezebel, a Phoenician princess and an ardent apostle of Canaanite Baʿalism. During the period of the Omrid dynasty (Omri, Ahab, Ahaziah, and Joram), two great crises arise: first, the attempt by the palace to wipe out the Yahwist religion in the north and replace it with Baʿalism, and second, the near extinction of the Davidic dynasty caused by Athaliah, Ahab's daughter (2 Kgs 11). Both crises are spearheaded by Jezebel.

The daughter of King Ethba'al of the Sidonians and priestess of the goddess Asherah ('Asthoreth/Astarte?), Jezebel is a zealous apostle of Ba'alism. She persuades Ahab to build a temple and altar to Ba'al (16:32), persecutes the followers of the religion of Yahweh (18:3–5), wages a personal war against Elijah (19:1–3), and arranges the murder of Naboth with cruel efficiency (21:7–15). She eventually dies at the hands of Jehu, the rebel general of the Israelite army (1 Kgs 9:30–37). Against Jezebel God sends the prophets Elijah and Elisha.

A cycle of stories about Elijah (1 Kgs 17—19) is now placed in the narrative about the northern kingdom. Elijah is from Tishbe, a city across the Jordan in Gilead. His mission is described as occurring primarily during the reign of Ahab and the religious crises caused by this king and his wife.

The stories of Elijah here and later those of Elisha have a character different from the rest of the books of Kings. Some of the episodes mention kings; others have no reference to the events of the day. They were probably developed in the circles that followed Elijah and Elisha. These circles of disciples concentrated on the actions of the prophets rather than on the words of their preaching, stressing especially their miraculous powers. In 1 Kings 17—19 we have five of the eight episodes preserved about Elijah (see also 1 Kgs 21; 2 Kgs 1—2).

17:1–6 *Episode 1: Elijah and the drought*

Elijah predicts a terrible drought as the opening salvo in his war to save Israel from Jezebel's influence. This natural disaster is quite ironic in the setting of Ba'alist fertility cults. Elijah hides from Ahab by the brook Kerith (17:1–7) in Transjordan where he is miraculously nourished like the Israelites in the desert (Exod 16:8–12).

17:7–24 *Episode 2: Elijah and the widow of Zarephath*

At Zarephath of Sidon he multiplies food for a desperate widow and her child (17:10–16). In the second half of this episode he raises the apparently dead child to life (17:17–24).

Elijah's action of stretching himself over the child suggests the practice of contact magic, whereby the sickness or health of corre-

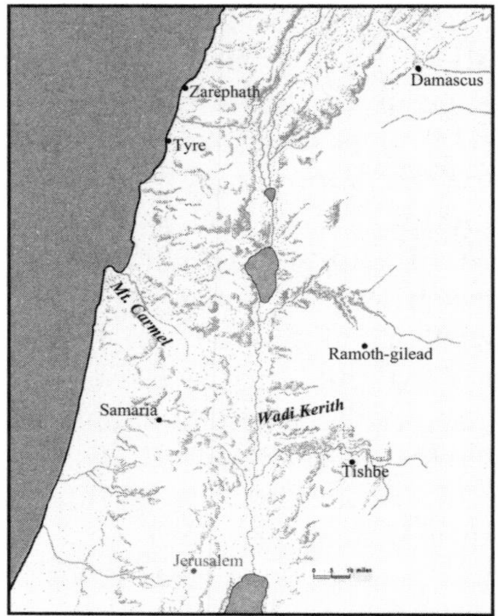

5F: Map of the Cities and Places of Elijah

sponding body parts was transferred from one person or object to the other (see Paul in a similar gesture in Acts 20:9–12). However, the restoration to life is attributed explicitly to Yahweh through Elijah's prayer (17:22). The gift of restored life leads the mother to confess, "The word of Yahweh comes truly from your mouth" (17:24).

18:1–46 ***Episode 3: Elijah and the prophets of Ba'al***

After three years of famine, Elijah confronts Ahab through Obadiah, the king's vizier (18:1–18). Elijah then confounds the prophets of Ba'al on Mount Carmel, probably a major Ba'alist shrine supported by Jezebel (18:19–46). Obadiah is at once a royal official and a faithful follower of Yahweh. His action of sheltering one hundred prophets from the wrath of Jezebel (18:4) shows his courage and gives us an insight into the phenomenon of prophetism in Israel, which here appears in the form of a prophetic guild. They are a distinct group, numerous, and needing protection. They parallel the "prophets of Ba'al" also mentioned in the story (18:19), showing that "prophetism" was in some ways a generic concept outside of Israel.

The confrontation between Elijah and the prophets of Baʿal on Mount Carmel is one of the great scenes of the Bible. In terms of human participants the odds are 450 to one. In terms of the power of the deities, no contest. Elijah has the twelve stones set up and the altar erected recalling the Exodus traditions (Exod 24:4–8). The challenge of Elijah to these prophets also echoes the challenge of Moses to the Egyptian magicians (Exod 7:8–22). Elijah ridicules the extreme human effort to get Baʿal to move.

In the background are "the people," whom Elijah addresses three times (18:15, 22, 30), marking out the progressive victory of Yahweh over Baʿal. Elijah's prayer is simple, mentioning the patriarchs like Moses in his prayer (Exod 32:13). In answer, "Yahweh's fire" explodes down and consumes sacrifice, altar, and water (18:36–38). "Seeing this, all the people fell prostrate and said, 'Yahweh is God! Yahweh is God!'" (18:39). Elijah thus succeeds in moving the people from straddling the fence (18:21) to a firm commitment to Yahweh. The main point of the story is this movement from religious half measures to uncompromising decision. The slaughter of the prophets of Baʿal again echoes the slaughter of the Israelites at the incident of the golden calf (Exod 32:25–28).

In the final scene, Elijah and Ahab have a meal together like friends and watch the end of the drought. The occasionally sympathetic picture of Ahab here and in other stories indicates an ancient source closer to the events than that of the later editors and their blanket condemnation of Ahab.

19:1–18 *Episode 4: Elijah at Horeb*

Threatened by Jezebel, Elijah flees for his life to Horeb, the Deuteronomists' name for Sinai, "the mountain of God" (1 Kgs 19:8), where we are given another great scene of the Bible. The mysterious experience occurs after the prophet is near death from exhaustion (19:4). He is strengthened by the bread and water from an "angel" (19:6–8), which allow him to continue on his journey, a return to the beginnings.

At the mountain of God, repeating the experience of Moses (Exod 33:18–23), he experiences a theophany. This theophany, however, occurs without the usual stage props for a typical theophany—no wind, no earthquake, no fire. He experiences God in "the sound of thin silence" (*qol damamah daqah,* 1 Kgs 19:12). God speaks through quiet unspectacular things. In the Bible as we have it now, Elijah on the mountain of God thus appears as the new Moses. In the New Testament Elijah together with Moses will represent the whole Old Testament, the Law and the prophets (see Mark 9:4 and parallels).

Elijah is given three jobs to do when he returns:

a. Anoint Hazael as king of Aram—which Elisha ends up more or less doing without actually anointing the Aramean king (2 Kgs 8:7–15)
b. Anoint Jehu as king of Israel—which Elisha ends up doing (2 Kgs 9:1–10)
c. Anoint Elisha as a prophet and successor—whom he in fact appoints but without anointing, which would have been an unusual way of distinguishing a prophet (2 Kgs 2:1–18)

The seven thousand in Israel who have remained faithful to God (1 Kgs 19:18) dramatize how God's power can prevail in *a remnant* (Amos 5:15; Mic 5:6–7; Isa 10:20–22). Paul in the New Testament recalls this text when he reflects on the mysterious ways of God that allow most of Israel to be blinded to the Gospel yet provide for success in the small number of Jewish Christians (Rom 11:4–5).

19:19–21 ***Episode 5 for Elijah and episode 1 for Elisha***

Elijah calls Elisha from his work with great urgency. Elisha then leaves a prosperous farm to follow Elijah and begins a prophetic career that lasts around sixty years. Unlike Elijah who was poor, Elisha is wealthy, has a personal servant, and cherishes social contacts more than Elijah. Elijah "appoints" Elisha through contact with his mantle, suggesting a way in which material things could contain divine power. Elisha leaves all things, including his family, to follow Elijah. The scene is echoed in the New Testament where Jesus calls his first disciples from their work (Mark 1:16–20) with the same urgency (Luke 9:59–61).

We break from the saga of Elijah to a narration of the Aramean (Syrian) wars (1 Kgs 20). In battle against Benhadad of

Damascus, Ahab appears in a favorable light. Actually, the name of Ahab here and in chapter 22 looks like it was added later. The history of wars at this time does not leave time either for this battle or that of chapter 22 at the time of Ahab. In any case, we see in this story the functioning of prophets. An unnamed prophet advises the king in military matters (20:13, 28). Another condemns Ahab for sparing the Aramean king (20:35, 37).

21:1–29 ***Episode 6: Elijah and Naboth's vineyard***

Chapter 21 returns to the saga of Elijah, who here accuses the king of sin, just as Nathan accused David (2 Sam 12:1–15). King Ahab had condoned the murder of Naboth, the Jezreelite, and seized his vineyard. Against Ahab and Jezebel, Elijah pronounces the judgment that runs through the entire books of Kings: "Because you have given yourself up to doing evil in Yahweh's sight, I am bringing evil upon you: I will destroy you" (21:20).

The story here dramatizes the link between the immoral fertility cults and social oppression. The focus is on the abuse of power and greed, but the editor roots the evil conduct of Ahab and Jezebel in their idolatry (21:25–26). Like David, however, Ahab repents, and God's judgment is deferred to Ahab's son (21:27–29; see 2 Kgs 9).

22:1–40 ***The war against Ramoth-gilead***

In a story that reflects literary affinities with chapter 20, kings Ahab and Jehoshaphat fight against Ramoth-gilead. This story describes a surprising cooperation between Judah and Israel as well as the role of prophetism in Israel. If the names of the kings were not added later to the story, the time would be around 853 BC, immediately after the battle of Qarqar, in which Ahab's army participated alongside of Aram and Egypt to stop the Assyrians, although the Assyrian annals describe it as a victory (see appendix 3). In light of the Assyrian menace, such an attack against Aram at this time would appear politically insane. In any case, according to the story, the attack fails and Ahab is killed as Elijah had prophesied (1 Kgs 21:19).

Sandwiched between accounts of the war (22:1–4, 29–38) is a story of prophetic intervention where conflicting prophetic voices advise the kings (22:5–28). Not to be confused with the literary prophet Micah of Moresheth, Micaiah son of Imlah stands alone against a large group of prophets denouncing their prophecies of victory as the utterances of "a lying spirit" in their mouths (22:22). The prophet of Yahweh stands against the "prophets of lies," as Jeremiah would later call them (Jer 23:9–32). These "prophets of lies" appear as part of the royal establishment rubber-stamping the king's opinions. In effect standing up against the king, Micaiah, like Jesus, suffers the indignity of a slap on the face and imprisonment (Matt 26:67 and John 18:22). He defends his word by appealing to his prophetic experience of the great council of God, giving in effect the foundation of authentic prophecy.

2 Kgs 1:1–18 ***Episode 7: Elijah and King Ahaziah of Israel***

With the opening of 2 Kings, we have two final stories about Elijah. In one, Elijah accuses King Ahaziah of Israel of the sin of consulting the Philistine god of Ekron, Baʿalzebub ("Lord of the flies"), and prophesies the king's death. The hairy garment and leather girdle of Elijah (1:8) provide the prophetic symbols that Mark uses to connect John the Baptist with Elijah (Mark 1:6; 9:11). The "fire from heaven," a symbol of divine judgment, warns us how not to approach a prophet (1:10–12; also see Luke 9:54–55).

2:1–18 ***Episode 8 for Elijah and episode 2 for Elisha: The ascension of Elijah***

The last Elijah episode describes the ascension of the prophet to heaven and the succession of Elisha to the prophetic office. The "double portion" of the prophetic spirit is an allusion to the double portion of an inheritance proper to the firstborn son in a family (Deut 21:17). The flaming chariot and horses along with the storm wind that gather Elijah up to "the heavens" (*ha-shamaim*) make for a scene that has captivated the religious imagination and led much later Jewish legends to speculate about where Elijah (along with Moses) went and when he will return (see Mark 9:2–13). Elisha then repeats Elijah's Jordan miracle (2:13–18).

The cycle of seventeen Elisha stories continues now, portraying the prophet especially as a wonder-worker. Several of the miracles that occur later in the series are similar to those of Jesus some eight hundred years later. Starting off the series, Elisha purifies a polluted spring, *episode 3* (2:19–22), and then destroys forty-two irreverent children, *episode 4*, in a "don't mess with a prophet" story (2:23–24).

3:1–27 ***Episode 5: Elisha and Jehoram of Israel***

The next Elisha story involves Jehoram of Israel (851–841 BC), the last of the Omrid dynasty. The war against Mesha, king of Moab, involves a coalition of Israel and Judah along with Edom. Unlike the story of Micaiah (1 Kgs 22:5–28), here the prophet supports the military campaign and predicts a water supply for the armies (3:20). The campaign is for the most part a success. However, "the Moabite Stone," dated between 840 and 820 BC, describes Mesha, king of Moab, *defeating* the son and house of "Omri, king of Israel" (see appendix 1).

The final lines of the story remain a puzzle. The king of Moab sacrifices his son—apparently to the god Chemosh, "and great anger (*qezef-gadol*) came against Israel" (3:27), resulting in Israel's withdrawal. Is this a trace of early storytellers believing that local god's like Chemosh had real power in their own lands?

A series of ten Elisha episodes now follow that have little connection with each other or with Israelite politics. Their disconnect from the flow of the political narrative in Kings and their reluctance to name rulers when they do appear in the story suggest that these stories were passed down and elaborated in prophetic circles. Their stress on wonder and miracle is typical of folklore. The parallels with the Elijah stories suggest that the followers of one prophet developed their stories from those of the other. The purpose of the stories apparently was not so much to record events as rather to depict the prophet so close to God that God's power would flow through the prophet into the world.

4:1–7 ***Episode 6: Elisha and the poor widow***

In the first of the ten episodes here, Elisha multiplies oil for a widow and rescues her from economic ruin. This is the first of the miracles directed to very specific human needs apart from the religious crisis in Israel, where the action of Yahweh as such

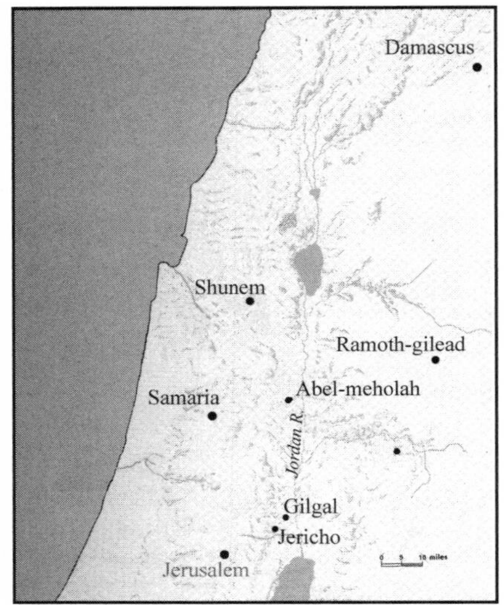

5G: Map of the Cities and Places of Elisha

recedes into the background, and agency appears more directly in the person of the "man of God."

4:8–37 ***Episode 7: Elisha and the Shunammite***

Elisha then helps a rather wealthy woman from the northern border town of Shunem by first removing her sterility so that she could conceive a son. The birth of a child as a reward for hospitality is a theme found in the patriarchal narratives (Gen 18:1–15). Several years later the prophet raises that child to life in a miracle that reflects Elijah's raising a dead child (1 Kgs 17:17–20, see also Mark 5:35–43).

4:38–41 ***Episode 8: The poisoned stew***

For a community of prophets, Elisha neutralizes a vegetable stew that was accidentally poisoned.

4:42–44 ***Episode 9: The multiplication of bread***

In a story that contrasts human resources and divine promise, Elisha multiplies bread for a large crowd. The story builds around the contrast between the views of Elisha's unnamed servant (apparently Gehazi) and that of the prophet himself (4:43). The servant expresses the very understandable attitude about the inadequacy of the resources to meet the need at hand. The prophet affirms his faith in the words of Yahweh, who operates powerfully with the limited human contribution. With its detail, including the prophet's command to the servant to feed the crowd, the barley loaves, and the food left over, the story clearly lies behind the Gospel narration of Jesus multiplying bread in Galilee (Mark 6:34–44 and parallels; John 6:1–15).

5:1–19 *Episode 10: The cure of Naaman*

In one of the several stories connecting Elisha with the king of Aram (Damascus), the prophet brings about the cure of Naaman, the army commander of the king of Aram (see Luke 4:27). The intent of both stories appears in Naaman's confession of faith (5:15) describing the uniqueness of the God of Israel on earth. Such monotheism implies the need for openness to those beyond national boundaries. The contrast in attitudes between the wise but unnamed king of Aram and the obtuse unnamed king of Israel suggests the same point.

6:1–7 *Episode 11: Recovery of the ax*

Elisha allows an iron ax head to float on the Jordan River after it had been accidentally dropped into the water by someone in a community of prophets. This is the community with whom Elisha apparently lived (6:1).

6:8–23 *Episode 12: The Aramean ambush*

Switching from a trivial, mundane issue to one of international warfare, Elisha assists an unnamed king of Israel against an unnamed king of Aram.

6:24–7:20 *Episode 13: The siege of Samaria*

Despite the hostility of an unnamed king of Israel (Jehoahaz?), Elisha predicts the end of some long and horrible siege of the city of Samaria by the king of Aram, here named Benhadad, probably Benhadad II (c.798–c.773 BC), the son of Hazael. The story also involves the death of a skeptical Israelite officer. It is not at all clear who the good guys are or the point of the story, except that Elisha is really in charge and the power of his prophetic words guides history.

8:1–6 ***Episode 14: The prediction of famine***

With a reference back to the Shunammite woman of *episode 7* (4:8–37), Elisha predicts a seven-year famine in the land, advising the woman to seek refuge among the Philistines. Then after the famine—apparently after Elisha's death—Gehazi the prophet's servant helps the woman recover her property in Israel.

8:7–15 ***Episode 15: Elisha and Hazael of Aram***

Again connecting Elisha with Damascus, the final story in this series of ten describes the prediction of the murder of Benhadad, king of Aram, by his servant, Hazael, the succession of Hazael as king, as well as Hazael's future ravaging of Israel. The Book of Kings later describes the oppressive victories of Hazael over Israel and Judah (8:28–29; 10:32–33; 12:17–18; 13:3, 22).

In its present sequence, the story follows *episode 13* (1 Kgs 6:24—7:20) about a King Benhadad II, *son* of Hazael, and is therefore clearly not in chronological order. The assassinated king here would have to be Benhadad I, reigning from the times of Asa and Baasha, around 880 BC (see 1 Kgs 15:16–20). The assassination would have occurred around 842 BC, implying a long reign of some 48 years for this Aramean king. An Assyrian inscription also writes of Hazael, a commoner, who seized the throne of Damascus. The king who "perished," in the event, however, is named Hadadezer (see appendix 3). This name is either an alternate throne name for Benhadad, or the name Benhadad may have been added to the biblical story (2 Kgs 8:7, 9).

However that may be, the intention of the story is to describe again the word of God spoken through the prophet directing history, even when the outcome involves great suffering for Israel.

9:1–37 ***Episode 16: Elisha and Jehu of Israel***

After briefly narrating the reign of two Judahite kings, Jehoram (848–841 BC) and Ahaziah (841 BC), the book returns to another story involving Elisha. The prophet sends a disciple to anoint Jehu king of Israel (841–813 BC), the founder of the fourth dynasty in Israel (Jehu, Jehoahaz, Jehoash, Jeroboam II, Zechariah). The commission of Elijah is thus completed (1 Kgs 19:15). After assassinating Jehoram of Israel (9:15–26) and Ahaziah of Judah (9:24–29), Jehu drives on to Jezreel, orders the execution of Jezebel (9:30–37), whom he had accused of religious "harlotry" (9:22) in the language that the prophet Hosea will insist on to describe the Ba'alist idolatry of Israel.

In the next stories, Jehu eliminates the remaining members of the house of Omri (10:1–11) and slaughters the priests of Ba'al (10:18–36). Despite the reforming zeal of Jehu's revolution (9:22; 10:18–30), the authors' judgment on this king is negative because he too followed in the "sin of Jeroboam" (10:31; see also Hosea's condemnation of Jehu's bloodletting, Hos 1:4). The military defeats mentioned in 10:32–33 echo the portrayal of Jehu on "the Black Obelisk" (see appendix 3) where he is pictured as bowing down in subjection to the Assyrian king, Shalmaneser III.

11:1–20 *Athaliah of Judah*

Athaliah (841–835 BC), queen mother after the death of King Jehoram of Judah, assumes the scepter of Judah, puts to death all her grandsons except Jehoash, who is hidden by his aunt Jehosheba (11:1–2). Six years later (11:4–12), with the help of "the Carians," apparently a private militia (11:4), and "the people of the land," probably a powerful rural gentry (11:14), the high priest Jehoiada restores Jehoash as king of Judah (835–796) and has Athaliah executed. Like Jezebel, her mother, she dies defiantly (11:13–16). Guided by the high priest, King Jehoash orders the temple of Ba'al destroyed and the Ba'alist priests executed.

This is all part of a covenant with Yahweh made by mediation of the priest Jehoiada, by which the people would be "Yahweh's people" (11:17). This covenant ceremony was perhaps also geared to renew the Davidic covenant broken by the usurpation of Athaliah.

13:14–21 ***Episode 17: The death of Elisha***

The final episode about Elisha describes his death. Jehoash is the last king to confer with Elisha, addressing him, "My father, my father!" (13:14). The life-giving power of the prophet appears in the last scene, where the bones of Elisha bring a dead man to life (13:20–21).

14:23–29 ***Jeroboam II of Israel***

In Israel Jeroboam II, who apparently reigns from 793 to 752 BC, becomes sole regent in 781 BC. He is summarily condemned by the authors (14:24) for following "the sins" of the first king of that name. Actually during his forty-year reign, Jeroboam II restored Israel's ancient boundaries from Moab to Hamath, north of the Sea of Galilee, and brought to Israel an economic prosperity rivaling that of the Solomonic era.

Israel's apostasy kept pace with her prosperity. It is during this period that the prophets Amos and Hosea warn Israel of the anger of God, although they are not mentioned in the Book of Kings. Six months after Jeroboam's death, his son Zechariah (753) is assassinated (15:8) and the dynasty of Jehu comes to an end.

The story mentions the prophet Jonah ben Amittai, whose utterances apparently encouraged Jeroboam (14:25). We can only assume he preached in the presence of Jeroboam. The Book of Jonah, written much later, is a fictitious story building on the scant memory about this prophet (see Jonah 1:1).

With the death of Zechariah, the northern kingdom enters a period of anarchy (15:8–31). Shallum (752 BC), the assassin of Zechariah, is himself assassinated after a one-month reign by Menahem (752–742 BC), who suffers the first Assyrian assault led by Tiglath-pileser III (named Pul in the text) sometime between 745 and 742 BC (15:19–20; see appendix 4). Menahem's son, Pekahiah (742–740 BC), is assassinated by Pekah (752–731 BC), who then counts the length of his reign back to the death of Zechariah. Although not mentioned here in the text of 2 Kings, the prophets Micah and Isaiah appeared in the southern kingdom of Judah. Isaiah in particular directed his preaching to the Judean kings, particularly to King Ahaz.

16:1–20 *Ahaz of Judah*

In Judah, Ahaz becomes king, apparently reigning from 734 or 730 to 715 BC. The indetermination of the official beginning of his reign might be due to the military interventions of Tiglath-pileser, the Assyrian king. At the start of his reign, well before 731 BC, he suffers an attack from Pekah of Israel aligned with Rezin, king of Aram. Aggravating the situation is the sin of Ahaz immolating his son, perhaps his only remaining son and heir to the Davidic throne (1 Kgs 16:3; 1 Chr 28:7 refers to the death of another son, Maaseiah).

This Syro-Ephraimite war is the background for Isaiah 7 and the "sign" of the male child, "Immanuel," given by Isaiah—not even mentioned here—to persuade Ahaz against any foreign alliance. Ahaz, nevertheless, invokes Tiglath-pileser, king of Assyria, and submits to him.

As the story is told in the books of Kings, Israel's destiny will be situated from now on in the wars and politics of the ancient Middle East. We know from Assyrian texts and inscriptions that King Ahab was involved in the battle of Qarqar against the Assyrians in 854 BC, and King Jehu paid tribute to Shalmaneser III of Assyria around 841 BC, although neither event is recorded in Kings. However, with Ahaz's elaborate gesture of fealty to the king of Assyria, Judah in effect loses its independence and becomes a client king in the Assyrian Empire.

In response to Ahaz's promise of loyalty, Tiglath-pileser in 733 BC invades the north, destroying Damascus and subjugating the kingdom of Israel, deporting the inhabitants of Naphtali, Gilead, and Galilee. Pekah of Israel is killed and replaced by the pro-Assyrian Hoshea, the last king of Israel (731–722 BC; see 15:29; and appendix 4). The result of Ahaz's alliance with Assyria is some compromise of the Jerusalem cult in deference to the Assyrian king (16:10–18).

17:1–23 *The end of the northern kingdom*

Hoshea would have come to the throne in the "second" (*shtayim*) year of Ahaz's reign, not the "twelfth" (*shtem 'esreh*) year as the text of 2 Kings 17:1 reads. After nine years, Hoshea of Israel revolts against the Assyrians. Successor to Tiglath-pileser in

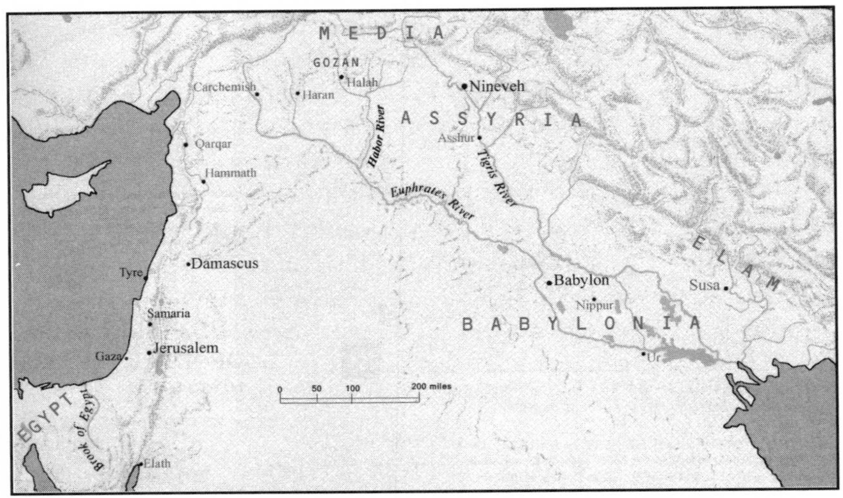

5H: Map of the Ancient Middle East

Assyria, Shalmaneser V is swift to retaliate. In 724 BC, Shalmaneser begins the siege of Samaria. In 722 BC. Samaria falls to Sargon II, successor of Shalmaneser. The remaining northern tribes are carried off to northern Assyria, to a city named Halah on the Habor River. The northern kingdom comes to an end (see appendix 5). The description of this attack is repeated in 18:9–12.

At the end of this part of Israel's history, the writers and editors pause as they did at the end of Solomon's reign (1 Kgs 11). They catalogue the sins of Israel, including the immolation of children (17:14–18). God deserted his people only because they first deserted him. Twice the authors stress the role of "the prophets" warning the people. They are not named here but are described as "servants" of God (17:13, 23). We saw the important roles of Elijah and Elisha from the ninth century. The mid-eighth century would have been the time for the prophets Amos and Hosea, but they are not mentioned in Kings. From their postexilic perspective, the Deuteronomist editors include Judah in their warnings (17:13, 19).

C. 2 Kings 18—25 / The End of the Southern Kingdom

The third and last part of Kings (2 Kgs 18—25) continues the history of the southern kingdom down to its destruction in 586 BC by the Babylonians. Here, as in the earlier parts of the history, the editors give extra space to those reigns in which the prophets or the Temple are involved, namely, the reigns of Hezekiah and Josiah. For the others, they are content to continue with the stereotyped summary formula.

18:1–7 *The reign of Hezekiah*

The first king after David to earn the unqualified praise of the authors is Hezekiah (715–686 BC), son of Ahaz. The reference to his accession "in the third year of Hoshea" (728 BC) could mark the beginning of some form of coregency with his father, Ahaz. This date may in fact be just four or five years after his birth, making Hezekiah around nineteen years old at his accession to the throne in 715 BC, not twenty-five years old as indicated in 18:2. The year 715 BC, the year of Hezekiah's reign as sole king, is based on our acceptance of the data in 18:13, describing the invasion of Sennacherib (701 BC) as occurring "in the fourteenth year of King Hezekiah," understood as measuring his sole regency. By strange exception, then, the twenty-nine-year length of Hezekiah's reign (18:2) would refer only to his governance after the death of his father, Ahaz. These calculations are important for the study of Isaiah and the possibility that Immanuel (Isa 7:14) or the "child born to us" (Isa 9:5) could be Hezekiah.

The praise of the writers for Hezekiah arises from his destruction of the "high places," "pillars," and "poles" forbidden by Deuteronomy 12:1–14 along with the other Ba‘alist cultic places. The purification included even destruction of the Mosaic bronze serpent (see Num 21:6–9) because of some form of abusive worship (2 Kgs 18:4). The praise "neither before him nor after him" any king like him (18:5) is an example of court hyperbole. The same will be said later of King Josiah (23:25).

The rebellion against Assyria described here (18:7) apparently refers to a widespread revolt that occurred at the death of the

Assyrian King Sargon II around 704. The dominion of Assyria over Judah was part of the treaty signed by Hezekiah's father, Ahaz, but involved a compromise of the Jerusalem cult (see 16:10–19).

18:13—19:37 The invasion of Sennacherib

Once the new Assyrian king, Sennacherib (704–681 BC), was firmly in control of his empire, he marched on Jerusalem. The year was 701. In this text we seem to have three accounts of the same events. The first in 18:13–16 describes a humiliating settlement, where tribute is paid and the attack called off. The second in 18:17—19:7 and the third in 19:9b–37 appear to be double theological accounts celebrating God's miraculous protection of Jerusalem.

In the second and third form the story of the invasion of Sennacherib and the siege of Jerusalem is the story of God's last-minute rescue of his holy city. The experience of the rescue left a profound mark on the theological imagination of Judah. The effect can be seen in many psalms celebrating the eleventh-hour rescue of Jerusalem by God (see Pss 46; 78). The point of these stories lies in the power of God to overcome the most intimidating enemies. Hezekiah's fidelity to Yahweh and his prayerful trust tapped into that power. Judah, however, came to believe that Jerusalem with its Temple was inviolable and indestructible, a belief that itself would be destroyed by the later prophets Jeremiah and Ezekiel (see Jer 7:1–15; Ezek 5:5–16). For the exiles and the Jews of later generations, Jerusalem will remain a focus and symbol of hope in God's salvation (see Ezek 40—48).

In the only appearance of a literary prophet in these books, Isaiah counsels Hezekiah not to be frightened by the Assyrian forces (19:6–7). Then in an elaborate oracle Isaiah taunts Sennacherib as exceeding the mandate that he had from God (19:21–34). As a result of the prophecy, "the angel of Yahweh" kills 185,000 Assyrian soldiers, "so that Sennacherib, king of Assyria, broke camp and went back home to Nineveh" (19:35–36).

The annals of Sennacherib give a picture of the attack corroborating the first form of the story here in Kings. The annals describe the Assyrian king as besieging Hezekiah "like a bird in a cage" and receiving enormous tribute (see appendix 6). Furthermore, the annals of Sennacherib describe only one attack.

More than likely, the second and third accounts of the siege with the miraculous divine interventions are the result of religious imagination. Storytellers embellished the sober account of Hezekiah's tribute. Yet Jerusalem was saved from the destruction that fell on many other important cities during this invasion. The storytellers had a faith in a God who can be present with his salvation even in somber and painful events. This may be a God who remains hidden to eyes that look only to the objective facts. This is a God who appears with his power to an imagination animated by faith—like that on the part of the prophet Isaiah in the story. The storytellers believed in the hand of God behind the military and political events. They told a story to dramatize that faith. Thus all three accounts of the siege find their way into the sacred writings of Israel.

21:23—22:2 ***The reign of Josiah***

The second king to receive unqualified praise is Josiah (640–609 BC), who ascends the throne after the long and wicked reigns of his grandfather, Manasseh (695–641 BC; see 2 Kgs 21:1–18), and father, Amon, cut short by assassination (641–640 BC; see 2 Kgs 21:19–16). As they had done for King Jehoash (11:12), the "people of the land" acclaim the child Josiah as king preserving the Davidic dynasty (21:24).

22:3-20 ***The reform of Josiah***

According to this text, Josiah's religious reform begins around 622 BC, the eighteenth year of Josiah's rule or after he had reached maturity. The crucial element of the reform is the finding of "the book of the Law" (*sefer ha-torah*) in the Temple (22:8). This unusual expression for the Law is the way Deuteronomy refers to itself (Deut 29:20) and may indicate some connection between the scroll found in the Temple and our present Book of Deuteronomy.

The intense concern shown here for this book or scroll as expressing the will of God (22:13) may mark the beginning of a faith that looked to official and sacred documents as a divine guide to decisions, at least in terms of public policy. Up to this point in the story, such a guide was mainly the spoken word of a prophet. References to the written divine law that appear in earlier stories (Josh 23:6; 24:26; 1 Kgs 2:3; 2 Kgs 14:6) look like anachronistic additions by the Deuteronomist authors. The next piece of evidence in this development of faith in "Sacred Scripture" will show up some 220 years later when Ezra reads "the book of the Law of Moses" aloud in one morning as part of the postexilic restoration of Israel (Neh 8:1–12).

To determine what to do about this book, King Josiah and the leaders of Jerusalem consult the prophetess Huldah (22:14–20), the last named prophet in this saga who forms a kind of inclusion with Deborah at the beginning of the saga (Judg 4—5). According to Huldah, the reform is too little too late to save Jerusalem (see 2 Kgs 23:26–27), but it does spare King Josiah from the humiliating defeat to come.

Curiously, the books of Kings ignore Jeremiah and Zephaniah, who were active at this time. Jeremiah, made bitter enemies with the Temple establishment (Jer 26). In the days of Josiah, Zephaniah decries Jerusalem as a rebellious and polluted city, whose leaders are treacherous predators (Zeph 3:1–4). Perhaps the Deuteronomist historians themselves felt little sympathy for these irritating firebrands.

23:1–27 *The reading of the Law*

Although the very presence of the book found in the Temple has an intense impact on the king and the leaders of Jerusalem, the binding force of the book is presented as based on a public covenant that then takes place at this time. After a public reading of the book, now called "the book of the covenant" (23:2), the king makes a covenant before Yahweh to observe "the ordinances, statutes, and decrees with their whole hearts and souls." This public act thus renews the covenant written in the book (23:3; see Deut 6:5 and 20).

The cultic reform that follows involved among other things the purification of the Temple from its Ba'alist defilements (23:1–7), the destruction of the high places in Judah (23:8–9), and the destruction of the Moloch shrine, Topheth (see Jer

7:30–34), outside Jerusalem (2 Kgs 23:10). These actions, especially the centralization of cult in Jerusalem, correspond fairly closely to the stipulations in Deuteronomy. It is from the perspective of this Josiahan centralization of cult that the whole Deuteronomistic history is written.

The removal of the high places near the cities of Samaria (23:19–20) suggests a major rebellion against Assyria, which governed Samaria as an Assyrian province but which was facing intense military pressure at home. Josiah appears to be attempting a reunification of all Israel around the Jerusalem Temple.

Culminating the reform, Josiah reinstates of the feast of the Passover (*pesach*), now apparently to be celebrated as a national pilgrim feast at a central sanctuary, as stipulated in Deuteronomy (16:1–8). The editor states that this feast was not totally new but had not been celebrated since the time of the Judges (see Josh 5:10–12). However, as we saw, the Book of Joshua, where the celebration is described, seems to be relatively late. Nevertheless, the association of Passover with the reign of Josiah in the late seventh century suggests a major development of the Exodus tradition at this time—which, however, left its footprint already in the Book of Judges (see Judg 6:13; 11:13, 16; 19:13).

23:28–30 *The death of Josiah*

The death of Josiah at the battle of Megiddo (609 BC) ended the reform. In a political switch of international alliances, Egypt under Pharaoh Neco moves from being the archenemy of Assyria to its ally, as the power of Babylon arises in the East. (The biblical Hebrew reads that Neco marched "against" the king of Assyria. This is a mistake.) Apparently without major allies, Josiah takes it on himself to stop Egypt and is slain. As a place where good battles evil and where evil at first prevailed, Megiddo enters into the religious imagery of Israel (see Zech 12:11; Rev 16:16).

What follows is a period of instability as foreign powers depose Davidic kings and replace them with others who will follow their orders. The kings remain in the Davidic line all from the family of Josiah. If we follow 2 Kings, these kings of Judah were related to each other according to the family tree shown below.

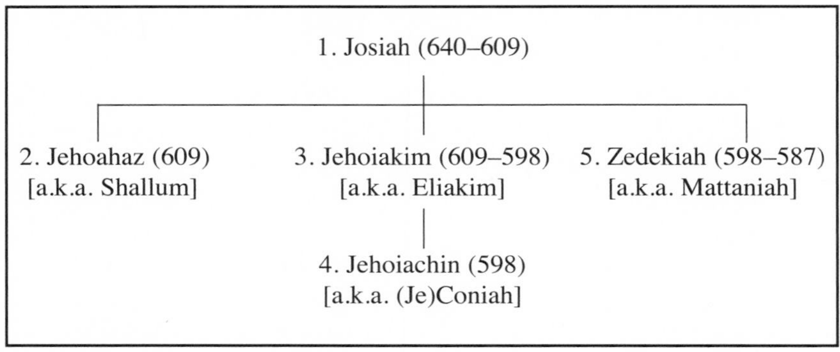

5I: Family of Josiah

23:31–37 *The reign of Jehoiakim*

Jehoahaz, son of Josiah, reigns briefly (609) and is deposed by Pharaoh Neco in favor of the pro-Egyptian Jehoiakim (609–598 BC). Jehoiakim's change of name from Eliakim emphasizes his status as vassal to Pharaoh. Jehoiakim is Jehoahaz's brother and appears in the Book of Jeremiah as the prophet's evil opponent (see Jer 36).

24:1–20 *The first Babylonian invasion*

In 605 BC, Nebuchadnezzar, king of Babylon, crushed the Egyptian-Assyrian army at the city of Carchemish, on the Euphrates (see Jer 46:2). The text relates how Nebuchadnezzar then attacked Jerusalem and captured it shortly after the death of Jehoiakim in 598 BC. Jehoiakim's son, Jehoiachin, succeeds him (2 Kgs 24:8–17). Jehoiachin and the major functionaries of Jerusalem (including the prophet Ezekiel) in the books of Kings are then led off captive to Babylonia. Nebuchadnezzar places a third son of Josiah on the Jerusalem throne, Zedekiah, the last Davidic king (598–587 BC).

25:1–30 *The second Babylonian invasion*

Zedekiah revolts against Babylon (against the advice of Jeremiah; see Jer 28). The result is disaster. Zedekiah is captured as he tries to escape (25:4–5) and apparently dies in Babylon (Ezek 12:12–13). All the glorious buildings of Solomon including the Temple are destroyed by fire and the walls of the city are

5J: Map of the Exile

torn down (2 Kgs 25:9–10). The second deportation leaves behind only some poor farmers and vinedressers (25:12).

A final rebellion of the remaining Jews against their Jewish governor (25:22–26) is described in fuller detail in the Book of Jeremiah (see Jer 40:13—41:18). The release of Jehoiachin from prison by the Babylonian king, Evil-merodach (562–560 BC), illustrates a theme that both Jeremiah and Ezekiel will orchestrate. God is with his people and will protect them in exile.

II. The Message of 1 and 2 Kings

A. Review of Themes

Like the books of Samuel, the books of Kings revolve around a wide range of themes. A listing of the most important ones found in our selected texts would include the following:

- The city and Temple of Jerusalem as the place of God's glorious "house" (1 Kgs 6:1–38; 8:1–13; 9:3; 2 Kgs 18:17–37)
- National destruction and exile as the consequence of the kings' failures (1 Kgs 9:6–9; 11:14–40; 13:1—14:20; 2 Kgs 17:1–23; 24:1–20; 24:20—25:26)

- The sins of the kings (1 Kgs 11:1–13; 12:26–32; 14:23–24; 16:25–26, 30–33; 21:1–29; 2 Kgs 14:24; 16:2–4; 23:37; 24:19)
- The key role of prophets (1 Kgs 1:11–48; 11:29–39; 12:21–24; 13:1—14:20; 17:19; 21:17–29; 22:6–28; 2 Kgs 1—9; 13:14–21; 22:14–20)
- The power of the prophets' words and touch (1 Kgs 13:19–32; 17:7–24; 18:36–38; 2 Kgs 1:12; 2:8; 3:15–20; 4:7; 13:20–21
- The evil of false prophets (1 Kgs 22:6–28)
- The written Law (2 Kgs 22:8—23:24)

B. The Theology of 1 and 2 Kings

The story from Solomon to Zedekiah follows a tragic line leading from the secure structures of Solomon to the abyss of chaos. The picture of the pillage and destruction of 2 Kings 25 contrasts with the majesty and splendor of 1 Kings 6—7, where the foundations of the Temple were laid in the atmosphere of optimism and joy. God had predicted that the throne of David would last forever and the son of David would build the Temple (2 Sam 7). When that Temple burnt in 587 BC and the last Davidic king was led blinded apparently to his death in Babylon, the atmosphere had changed to horror and dejection. For all the divine promises of indefectibility, the sacred institution failed and collapsed.

The story of Kings is compiled in exile. We must imagine religious leaders struggling to understand the ruins of three-and-a-half centuries of tradition, trying to find God in the chaos of this long history. In story form, their efforts came back over and over to three elements: the kings, the Temple, and the prophets. In each of these elements and in their interplay, there appears a basic tension between divine promise and permanence, on the one hand, and divine transcendence and mystery, on the other. Through that interplay the authors attempted to express a deep faith in a time of disaster.

1. The Kings

In the books of Kings, the divinely appointed monarch represents the institutionalized promise of divine protection. The monarchy, especially the Davidic monarchy, was sacred. It flowed from the sacred promises to David, which led God to overlook much in the life of later kings (1 Kgs 8:25; 9:5; 11:32–36; 15:4; 2 Kgs 8:19). Israel's leaders were God's anointed, even God's sons (1 Sam 7; Ps 2), who often exercised priestly functions (2 Sam 6:13; 1 Kgs 3:3–4; see Ps 110). Saint or sinner, the king marked a place in history and human order where God enters. The monarchy, especially the Davidic monarchy, was a type of incarnation of God in history.

Yet, more than any other element in Israel, the king represented the paradox of the sacred/sinful institution. The northern kings are condemned as a whole. The sins of the southern kings return again and again. Every once and a while, kings like Hezekiah or Josiah evidence deeply rooted integrity and personal holiness. Yet the holy kings are followed by wicked sons. Just when it looks like progress is being made, the successor undoes it all.

2. The Temple

The paradox of permanence and mystery appears also in the Temple. The first part of Kings is dominated by Solomon's construction of the house of God with its precious furnishings. It is the place filled by God's glory, the place where God intends to dwell (1 Kgs 8:10–12). The meeting tent was mobile, transitional, and perhaps a bit flimsy. The massive stones of the Temple conveyed permanence. As Solomon explains to God, "I have truly built you a princely house, a dwelling where you may abide forever" (8:13). The Temple had survived the siege of Sennacherib (2 Kgs 19). How could God let his house be destroyed? It seemed that the Jerusalemites could always count on an eleventh-hour rescue.

The last part of Kings moves inexorably to the action of Nabuzaradan, representative of the king of Babylon: "He burned the house of Yahweh...every large building was destroyed by fire" (2 Kgs 25:9). The writer then lists the magnificent structures, furnishings, and appointments provided by Solomon and his successors and describes how they were destroyed and pillaged (25:13–17).

Along the way, we hear of abuses in the Temple. Along the way, the Temple is stripped of its wealth and grandeur. In the end, like the ark in the story of Eli (1 Sam 4), the Temple is no guarantee of God's blessing. Yet in their faith, the authors of Kings could picture the smoking rubble of the Temple and find God.

3. *The Prophets*

The prophets provided the otherworldly or transcendent presence of God. Generally they were not part of the power structures of society. They could therefore unmask the comfortable yet idolatrous compromises of their contemporaries. Their message could not be controlled. Their preaching represented God intervening in the course of sacred politics.

Although they experienced human weakness, their wonder-working power represented God's power in this world. The miracles of Elisha—healing lepers, providing food and rain, even raising the dead—were not just entertaining fables of magic. They were stories describing a locality or space of salvation around the person of the prophet. Other stories of death described a punishing judgment of God against the prophet's adversaries. In all cases, the salvation and the punishment were immediate and earthly, not eschatological. The salvation that came through the prophets often came through their physical presence and sometimes their touch. Thus the space of salvation was limited. Not all lepers were cured. Not all mothers received their children back from the dead. However, the limits were not coextensive with the boundaries of Israel. The widow of Zarephath, and the Syrian leaders Naaman and Hazael are assisted by Elijah and Elisha.

For all his saving activity, however, Elijah draws intense opposition and experiences intense frustration. He is given divine help on his way to Mount Horeb, but only after he prays for death as he suffers the brunt of Jezebel's hatred. "Prophets of lies" in the king's court drown out the message of Micaiah the true prophet of Yahweh. The power of God operated in weakness.

4. *Faith in a Time of Disaster*

The theologians in exile insisted on how the most absolute of promises are conditioned on fidelity to God, especially on the part of the leaders. God is faithful to his promises, but he will not allow himself to be manipulated by his promises—as understood by human beings. The foundational promises do not provide a magic power over God. They remain grace, a reality over which only God is in control. The destruction of Jerusalem was not some accidental quirk of history. Rather, it manifested the very nature of God.

Defeat, disaster, death, and destruction in Kings describe God's way of dealing with the sin of his people and their king. What is most treasured on the worldly level is stripped away. God thus deals with sin on its own level, that of death and destruction. Israel is first divided and then reduced in size and glory to an almost insignificant entity among worldly powers.

In exile and stripped of all worldly trappings and glory, Israel will be able to understand itself only as God's people. The Temple was destroyed, but not before "the book of the covenant" was discovered in it and rescued for posterity. With the monarchy, the priesthood, the Temple, and all political power stripped away, the faith of Israel turns to God alone. It reflects on what it means to be a sacred institution and to fail. It reflects on what it means to lie stripped and poor before God. It could stare into the abyss of chaos.

Beyond that worldly level, hope arises. This history ends with the encouraging notice concerning the freeing of Jehoiachin from prison (2 Kgs 25:27–29). Israel will continue in a more spiritual form after the Exile. The prophetic word will endure long after the last king disappears. Like good King Josiah, postexilic Israel will focus on the Law and the covenant with its principles of social care and justice.

6

The Message of the Deuteronomist History

If we picture the Deuteronomist writers in exile, hearing of the abject destruction of their country and Temple, seeing nothing yet of any return from Babylon, then we can see the very effort to create this long consecutive history as a profound act of faith. They believed in the goodness and justice of God and therefore felt they could look squarely at these six hundred years of sad and sinful history and make sense of it.

This story had to be told and recorded. Israel lived in history. The next generation could forget, and the identity of Israel could be lost. The injunction to pass the tradition on was one of the fundamental principles of Deuteronomy (Deut 6:7, 20). It is easy to forget. However, as a people of faith, Israel's identity meant remembering its relationship with God, not just abstractly but concretely in the historical turning points and moments of crisis.

I. The Historical Epic

Like most peoples, Israel told stories of its origins and of its God. Unlike most peoples of the ancient world, Israel here included stories of its more recent past and of the critical periods leading up to its present situation, stories that filled in the gap between the ancient origins and the present, including stories of its failures. These stories were placed in a sequence that covered some six hundred years. Israel had developed a historical consciousness. With its memories of the past and promises for the future, the extended flow of history became a way of understanding God and his plan for Israel.

The writing of this epic was a prophetic action. Only a divine perspective, it would seem, could embrace six hundred years. No human family or other "collective memory" could remember the actions of God founding, guiding, and even punishing an entire nation. Assuming this divine perspective, the narrator is in some way, like Micaiah ben Imlah, standing in the "council of God" (1 Kgs 22:17–28) as he speaks to the people.

The resulting epic is not however a story about God in heaven like so many ancient myths of the gods. Rather, it is a story about human choice on earth and responsibility for that choice. It is the story of weak human beings and their decisions. It is therefore a story of radical contingency and God's love and fidelity in and through that radical contingency.

This was a story rooted in origins. If the Book of Deuteronomy originally led off this epic, the story began on the plains of Moab with Moses leading the people to choose Yahweh. We see the choice again under Joshua, shortly after the new beginning marked by crossing the Jordan. Joshua poses the fundamental issue for Israel:

> If it does not please you to serve Yahweh, decide today whom you will serve, the gods your fathers served beyond the River or the gods of the Amorites in whose country you are dwelling. As for me and my household, we will serve Yahweh. (Josh 24:15)

The story thus starts with purpose and intention. A new epoch has in fact begun. After crossing the Jordan River, the Israelites began to live "from the produce of the land" (Josh 5:12). Human responsibility and enterprise enter the picture. The hand of God had led and fed in the desert. Now in the land "flowing with milk and honey," the chosen people must grow as a child grows through adolescence into adulthood. The people must choose. God will not do it for them, and the choice is between life and death (Deut 30:15).

Entrance into the promised land, however, was not a return to Eden and its innocence. Sinfulness and rebellion grew along with the momentary faithfulness and justice of some. By portraying human weakness and sinfulness as the sequel to divine promise and choice, the Deuteronomists give us a history of struggle. The story is a story of ambiguity and fumbling, of combat and wrestling, almost as though Jacob's wrestling with God (Gen 32:23–33) was a paradigm for Israel and Jacob's limp a symbol of the spiritual disability of God's people.

The Deuteronomists stress the divine promises to David and his dynasty, which was to last forever. Yet the promises of God did not remove the dynasty from the contingency of history. Divine promises do not guarantee future success measured in human terms. The promise of indefectibility cannot be used against God in some form of arrogant presumption. As the books of Kings stress, these promises imbedded in history remain conditioned on fidelity to God, especially on the part of the leaders, a fidelity that failed.

The God of Israel does on occasion appear in these earthly dramas. For all its brutality, the conquest of the land is narrated as the fulfillment of God's promises. Rescue from Canaanite harassment and subjugation is told as the action of God "raising up a savior." The foundation of monarchies and the establishment of dynasties happened as anointings by prophets and promises by God. Even the miracles of Elisha remind us of the divine power always present on a deeper level of the epic. The stories would still be told in terms of human decisions and other historical contingencies, but somehow behind the scenes was God who guided the events and sometimes instructed the actors. God acted in human history.

II. Sin and Faith in God

Why tell a story that stresses such high hopes in the beginning and ends in sin and disaster? Why tell a story of fumbling kings and military defeats that so thoroughly dilute the moments of glory and goodness in the history of Israel? What were authors in exile trying to do by telling this story to a people whose only realistic hope was to forget its tradition and be assimilated into the rich Babylonian culture?

Sin predominates this whole period, which is colored by the sad note of the final chapter. For the Deuteronomists, understanding the portrayal of human sinfulness was especially connected with the leaders and the holy institutions in which those leaders exercised and passed down their power. The majority of the judges were brutal. David would inaugurate his reign with adultery and murder. Solomon, the "son of God," would oppress his people for his own grandeur. The stories of the kings are stories of the weak and the evil, with a mention only here and there of the very holy.

Given these vicissitudes, was the God of Israel as fickle as the deities of the Near Eastern myths? Throughout the epic story, the Deuteronomists again insist that God was faithful to his covenant obligations. Did God cease to love his people? The Deuteronomists insist this was not the case. God, however, was a jealous lover (Deut 5:9; 6:15). He demanded an exclusive relationship. As the prophets would later say, God would not tolerate other gods. And when such infidelity occurred, God was ready to root up and tear down what he had planted and built.

In a history dominated by sin, the people of God may lose king and Temple. Yet God is above the vicissitudes of history. Faith in the God of history is a faith that draws his people beyond history, where truth and justice are uncompromised. Perhaps the failures and mistakes could be looked at with cold honesty because Israel saw its life rooted not in its own endeavors but in a transcendent God who was angered but not diminished by the sins of Israel. "To serve Yahweh" is to commit oneself to God's truth and justice.

On its deepest level, the Deuteronomist history is thus a testimony to faith in God's goodness and justice, a testimony that history is not a narration of the absurdity of life. For all its struggle and disappointments, their life was worth the struggle. This was an act of faith because all the evidence spoke to the contrary. Good kings like Josiah suffered military defeat. The northern tribes then the southern were conquered and scattered in foreign lands. The Temple of Yahweh lay in cold and dusty ruins. However, in the land of Babylon where no national future could be planned or even seen, the Deuteronomists clung to a faith that it was good to be an Israelite. It was good because God remained the God of Israel. Life was good. For all the sinfulness, it was good to be God's people.

King David, for all his paradigm character, could appear with his sins because the real paradigm was God and his Law. A hero like David was more important as a model of repentance, a person who could recognize his failure and then turn back to God for mercy. A major role of prophets like Nathan and Elijah was to confront the kings with their shortcomings and call them to repentance. In this sense, God is the God of human ambiguity and fumbling. God is the God of forgiveness.

III. Hope for the Future

The picture, however, is not all bleak. Occasionally as with Joshua, David, Josiah, and Hezekiah, we see the beauty of lives reflecting the presence of God. For all his sinfulness, David remained an image of fidelity. Over and over again, the Deuteronomist measured the successive kings by the standard of David (1 Kgs 3:3; 9:4; 11:4, 6, 33, 38; 14:8; 15:3, 5, 11; 2 Kgs 14:3; 16:2; 18:3; 22:2). Eventually, David becomes a symbol of hope, a symbol of God's fidelity even in the midst of destruction and exile.

History ebbs and flows according to a mysterious obscurity that frustrates human understanding. The biblical storytellers, however, elicit a heartfelt commitment to a divine purpose, if seen only in retrospect. The stories of the past suggest a divine purpose. Beginnings look for endings. For the Israelites, however, endings must also look to beginnings. Gazing at the past, the Israelites would have to back into the future. The future would echo past promises. Soon the Israelites would expect a new Exodus, a new David, and a new covenant as their hope for the future.

Centuries later a son of David and one greater than Solomon (Matt 1:1; 12:42) would proclaim the coming of the kingdom of God (Matt 4:17), which will demand producing the fruit of justice (Matt 21:43). When Jesus appeared between Moses and Elijah (Mark 9:4 and parallels), he showed how much he belonged to this epic of God's kingdom on earth. Again faced with crucifixion and the burning of the Temple, those "awaiting the kingdom of God" would look beyond history to the coming of a Son of Man seated on his glorious throne inviting the just, "Come, you who are blessed by my Father. Inherit the kingdom prepared for you from the foundation of the world" (Matt 25:34).

PART II

The Chroniclers' History

7

Introduction to the Chroniclers' History

Sometime after the Babylonian Exile, a group of scribes decided to rewrite the history of the kingdoms up to the Exile along with the story of the difficult restoration of Israel after the Exile. The results are 1 and 2 Chronicles and the books of Ezra and Nehemiah. The apparent motive for this major work was to assist in the reconstruction of Israel after the Exile.

The Deuteronomist history had insisted on the infidelity of the kings, providing an understanding of the destruction of Jerusalem in 587 BC and the deportation of the Jews into Babylon as a punishment for infidelity to the covenant. For some, this depressing history could easily blast beyond repair all hopes Israel had for a glorious future. The Chroniclers, therefore, decided to modify this depressing picture. After all and against all expectation, Israel still existed and had a future.

The Chroniclers' history returns to two sources of Israel's hope: (a) the Temple in her midst where God can be worshiped by sacrificial ritual and (b) the Davidic dynasty "established forever" as a part of God's kingdom (1 Chr 17:14), even though at the time of the writing no descendant of David ruled as king in Israel. These bases of hope were tightly connected with each other in the Chroniclers' theology, which portrays David carefully preparing the building of the Temple before consigning the task to his son Solomon (1 Chr 22—29). In Ezra, the story of the rebuilding of the Temple is attributed to the work of Zerubbabel, the last descendant of David described in this history (Ezra 5), and then mention of the dynasty disappears. The Davidic dynasty with its promises and hopes is subsumed into the religious institution of the Temple.

Many elements of style and perspective bind 1 and 2 Chronicles with Ezra and Nehemiah. The four books form a coherent whole, beginning after a series of genealogies and summaries with the story of David in the tenth century BC and continuing through the formation of the Judaism of the Persian period, probably as late as the fourth century BC. The style and interests of these works in turn reflect those of the priestly strand of the Pentateuch.

Other differences in emphasis suggest another hand in the writing of Ezra and Nehemiah, allowing the question of whether Ezra and Nehemiah were written after or before Chronicles. Clearly the books grew through many additions and editions. The final form of this collection, probably stemming from the around 350 BC, shows enough cohesion that we will refer to the group responsible for its writing as "the Chroniclers."

In the Greek Bible, which arranged books mostly by content, these postexilic books were placed after the books of Kings (or "Kingdoms" as they are called in Greek), where they are found today in most English translations. The Hebrew Bible, however, arranged books by the order of their canonization and placed these books in the third major part, "the Writings," where Ezra and Nehemiah now appear before Chronicles.

Chronicles closely parallels Samuel and Kings, and the distinctive perspective of Chronicles can best be seen by a comparison with Samuel and Kings, a distinctiveness that in turn helps us understand better the purpose of postexilic theology. Ezra and Nehemiah also are a major source of information for the history of Israel after the Exile.

This is the period of intense literary activity for Israel, the period when our Bible begins to take shape. Oral and written traditions from the time of the monarchy were somehow preserved in the period of devastation and displacement. Patriarchal and Exodus traditions (J and E) were preserved and integrated into a distinctive tradition concerned about religious and priestly matters (P). Soon the Book of Deuteronomy would be detached from the Deuteronomistic history and fused with these patriarchal and Exodus traditions to form what we know as the Torah (Pentateuch). Nehemiah may refer to this form of the Torah (Neh 8). The preachings of exilic prophets, like Ezekiel and Deutero-Isaiah, will be written down by disciples. Some become self-standing "books"; others are incorporated into existing written prophetic works. In the period immediately following the return from exile, other preachers will continue the prophetic tradition, like Trito-Isaiah, Haggai, and Zechariah, preaching that in some cases will become additional "books," in other cases, enlarging existing "books." The loss of political and economic power appears to have turned the Jews (now known by their Judean homeland) to the spiritual and literary.

8
1 and 2 Chronicles

I. Overview

The Chroniclers' intention clearly appears as we note the changes and omissions they made to their principal sources, the books of Samuel and Kings. The Chroniclers frequently copy word for word many sections from these books. At times they tap into other sources of information, providing supplements to our knowledge of ancient Israel. In 1 Chronicles 1—9, all of Israel's history from Adam to Saul is summed up in a series of genealogies. The death of Saul is mentioned (1 Chr 10), but only as a prelude to the career of David, with whom the remainder of 1 Chronicles is concerned. In 2 Chronicles, the authors all but ignore the northern kingdom and devote themselves to the kings of David's dynasty. The Chroniclers delete from their sources whatever might depict David in anything but the kindest light. Apart from the census story, David's sins, the revolts of his people against him, and his weaknesses are all passed over. He appears as the ideal king. Solomon receives a similar treatment.

The emphasis in Chronicles is not only on David and his dynasty but also on the relationship of the Davidic kings to the Temple of Jerusalem. Second Chronicles 2—7 is dedicated to a minute description of the building and dedication of Solomon's Temple. In 2 Chronicles 10—36, the lion's share of space goes to the kings who concerned themselves with the Temple and its personnel.

From this comparison we can identify the literary form of Chronicles as a kind of theological history, a loosely historical narrative that elaborates ancient texts in order to edify, teach, or explain some question of importance at the time of the writers.

The Chroniclers' history verges on the midrashic in the way it selects, emphasizes, and imaginatively embroiders the data taken from Samuel and Kings.

From the amount of space given to the Temple, Temple worship, and the Temple personnel, the Chroniclers' obvious intent was to tell the story from the point of view of priestly or liturgical functions. From the amount of space given to David and his dynasty, it is equally clear that their principal intent was to emphasize the liturgical significance of David and the important part that the Temple was meant to play in the life of Israel. Chronicles appear to be intent on emphasizing the hopes of Israel and the ecclesiastical nature of the nation.

Later divided into two books, the Chroniclers' history falls into four distinct parts:

1 Chronicles 1—9:	Genealogies from Adam to Saul, with emphasis first on those of Judah and David (2—4); secondly on those of the priests, Levites, and other Temple personnel (6 and 9)
1 Chronicles 10—29:	David's reign, with emphasis on the king's liturgical achievements: his transfer of the ark to Jerusalem (15—16), his desire to build the Temple (17), and his preparations for the Temple's construction and its liturgical personnel (21—28)
2 Chronicles 1—9:	The reign of Solomon, with emphasis on matters liturgical: the preparation, building, and dedication of the Temple (2—7)
2 Chronicles 10—36:	The history of the kings of Judah, with emphasis on those who lavished time and attention upon the Temple: Asa (14—16), Jehoshaphat (17—21), Hezekiah (29—32), and Josiah (34—35)

II. Significant Passages in 1 and 2 Chronicles

A. 1 Chronicles 1—9 / Genealogies

As in the priestly strand of the Pentateuch, concern for genealogies is really a concern for legitimation. These lists are not like modern genealogies, but rather expressions of faith in the grand plan of God. By means of genealogies, the authors present links that go back to Adam (1 Chr 1:1), thus summarizing the whole patriarchal history—which must by now have been written down in some form, giving the first forms of our Book of Genesis.

3:1–24 *The descendants of David*

Chapter 3 picks up David's genealogy interrupted after 2:17. We hear first about the sons of David (3:1–9). With some variations in the names, this list seems to come from 2 Samuel 3:25 and 5:14–15. The next paragraph (3:10–16) follows the descendants of Solomon who ruled as kings of Judah.

The last paragraph (3:17–24) describes seven or eight generations after Jeconiah, named Jehoiachin in 2 Kings 24, the last surviving Davidic king with descendants. The first generation includes Shealtiel, Pedaiah, and Shenazzar, who is probably the Sheshbazzar named in Ezra 1:8, 11; 5:14–15, the Davidic prince who led the first group of captives back to Israel. The second generation includes Zerubbabel, described here as a son of Pedaiah, but as the son of Shealtiel in Ezra, Nehemiah, and Haggai, where he has a leading role in rebuilding the Temple (Ezra 3:2, 8; 5:2; Neh 12:1; Hag 1:12–14; 2:2–23). From Zerubbabel, five or six generations continue the Davidic heritage (3:19–34), depending on how we read a partially corrupt text (3:22). The Davidic line seems to be passed through Hananiah (3:19), the father of Shecaniah (3:21), the father of Shemaiah (3:22), either the father or brother of Neariah (3:22), the father of Elioenai (3:22). The last generation names seven sons (3:24), and nothing is said about which son then carried the Davidic heritage. These seven or eight generations take us to roughly 400–350 BC, probably the time of the Chroniclers.

This effort to keep track of the Davidic family into the time of the writing suggests that the Chroniclers continued to place their hopes in some form of restoration of the Davidic dynasty. The Chroniclers reemphasize the eternal nature of David's dynasty as expressed through the prophecy of Nathan, "His throne shall be firmly established forever *('ad 'olam)*" (1 Chr 17:14; 1 Sam 7:16).

Both Matthew and Luke are concerned to show Jesus as a royal descendant of David through Zerubbabel. However, neither Matthew's nor Luke's genealogies of Jesus mention any of the descendants from Zerubbabel listed in Chronicles (Matt 1:13–16; Luke 3:23–27).

B. 1 Chronicles 10—29 / David and the Temple

God's covenant with David (especially 1 Chr 17) dominates the entire work of Chronicles, eclipsing the promises to Abraham and the Sinai covenant. David is the ideal king. He does not build the Temple, but he arranges the details of its building and its functioning (1 Chr 22—28). Solomon first receives the plans for the Temple from David (1 Chr 28:11) and then executes the construction (2 Chr 3). For the Chroniclers the Temple is a Davidic Temple.

15:1–29 ***David brings the ark to Jerusalem***

After telling the story of David's consolidation of power and his establishment of Jerusalem as his capital (1 Chr 11—14)—drawing on 2 Samuel 5—the Chroniclers now turn their attention to their primary concern, David's organization of religious matters. The first stage of David bringing the ark to Jerusalem, the movement from Kiriath-jearim to the house of Obededom (1 Chr 13:1–14; 2 Sam 6:1–11), was moved ahead in the narrative to show how David's success (1 Chr 14; 2 Sam 5:11–25) is linked to his worship of Yahweh. The second stage of the ark's progress to Jerusalem is then here described with great religious pageantry (1 Chr 15).

Whereas 2 Samuel 6:15 describes David "and all the Israelites" as bringing up the ark, the Chroniclers are careful to specify the role of the Levites in carrying the ark: "No one may carry the ark of God except the Levites" (15:2). This instruction shifts the privilege of carrying the ark from the priests (1 Kgs 8:3–4) to the Levites (see also 2 Chr 5:4). Before the narrative taken from 2 Samuel 6:12–19 is resumed, we hear of further instructions to the Levites on their responsibilities (1 Chr 15:4–15), with special attention to the Levitical musicians (15:16–24). Following these liturgical rules is key to avoiding the wrath of God bursting out on the people (15:13). The political significance of the event fades behind the religious ritual.

17:1–27 *The divine promise to David*

The Chroniclers use 2 Samuel 7 to describe the eternal covenant of God with David. The words in 1 Chronicles 7 often follow word for word the account in 2 Samuel. But several subtle changes are made. The reference to coming out of Egypt is dropped (1 Chr 17:6; compare 2 Sam 7:6). The promise of perpetuity of reign is explicitly related to Solomon's government, with a reference to God's kingdom: "I will maintain him in my house and my kingdom [*malkuti*] forever, and his throne shall be firmly established forever" (1 Chr 17:14; compare 2 Sam 7:16). David's response in Chronicles then alludes to the promise of God for David's family "reaching into the distant future [*l*^{e}*merachoq*]" (2 Chr 17:17). The stability of the Davidic line is thus reinforced. At the same time we see the beginning of several references to the kingdom of God.

21:1—22:1 *The census, the plague, and the altar*

Following the detached episode of 2 Samuel 24, the Chroniclers by rare exception include a sin of David, his census. The story is needed because of its connection with David's erection of the altar of holocausts, which connects David to the building of the Temple. The connection between Ornan's (Araunah's) threshing floor and the Temple is made clear in 22:1. God's acceptance of David's offering is shown by his sending "fire from heaven" (22:26), a divine gesture reminiscent of Elijah on Carmel (1 Kgs 18:38; see also Lev 9:24), to be repeated at the dedication of the Temple (2 Chr 7:1).

As the story begins, the Chroniclers introduce a change. It is not Yahweh who incites David to sin (2 Sam 24:1), but "Satan." Satan first appears in postexilic literature as an angel in God's court who tests or accuses human beings (Job 1:6–12; Zech 3:1–2). The Hebrew noun, *satan*, means an "adversary." In later apocalyptic literature, Satan becomes an anti-God creature, whose work is to dishonor God and destroy his work. Like the theologians of the postexilic period, the Chroniclers introduce Satan here to avoid attributing evil to God.

22:2–5 ***David's plans for the Temple***

The next eight chapters, 22—29, are unique to Chronicles. The religious details here look much like the cultic laws of the Torah. They are explicitly described as part of David's instructions to Solomon in 22:12 (see also 16:40). Very important for the Chroniclers' theology is David's role in the building of the Temple. David basically designs the Temple and arranges for all the building materials. In effect this is David's Temple. Thus the hopes connected with the Davidic dynasty are melded with those linked to the Temple.

28:11–19 ***David hands the Temple plans to Solomon***

With David handing "the plans" (*tabnit*) of the Temple to Solomon, the continuity of work between the two kings is established. These plans or patterns include the division of work between priests and Levites, the liturgical vessels and appointments of the Temple (28:13–18), and all else that "he had in mind" for the Temple (28:11). The priestly strand of the Torah places all these determinations as coming from Moses (Exod 25:9–30). In Chronicles, not just the buildings but the entire Temple worship is now seen to be rooted in David, who, by the way, commits all these plans "to writing...by the hand of Yahweh" (28:19), an echo again of the postexilic concern for following "the book," but also an insistence of the replacement of Moses by David as the person responsible for the written word of God (compare Exod 31:18).

C. 2 Chronicles 1—9 / Solomon and the Temple

Involved in none of the court intrigues and few of the moral failings described by 1 Kings, Solomon succeeds his father David. While Solomon's wisdom is again celebrated (1:7–12; 9:1–8; see 1 Kgs 3:5–15; 10:1–13), Solomon's famous judgment between the two prostitutes (1 Kgs 10:16–28) is passed over in silence. The Chroniclers also appear to avoid references to Egypt and the Exodus tradition found in Kings. Moses and the Exodus tradition (Sinai covenant?) have taken a backseat to David and the promise of an eternal dynasty. In this section, the Law appears as Solomon's guide (6:16).

2 Chr 2:1–15 *Preparations for the Temple*

This chapter is a rewriting of 1 Kings 5:15-31. The description of the Temple that Solomon proposes to build is not only "to honor Yahweh, my God" (1 Kgs 5:19), but also "to consecrate it to him, for the burning of fragrant incense in his presence, for the perpetual display of the showbread, for holocausts morning and evening, and for the sabbaths, new moons and festivals of Yahweh our God" (2 Chr 2:3). The Chroniclers avoid describing the Temple as the place where God dwells. The exilic prophets had effectively made the point that God cannot be confined to a building (2:5; see Jer 7; 26; Ezek 10:18–19; 11:22–23). Rather, the Temple is the place where people worship God, where they offer sacrifice and celebrate feasts.

Huram (Hiram), the king of Tyre, starts his prayer of praise with the blessing found in 1 Kings 5:21 but then continues to confess Yahweh as "the God of Israel who made heaven and earth" (1 Chr 2:11). Far from being affronted by Solomon's religious declaration in 2:4, Huram, the Gentile king, is actually drawn into the circle of the faithful as he fulfills a part of God's plan.

7:1–11 *Completion and dedication of the Temple*

The Chroniclers follow the narrative of 1 Kings 8:54–66, elaborating on the liturgy of the dedication. In the first verse, the Chroniclers interrupt the account with the same description that they had made earlier regarding David's sacrifice on Ornan's threshing floor (1 Chr 21:26): "fire came down from heaven and consumed the holocaust and the sacrifices" (7:1; see 1 Kgs 18:38). The Chroniclers also add a description of the inability of the priests to enter the Temple because of the "glory of Yahweh" filling the house (7:2; 5:14; 1 Kgs 8:10–11), a description that echoes the dedication of the desert meeting tent (Exod 24:16; 40:34–35).

D. 2 Chronicles 10—36 / The Kings after Solomon

Following 1 Kings 12 to 2 Kings 25, the Chroniclers provide a brief sketch of the successors of Solomon down to the destruction of Jerusalem. Unlike the authors of Kings, however, the Chroniclers have little interest in describing the events of the northern kingdom. Even Elijah and Elisha withdraw from view.

13:1–23 ***The reign of Abijah***

Dismissed as a wicked king by the Deuteronomist historians, Abijah (named Abijam in 1 Kgs 15:1–8) becomes one of the good kings in the Chroniclers' account. With an army half the size of the enemy, he defeats Jeroboam of the north (2 Chr 13:3, 13–18) and lives longer than his evil rival (13:20–21), because he "relied on Yahweh" (13:18). As a consequence of this good behavior, "God defeated Jeroboam and all Israel before Abijah and Judah" (13:15).

The Chroniclers insert a speech into the account of Abijah. In reality, the speech is a proclamation of the Chroniclers' theology. It describes God's "covenant in salt" with David (13:5) that must be recognized. Here we hear also of "the kingdom of Yahweh *(mamleket Yhwh)* in the hands of the sons of David" (1 Chr 13:8). The speech condemns the northern perversion of cult, describing Jeroboam's golden calves (1 Kgs 12:28) precisely as idolatrous "gods" (13:8) and insists that the real priests and Levites actually left the northern kingdom (13:9; see 11:14). In Judah alone can one find the correct cult, an advantage that spills out into miraculous military success. This taunt speech is patterned on older ones (Judg 9:7–20; 1 Sam 17:45–47).

Chronicles jumps completely over 1 Kings 17—21 to focus on Jehoshaphat (who never jumps; 2 Chr 17—20), repeating with a few modifications the story of the botched attack on Ramoth-gilead (18:1–34; see 1 Kgs 22:2-38) and the summary account of Jehoshaphat's rule (20:31–37; see 1 Kgs 22:41–51). The Chroniclers' modifications follow their basic theology and purpose. For example, in the battle of Ramoth-gilead, King Jehoshaphat is saved, not simply by being recognized from "his battle cry" (1 Kgs 22:32), but because "Jehoshaphat cried out and Yahweh helped him" (2 Chr 18:31).

17:1–9 ***Jehoshaphat's zeal for the Law***

The description in 2 Chronicles 17 of Jehoshaphat's dedication to the Law has no parallel in Kings. Later, Chronicles will repeat the story in 2 Kings 22:8–13 of the discovery of the "book of the Law," which supposedly occurred some 233 years later under Josiah's reform (2 Chr 34:14–18). Hence, the reference to "the book of the Law" in this story (17:9) appears anachronistic. However, it fits well the deep concern for the Law found throughout Chronicles. The Law becomes the guide and standard for kings (15:3; 17:9; 23:18; 25:4; 31:3, 21; 33:8; 35:26) and for the priests and Levites (30:16; 31:4).

In this story, the Law is taught to the people. We see here the beginning of an explicit sense of national identity based on common popular observance of the Law. Rabbinic Judaism with its focus on a written text appears to be projected back to the time of Jehoshaphat. In effect, this and other stories about the importance of the written book of the Law in Chronicles seem to reflect the mid-fourth century when Chronicles was written, as we will see in our study of Ezra and Nehemiah.

19:1–3 ***Jehu, the seer***

The only rebuke of Jehoshaphat in the Chroniclers' material is that from Jehu, son of Hanani, the "seer," who scolds the king for cooperating with Ahab in the battle of Ramoth-gilead (19:1–2). Jehu is one of the few prophets who appear in Chronicles.

20:13–20 ***Jahaziel the Levite***

The successful military campaign described in 2 Chronicles 20 has no parallel in Kings. The description of that campaign, however, follows the pattern of the story in 2 Kings 3, with a change of the names of the persons involved. In the Chronicles account, Jehoshaphat replaces both Jehoram of Israel and the unnamed king of Judah in the Deuteronomists' account. The spirit-filled Levite, Jahaziel, in Chronicles replaces the famous Elisha in Kings, who is totally ignored in Chronicles. In both stories, God provides victory over the enemies. In this story, the Chroniclers show the influence of Isaiah 7:9 (see 2 Kgs 19:6) when they proclaim through the mouth of Jehoshaphat, "Trust in Yahweh, your God, and you will be found firm." This proclamation also includes an unusual emphasis on the prophets, "Trust in his prophets and you will succeed" (20:20).

After skipping all the material in 2 Kings dedicated to Elisha (2 Kgs 2—8), 2 Chronicles 22 picks up more or less the stories of the Judean kings from 2 Kings 8:24, including references to 2 Kings 9 (2 Chr 22:7, 9), 2 Kings 10 (2 Chr 22:8), longer rewritings of 2 Kings 11 (2 Chr 22:10—23:17), 2 Kings 12 (2 Chr 24:1–14, 23–27), 2 Kings 14 (2 Chr 25:1–13, 17–27); 2 Kings 15 (2 Chr 26:1–4, 19, 21, 23; 27:1–3, 7–9), 2 Kings 16 (2 Chr 28). Material added in this section often deals with the Levites and the Temple (for example, 2 Chr 23:18–21; 26:16–18) or additional material about the Judean kings (for example, 2 Chr 24:15–22; 25:14–16; 27:4–6). In this section there are surprising but brief references to the familiar prophets, Elijah (21:12) and Isaiah (26:27), along with the otherwise unknown Oded of Samaria (28:9–11).

The Chroniclers then dedicate four chapters to the reign of Hezekiah (chapters 29—32). They begin their story of this good king by tapping into 2 Kings 18:1–5, the beginning of his reign and the initiation of his religious reform (29:1–3). However, the Chroniclers will then add about one hundred verses elaborating on the religious aspects of Hezekiah's reform (29:4—31:21).

29:4–30 *The religious reform*

What is most characteristic of the Chroniclers' purpose is the detailed account of Hezekiah's religious reform. Hezekiah summons the priests and Levites (29:4) but speaks only to the Levites (29:5–11). The public confession of past sins resembles Nehemiah 9:2. While the priests alone enter the interior of the Temple

(29:16), the Levites do the bulk of the work of "sanctifying," that is, cleansing the Temple (29:12–17). The rites of expiation performed by the priests follow closely the prescriptions in Leviticus 4. One of the most emphasized functions of the Levites is singing. We see references to their musical instruments (29:25) and to their songs of praise (29:30), in both cases with explicit links to David. Continuity with David comes also through the Levites.

30:1–27 ***Celebration of the Passover***

After the rites of Temple purification, Hezekiah organizes the celebration of Passover in Jerusalem. The Chroniclers are drawing from stories about the later King Josiah, who according to 2 Kings was the first king to celebrate the Passover since the time of the judges (2 Kgs 23:21–23; see 2 Chr 35:1–19).

Just as Hezekiah offered the sin offerings earlier "for all Israel" (29:24), so here he invites "all Israel and Judah," even "Ephraim and Manasseh," to come to the feast (30:1). A remarkable "ecumenical" flexibility appears regarding those from the north who were not ritually "cleansed." Insisting on the importance of "seeking God" over the requirements of "holiness," the prayer of the king satisfies for the cultic infraction (30:18–20). The result: "There was great rejoicing in Jerusalem, for since the days of Solomon, son of David, king of Israel, there had not been the like in the city" (30:26).

The Chroniclers end their story of Hezekiah (32:1–22) by returning to the invasion of Sennacherib as found in 2 Kings 18:13, 17–37; 19:35–37. The Chroniclers, however, skip over the humiliating tribute paid by Hezekiah to Sennacherib (2 Kgs 18:13–16) and reduce the role of the prophet Isaiah in the war (2 Kgs 19:1–34) to saying a prayer (2 Chr 32:20).

Continuing the story after the death of Hezekiah, the Chroniclers retell the evils of King Manasseh (2 Chr 33:1–20; see 2 Kgs 21:1–18), adding a curious positive description to the story (33:11–17), perhaps to explain his long life and reign. Josiah's reform is rewritten from 2 Kings 22—23 (2 Chr 34—35). To the description of the battle of Megiddo (35:20–24), the Chroniclers add Josiah's refusal to listen to the prophetic words of Neco—perhaps to explain the sudden end of his life and reign.

36:1–23 ***The end of the kingdom***

The last three kings, Jehoiakim, Jehoiachin, and Zedekiah, are condemned as evil (36:5–14). Contrary to 2 Kings 24:6, the Chroniclers describe Jehoiakim as taken prisoner by Nebuchadnezzar (36:6). The general theme of Chronicles is to blame the last kings of Judah for the wrath of God. However, in this text the authors give a general condemnation of the people as not listening to the prophets, similar to the judgment passed on Israel by the Deuteronomist historians:

> Early and often did Yahweh, the God of their fathers, send his messengers to them, for he had compassion on his people and his dwelling place. But they mocked the messengers of God, despised his warnings and scoffed at his prophets, until the anger of Yahweh against the people was so inflamed that there was no remedy. (2 Chr 36:15–16; see 2 Kgs 17:13–18)

Jeremiah is mentioned by name three times (36:12, 21, 22). On the other hand, the Chroniclers make no mention of Jehoiachin's release in Babylon (2 Kgs 25:27–30). In its place now at the end of the book are two verses that describe the edict of Cyrus, king of Persia, allowing the Jews "to go up" to Jerusalem and rebuild the Temple (2 Chr 36:22–23). These two verses are identical to the opening verses of the Book of Ezra (1:1–3). In the Hebrew Bible these verses are the final words of the whole Bible.

III. The Message of 1 and 2 Chronicles

A. Review of Themes

The significant passages from the books of Chronicles signal the following themes as important:

- King David as the key to a right relationship with God (1 Chr 3:1–24; 15:1–29; 21:15–22:1; 2 Chr 13:5)

- The important role of Levites in the life of Israel (1 Chr 15:2–24; 2 Chr 7:6; 13:9–10)
- The Temple of Jerusalem as the central element for the worship of God (2 Chr 2:1–15; 7:1–11)
- The Law as a standard of behavior for the kings and the people (2 Chr 17:9)
- The replacement of prophecy by Levitical office (2 Chr 20:13–19)
- The assembly of Israel (1 Chr 13:2, 4; 28:8; 29:1, 10, 20; 2 Chr 1:3, 5; 6:3, 12–13; 7; 8; 20:5, 14; 23:3; 24:6; 28:14; 29:23, 28, 31–32; 30:2, 4, 13, 17, 23–25; 31:18)

B. The Theology of 1 and 2 Chronicles

Like the prophets, the Chroniclers console and encourage their people in difficult and discouraging times. The reconstruction of Israel after the Exile involved daunting obstacles ranging from inadequate land and resources to political hostility from neighboring peoples (see Ezra 4; Hag 2:3). To respond to these difficulties, the authors of Chronicles tell the story of the past. Although God may appear to be absent or unconcerned in the present time of pain and failure, the larger picture of history can retune one's faith to God's wavelength. The Chroniclers present that larger picture.

The Chroniclers do so by idealizing the picture. In their version of salvation history, the Chroniclers do not give us the same sense of historical contingency and unpredictability as we find in the Deuteronomist history. Rather, the Chroniclers iron out history into a pattern. Good kings have prosperous reigns; bad kings face disasters. On the surface, things may change radically; on a deeper level, the firm rock of God's plan holds things stable. As King Jehoshaphat exhorted the Judahites and inhabitants of Jerusalem, "Trust in Yahweh your God, and you will be found firm" (2 Chr 20:20).

God's plan for the Chroniclers is intimately connected to the written book of the Law, the supreme guide for Israel. Although the Chroniclers remain faithful to the Deuteronomist story of the discovery of the book of the Law under Josiah around 622 BC, this book of the Law plays a dominant role in the decisions of the earlier kings, other officials, and the people in general.

The Chroniclers' message is to look for signs of hope. Those signs hover around two institutions, the Davidic dynasty and the Temple built by the Davidic kings. The kings were not all that bad. The disaster of 587 BC occurred mostly because of the sinfulness of the last individual kings just prior to that Babylonian invasion. But as late as King Hezekiah, the virtue of the king led to peace and prosperity for the people. As the Chroniclers' genealogy points out, a shadow of that dynasty remains in the descendants of David still with the people (1 Chr 3:17–24).

At the time of the writing of Chronicles, the Temple and its cult had begun again. The authors saw in the scrupulous observance of rituals the key to a right relationship with God and to success as a people. The identity of the Israelites became centered in cult. Commissioned directly by David, the Levites appear as the guardians of that cult. In many ways, the Levites replace the prophets in the Chroniclers' view.

The glory of this second Temple was perhaps only a shadow of that of the original (see Ezra 3:12; Hag 2:3). Nevertheless, through that Temple the people could experience the "everlasting mercy" of God to his people. Kings are evaluated by their contribution to the Temple. Through that Temple the people regained continuity with the Davidic kings who built and reformed it.

9
Ezra and Nehemiah

I. Overview

Ezra and Nehemiah taken together give us a continuation of Israelite history into the postexilic period, the period when the Jews in Babylonia were allowed to return to the land of Israel to rebuild their Temple and their city. We have here a glimpse into "the Persian period," when Israel accepted the domination of a foreign, Gentile empire and sought to understand itself in terms of its spiritual heritage.

The books of Ezra and Nehemiah actually consist of a compilation of many different documents, memoirs, census lists and other lists, genealogies, letters, and other "official" documents. Some of the narrative accounts are written in the first person, thus suggesting something like "memoirs." Others are third-person descriptions. Most of the texts are in Hebrew. A few are written in Aramaic, particularly those that have the form of a letter to or from the Persian government. All this diverse material now comes together without great concern for chronological sequence to form a unified exhortation to reconstruct Israel after the Exile.

In the Hebrew Bible, the two books are joined under one title, Ezra Nechemya; however, chapters and verses begin again from scratch at the point where we separate the two books. In the Greek Bible, the two books are also combined in twenty-three consecutive chapters as Esdras II (or B). Esdras I (or A) of the Greek Bible, a second-century BC collection of stories from 2 Chronicles, Ezra and Nehemiah, plus other stories, is included in the Orthodox canon. We will study what are found in all three canons as Ezra and Nehemiah.

At some point these books were edited and joined to the books of Chronicles to continue the historical narration of Israel through the Exile into the period of reconstruction extended into the fourth century BC. (In the Hebrew Bible, they precede the books of Chronicles.) Much of the content and style of both Ezra and Nehemiah connects well with the books of Chronicles. The historical descriptions of Ezra 1—3 follow closely on 2 Chronicles and may very well have originally been the continuation of that work. Like Chronicles, Ezra and Nehemiah are filled with lists of names that apparently functioned to give special legal status to those listed. Like Chronicles, these books throughout are deeply concerned about the Jerusalem Temple, placing great emphasis on the Levites and liturgical reform. These books also share the theology of Chronicles about the importance of each generation in solidarity with its leadership taking responsibility for sins and living in fidelity to the Law of God. Just as Hezekiah and Josiah made public confessions of sin (2 Chr 29:6–11; 34:21), so Ezra repeatedly confesses the sins of the people (Ezra 9:10–15; Neh 9:1–3; 11:33–37). On the basis of this similarity, we will consider the Chroniclers' history as including these two books.

Differences between the books of Ezra and Nehemiah and the books of Chronicles, however, warn us not to picture this continuation of Israelite history into the postexilic period as the work of one hand. Unlike Chronicles, these books give very little attention to the Davidic dynasty. Brief mentions of Sheshbazzar and Zerubbabel bring down the curtain on the Davidic dynasty. Further differences include an interest in the Exodus and Sinai (see Neh 1:7–8; 9:9–15). The "ecumenical" flexibility found in the story of Hezekiah (2 Chr 17—20) disappears in the legal rigorism of Ezra and Nehemiah (see Ezra 2:62–63). This complex relationship to Chronicles might be best understood in terms of the various sources used by the editors of Ezra and Nehemiah.

The chronology reflected in the narrations of Ezra and Nehemiah is that of the Persian Empire of the fifth and fourth centuries BC. The principal dates of that period are as follows:

538	The edict of Cyrus allowing the Jews to return
c. 535	The expedition and "governorship" of Sheshbazzar
529–522	The reign of Cambyses
522–485	The reign of Darius I
520	The preaching of Haggai, the prophet; the work of Zerubbabel, the prince, and Joshua, the priest
520–515	The preaching of Zachariah, the prophet
515	The dedication of the second Temple of Jerusalem
485–465	The reign of Xerxes I
465–424	The reign of Artaxerxes I
445–433	The first mission of Nehemiah
431ff.	The second mission of Nehemiah
424–404	The reign of Darius II
404–358	The reign of Artaxerxes II
398	The most likely date for the work of Ezra
350(?)	The writing/editing of the Chroniclers' history

The chronology within the narrations of Ezra and Nehemiah is confusing because the dating of the work of Ezra is not clear from the text. The work of Ezra the priest is dated from the seventh year of Artaxerxes (Ezra 7:7), who probably should be identified as Artaxerxes II (404–358 BC). Ancient documents make no distinction in the names of successive rulers with the same name. Far fewer problems arise if we see Ezra's work as some fifty years after that of Nehemiah, despite the appearance of Ezra before Nehemiah in the narration.

In effect, the historical chronological sequence is found by jumping around the major parts of these two books. If placed in chronological sequence, the chapters would be in the following order:

Ezra 1—6:	Return from exile and building the Temple	538–515 BC
Nehemiah 1—7; 12:27–4:	Nehemiah's building the city walls; the dedication of walls	445–433 BC

Nehemiah 13:	The second mission of Nehemiah dealing with religious reforms	431–??? BC
Ezra 7—10; Nehemiah 8:	Ezra's religious reform; the solemn reading of the Law	398– ??? BC

Chapters such as Nehemiah 9; 10; see 11; 12:1–26 are sort of timeless descriptions of ceremonies and lists that could have their historical setting at any number of times.

The present arrangement or order of the books appears to be based on the effort to describe Ezra and Nehemiah in parallel ways, to show the complementarity of their work. We will follow that order. The authors apparently wanted also to show the parallel between the work of these postexilic leaders with the great kings of the past who were responsible for the first Temple.

II. Significant Passages in Ezra and Nehemiah

A. Ezra 1—6 / The Return of the Exiles

1:1–11 *The return from exile*

As mentioned earlier, 1:1–3 repeats the last verses of 2 Chronicles, describing the edict of Cyrus in 538 BC that allowed the exiled Jews to return home. Cyrus, the king of Persia (559–530 BC), captured the city of Babylon without a fight in 539 BC. What else we know of Cyrus the Great from history more or less fits the text of Ezra 1 if we allow for intense idealization. A baked clay inscription from the time of Cyrus reads:

> I am Cyrus, king of the world, great king, legitimate king, king of Babylon, king of Sumer and Akkad, king of the four rims (of the earth), son of Cambyses....I returned to sacred cities on the other side of the Tigris, the sanctuaries of which have been ruins for a long time, the images which (used) to live therein and established for them permanent sanctuaries. I (also) gathered all their (former)

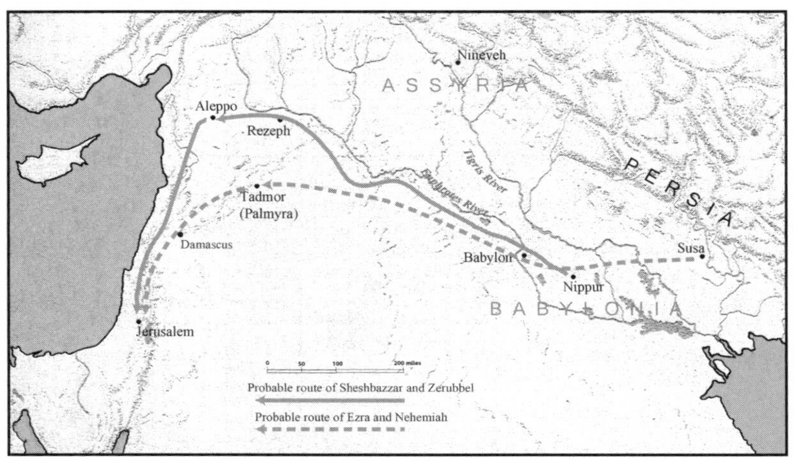

9A: Map of the Return from Exile

> inhabitants and returned (to them) their habitations....May all the gods whom I have resettled in their sacred cities ask daily Bel and Nebo for a long life for me and may they recommend me to Marduk. (*Ancient Near Eastern Texts Relating to the Old Testament*, ed. James B. Pritchard, 3rd ed. [Princeton, NJ: Princeton University Press, 1969], 316)

Cyrus thus may not have recognized "Yahweh, the God of heaven" quite as explicitly as presented by Ezra 1:2. He seems, nevertheless, to have the idea that there were many gods, and as emperor he needed to be loyal to them all. It is quite possible he spoke about Yahweh in such terms. Deutero-Isaiah wrote about Cyrus as Yahweh's "anointed one" (Isa 45:1).

The reference to "silver, gods, goods, and cattle" (1:4) sounds like an allusion to the goods that the Israelites collected at the time of their Exodus (Exod 11:2; see Dan 5:2). This return from Babylon looks like a new Exodus (see also Isa 40:3–5). Sheshbazzar, the fourth son of Jehoiachin (Shenazzar of 1 Chr 3:18), leads the first caravan of repatriates back to Israel. While the title "king" (*melek*) is frequently applied to the Persian ruler,

Sheshbazzar is discreetly called "prince" (*nasi'*; 1:8). Later he will be called "governor" (*pechah*; 5:14).

3:1–13 *Building the altar*

The first major task of the restoration was to construct a new Temple, starting with the altar of sacrifice. A new set of leaders now appear, Jeshua (Joshua), the high priest, and Zerubbabel, the Davidic prince (3:2; see Hag 1:12; 2:23; Zech 3:8; 4:11; 6:12).

Here as well as in Haggai and Zechariah, Zerubbabel is described as the son of Shealtiel, not Pedaiah as Chronicles lists him. The Davidic family from Jehoiachin appears in the diagram below.

We get the impression that all liturgy had ceased in Jerusalem by this time, although Jeremiah 41:5 describes sacrificial offerings continuing for some time after the destruction of the Temple by Nebuchadnezzar. Through the combined leadership of priest and prince, the official sacrificial worship of Yahweh is restored (3:3–6).

Work then turns to rebuilding the Temple around the altar. The mention of the "stonecutters and carpenters," cedarwood from Lebanon, even the port of Joppa, all function to set this effort in parallel with the building of the first Solomonic Temple (1 Chr 22:1–5; 2 Chr 2:8–15). The foundations are laid under the supervision of the priests and Levites. As the small size of the new Temple is traced on the ground by the laying of foundations to the musical accompaniment of priests and Levites, there results a "clamor," a mixture of sorrow and joy (3:12–13). Haggai 2:3 sug-

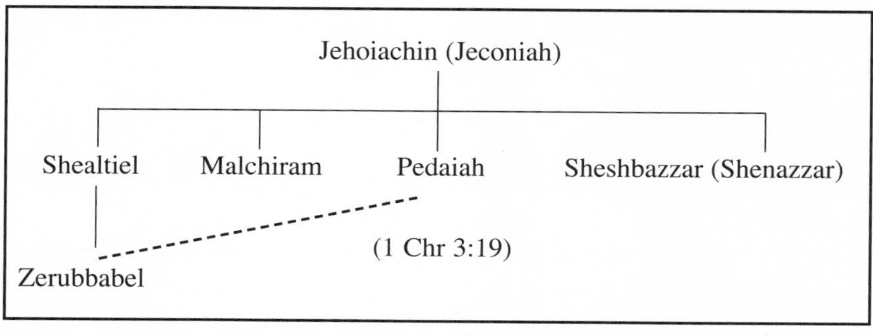

9B: Family of Jehoiachin

gests that the second Temple was a great disappointment when compared to the glorious Temple of Solomon.

4:1–5 ***Interruption of work on the Temple***

The "people of the land" (4:4) here appear to be the few Jews who remained in Israel during the Babylonian Exile (2 Kgs 25:22) as well as the foreigners who were settled in Israel by the Assyrians (2 Kgs 17:24–34). Rebuffed by Zerubbabel, Jeshua, and the leaders of Israel (4:3), this group becomes "the enemies of Judah and Benjamin" and effectively blocks further work on the Temple.

4:24—6:22 ***Resumption and completion of the building***

Work on the Temple resumed around 520 BC, the second year of Darius I of Persia. The Chronicler names the prophets Haggai and Zechariah (4:1) along with Zerubbabel and Jeshua (4:2) as leading the effort. The books of these two postexilic prophets detail further the efforts to build the Temple (see below). Both Haggai and Zechariah stress the continuing role of both Zerubbabel and Jeshua, hinting at hopes in the reestablishment of the Davidic dynasty through Zerubbabel (see Hag 2:23; Zech 3:8; 4:14). In contrast, the books of Ezra and Nehemiah ignore both Zerubbabel and Jeshua once the Temple is rebuilt and insist on Jewish leadership passing to priestly circles—perhaps because of Persian censorship.

Writing in Aramaic (5:7b—6:18), the Chronicler presents the "official" correspondence between King Darius I (522–485 BC) and his governor of the province where the Temple was being rebuilt. These documents establish the legality of the building effort and secure financial help from the Persian government. Continuing in Aramaic, the Chronicler then describes the completion and dedication of the Temple in 515 BC, all according to "the book of Moses" (6:18).

Completing the account of the reestablishment of Judaism, the Chronicler shifts back to Hebrew and narrates the feast of Passover, described as a sacrificial killing performed by the Levites, much like the Passover celebration after Hezekiah's reform (2 Chr 30) and Josiah's reform (2 Chr 35:1–19; 2 Kgs 23:21–23). Unlike the liberal attitude at the time of Hezekiah, legal exactitude here enforces a strict exclusivism, especially as regards the "uncleanness of the peoples of the land" (6:21).

B. Ezra 7—10 / The Return and Reform of Ezra

If we follow the sequence of the biblical text, then we must now jump about 120 years ahead to 398 BC, the seventh year of King Artaxerxes II (404–358 BC). Much of this section is in the first-person singular, making it look like the "memoirs" of Ezra, the priest and scribe. Putting first-person statements in the mouth of a famous person (see the Cyrus text above regarding 1:1–11) was a typical Old Testament rhetorical technique.

7:1–10 *Ezra's background*

Ezra's priestly genealogy ties into the high priestly genealogy through his ancestor, Seraiah, the last functioning high priest before the exile (2 Kgs 25:18; see 1 Chr 5:29–41). His claim to fame, however, is his education, "well versed in the Law of Moses." As such he is called a "scribe" (*sofer*, 7:6, 10). Ezra is named one of a class of authorities growing in importance in Israel, charged with studying and expounding the Law. More and more they appear as successors to the prophets. The expression, "The hand of Yahweh was on him" (7:6), may be a way of showing continuity with a prophet like Ezekiel (see Ezek 1:3; 3:22).

Appended to the introduction to Ezra is an Aramaic document describing Ezra's legal authority from the Persian king to enforce "the law of your God" (7:14) even by using the death penalty (7:26).

9:1–5 *Denunciation of mixed marriages*

Ezra's authority focuses on enforcing strict exclusivism in Jewish society. Attention here focuses on the evil of marriages with non-Jewish spouses.

The Mosaic Law against mixed marriages is not clear. Prohibitions such as Exodus 34:16 or Deuteronomy 7:3–4 denounce mixed marriages because of the danger of foreign spouses leading families away from the Israelite faith. These marriages are not denounced per se. In fact, Deuteronomy sets rules for marriages of Israelites and non-Israelite captives. Furthermore, the early traditions about the mixed marriages of heroes from Moses to David would have made such a blanket condemnation in the past rather difficult.

10:1–17 ***The people's response***

After a public confession of collective guilt like that of 9:6–14 (see also Bar 1:15—2:10), a great assembly (*qahal*) is gathered of all Israel, and covenants are made at which the people voice full acceptance of this rule of marital purity. This assembly of Israel appears at strategic moments in the story. Israel becomes most Israel when it is gathered. The agreement is to dismiss all the foreign wives and all the children born to them (10:3.44). Enforcement of this decision is to be in the hands of local magistrates and elders (10:14).

The authors of Ezra here obviously approve of this decision, seeing it as protecting the faith from syncretism by creating a barrier to other peoples. In fact, protection of the faith has completely eclipsed care for other human beings. The Judaism of Ezra embraces a ghetto mentality.

Also apparently written about this time, the Book of Ruth celebrates the holy marriage of Boaz, David's great-grandfather, to Ruth, the *Moabite*. The author of Ruth appears to be protesting the policies of Ezra, as does the author of Jonah.

C. Nehemiah 1—7 / The Return and Work of Nehemiah

As we move into the Book of Nehemiah, we must back up some fifty years to 445 BC, the twentieth year of Artaxerxes I (465–424 BC). The narrative is about Nehemiah, the counterpart to Ezra in these stories of postexilic reconstruction. Like the narratives about Ezra, this section is in the first-person singular. These chapters are thus presented as the memoirs of Nehemiah. Unlike the priest Ezra, Nehemiah is a layperson, whose main work is the reconstruction of the walls of Jerusalem. He appears to be an able politician of deep faith and a powerful speaker who knows how to persuade people and neutralize opposition.

1:1–11 ***Nehemiah's background and prayer***

Nehemiah, a powerful Jewish member of the Persian court (1:11, "cupbearer to the king"), learns about the difficulties and discouragement faced by the Jewish repatriates (1:3). The damage to the walls and gates of Jerusalem described here appear to be recent events and may be connected to the hostility described in Ezra 4. Nehemiah's prayer, echoing Deuteronomistic theology, follows the form of the familiar public confession of guilt.

2:1–20 ***Appointment by the king***

Demonstrating the political art of "perfect timing," Nehemiah receives the necessary "papers" along with some military force to travel to Jerusalem and assist the discouraged Jews. After some careful "fact-finding" (2:11–16) and after shoring up his base of support (2:17–18), Nehemiah confronts his political adversaries, Sanballat, Tobiah, and Geshem, as he gets the leaders of the Jews to begin work on the walls of Jerusalem (2:19–20).

Anti-Samaritan sentiment continues throughout the book. Sanballat and Tobiah remain rivals of Nehemiah, attempting to subvert at every turn his efforts to restore Jerusalem's position of strength (Neh 4:1–2; 6:1–2, 14, 19; 13:4–9). A Jewish writing from the island of Elephantine in southern Egypt dated 407 BC mentions a Sanballat as the Persian governor of Samaria (Pritchard, *Ancient Near Eastern Texts*, 492). Tobiah may have been the governor of Ammon, assuming that the description "servant" (2:10, 19) indicated a public official.

4:1–17 ***More enemies***

Adding the people of Ashdod to the list of enemies, the Chroniclers now picture Nehemiah and his followers surrounded in Jerusalem. Here Nehemiah proves himself both an able civic and military leader who can motivate people to great efforts in time of struggle with a "praise the Lord and pass the ammunition" exhortation (4:6–8).

5:1–13 ***Nehemiah's social program***

Before narrating the successful conclusion of the building project, the Chroniclers interject a picture of Nehemiah as protector of the poor. He deals with oppressive debt by exhorting the powerful "nobles and magistrates" to forgive the debts they held against the poor and thus show fidelity to the Law (see Deut 15:1–11; 23:20; Lev 25). Again we hear of Israel as a great assembly, agreeing to reform this social evil (5:13).

6:1–19 ***The building of the walls***

The building narrative picks up from chapter 4 and describes the completion of the project. Nehemiah avoids what appears to be an attempt to assassinate him (6:1–4) and then to accuse him of treason (6:5–9). He also sees through the attempt of his enemies, using the prophets of the time to lure him into the trap of entering the *hekal* of the Temple (6:10–14) and thus break faith with the priests (see 2 Chr 26:16).

The work is finished around the end of August, resulting in a political defeat for Nehemiah's enemies. The text describes the work as taking only fifty-two days (6:15). Josephus, the Jewish historian of the first century AD, claims it took a more credible two years and four months (*Antiquities*, XI, 8).

D. Nehemiah 8—13 / More on Ezra and Nehemiah

This last section provides a parallel between Ezra and Nehemiah as religious reformers. The order of the texts, however, requires that we first jump ahead to the time of Ezra and then back to the time of Nehemiah.

8:1–18 ***Promulgation the Law***

The story about Ezra is told in the third person. The scene is centered on Ezra publicly reading "the book of the Law of Moses" (8:1), also described as "the book of the Law of God" (8:8). All the "men, women, and children who could listen with understanding" are gathered in the assembly (8:2; see Josh 8:34–35). Ezra "read plainly...interpreting it so that all could understand what was read" (8:8), perhaps giving an Aramaic translation, or *targum*. The Levites are closely associated with this education in the Law (8:7, 9, 11, 13). The naming of Nehemiah as participating at this event (8:9) is probably a later addition—for one thing, the extra name along with mention of the Levites does not fit the grammar of the sentence.

Ezra's reading took about six hours (8:3). The description here could well be the promulgation of the recently edited Torah, the five books of Moses. If so, this would be the time when the J, E, P, and D traditions came together to form this Pentateuch. Six hours is not enough time to read aloud the entire Pentateuch. Perhaps this was only the first installment of seven days of reading (8:18). From this time on, Judaism is a religion of the book, a religion revolving around the Torah—which is supposed to bring rejoicing and celebration (8:9–11).

The episode concludes with a renewal of the feast of Booths (8:14–18; see Lev 23:33–43; Deut 16:13–15).

13:1–30 ***Nehemiah's second mission***

In the year 433 BC, the thirty-second year of Artaxerxes I (465–424), Nehemiah apparently returned to Susa—after the events described in 12:27–43 and 7:1–5. He received permission to return to Jerusalem when he hears of the return to power of his political enemy, Tobiah (13:7–8). Once in Jerusalem, Nehemiah neutralizes the house of Tobiah in regard to the Temple (13:9), reestablishes the support of the Levites (13:10–13), reestablishes the Sabbath rest (13:15–22), forbids future mixed marriages (13:23–27; see Ezra 9—10), and weakens the influence of Sanballat's family in regard to the high priesthood (13:28–29). These and other religious reforms (13:30–31) place Nehemiah in close parallel with Ezra.

III. The Message of Ezra and Nehemiah

A. Review of Themes

The selected passages above insist on the following themes:

- Return and restoration of past institutions (Ezra 1:5–11; 3:1–13; 6:19–22)

- Opposition, hostility, and suffering (Ezra 4:1–5; Neh 2:10, 19–20; 4:1–17; 6:10–14)
- Concern for imperial authority (Ezra 6:1–12; 7:14; Neh 1:11; 2:1–9)
- The written Law (Ezra 6:18; 7:6, 10; Neh 8:1–18)
- Exclusion of outsiders from cult and community (Ezra 6:21; 9:1–5; Neh 13:23–27)
- The assembly of Israel (Ezra 10:1, 8, 12, 14; Neh 5:13; 8:2, 17; 13:1)
- National confession of guilt and profession of obedience to the Law (Ezra 10:1–15)
- Protection of the poor within the community (Neh 5:1–13)

B. The Theology of Ezra and Nehemiah

If we read Ezra and Nehemiah from the perspective of an Orthodox Jew today, we would find full support for a position of exclusivism, a need for ramparts around the community, and a strict observance of the Law's most minute prescriptions. If we read these books from the perspective of a Jew or Christian brought up in liberal individualism, we would probably be shocked and repelled by the message of Ezra and thus faced with a dilemma. How can we pick and choose what we like about the message of Ezra and Nehemiah?

The way out of the dilemma is context and through the context to see a reality that is perhaps only imperfectly touched by this exclusivism and legalism. One context is the historical setting, one of dangerous opposition and conflict. Israel was faced with utter destruction. The Temple was in rubble; Jerusalem, in ruins; the Davidic dynasty, finished. The "holy kingdom" of God seemed no longer to exist. Israel became a small and poor province in the powerful and glorious Persian Empire. Should Israel give up its belief that she is God's chosen people? Ezra and Nehemiah urge Israel never to give up that belief.

Another context for understanding the rigorism of Ezra and Nehemiah is the Bible as a whole. Other books in the Old Testament canon stand in stark contrast with the exclusivism of Ezra and Nehemiah. The Book of Ruth describes the holy marriage of Boaz the Jew and Ruth the Moabite. Jonah satirizes the narrow and bigoted attitude of Jews who do not want pagan Assyria to be blessed. Deutero- and Trito-Isaiah preach an openness of Israel to the world. For Christians, the Gospels and Paul teach that the Law is a Law of love, and love excludes no one. Ezra and Nehemiah must be read in a dialectic with these conflicting texts. Within that dialectic, the message of Ezra and Nehemiah appears to be the importance of the believing family. More than in armies or through a powerful clergy, it is in the believing family that the faith is preserved and passed down.

As the story in Ezra and Nehemiah unfolds we see a new form of leadership, not based on a dynasty but on priestly leadership. Ezra, the priest, and Nehemiah, the imperial "cupbearer," exercise their authority to resolve the people's problems. They do not act for their own glory. They do not pass their roles down to their children. After they have performed their governing tasks, they disappear. In effect, we see here a "rise-to-the-occasion" leadership, somewhat like the judges of old.

For better or for worse, a new feeling about the Law manifests itself. In place of a *torah* of covenant loyalty directed primarily to the king, the Law becomes a code of conduct directed to every individual, based on a need for social identity. People know they belong to Israel by the way they keep the Law. This shift in the sense of law seems to be a natural defensive reaction in times of destruction. It happens again when the Romans destroy the Temple in AD 70. Circling the wagons and demanding conformity within the besieged community might be appropriate for a weak and ridiculed people. It is another matter when such demand for conformity is used by a powerful and respected group.

In Ezra and Nehemiah, the Temple takes center stage. Building the second Temple will be easier than reinstating the Davidic dynasty. Israel moves from being a political force to being a religious force. Wielding no army or foreign policy, Israel exists at the pleasure of the Persian Empire and must find its strength within the context of that secular political power. Whether historical or not, the curious confession of faith on the part of Cyrus that introduces these two books (Ezra 1:2–3) describes the new relationship of Israel to its secular world. To the degree Israel can in fact draw other peoples and rulers to a recognition of "the God of heaven," to that degree it survives in peace.

Somewhat parallel with the stress on the Temple liturgy is another facet of Jewish religious life that takes on prominence in Ezra and Nehemiah, the religious assembly (*qahal*). The Israelites of the story assemble as a whole people to acknowledge their guilt regarding mixed marriages (Ezra 10:1, 8, 12, 14). They also assemble all together to proclaim their determination to end the oppression of the poor (Neh 5:13). And as a great assembly they listen to the reading of the Law (Neh 8:2) and celebrate the feast of Booths (8:17). It is from "the assembly of God" that the Jews exclude Ammonites and Moabites (13:1). The image here of the repatriated Jews assembling as a whole people clearly reflects the image of the great "day of assembly" at Horeb according to the Deuteronomistic theology (Deut 18:16; see 5:22; 9:10; 10:4; 23:1–3).

Very likely also this image of the assembly reflects the development of the synagogue during the Exile, when Jews could not offer sacrifices or engage in other forms of Temple liturgy, but they could gather to listen to the Law and pray together. In the Septuagint, the second-century BC translation of the Old Testament, the Hebrew word, *qahal*, was usually translated by the Greek, *synagogê*, and less frequently also by *ekklêsia*. In effect, with their stress on the assembly of Israelites, Ezra and Nehemiah seem to be laying the foundation for the great congregational stress of later rabbinic Judaism and Christianity.

Ultimately, the message of Ezra-Nehemiah is a message of hope. Out of utter destruction and rubble comes new life. As Ezekiel had predicted decades before Ezra and Nehemiah, the "dry bones" of Israel come alive with "the spirit" of God (Ezek 37). Life out of death becomes the pattern of God's grace.

10
The Message of the Chroniclers' History

The Chroniclers no longer feel the need to look into the abyss and search for God in the darkness of dashed hopes. That abyss, at least now, is covered by a thick ice sheet, called the Persian Empire. Things seem to be working out and attention turns back to encouraging things on earth. Looked at as a whole, the Chroniclers' history develops around three institutions, the Temple, the Law, and the Davidic dynasty. We need to reflect briefly on how this triple focus touches on God and his presence, seeing in these foci connections to the New Testament.

I. The Temple

For the Chroniclers, the life of the people revolved around the Temple. From the elaborations of David's role in the Temple (1 Chr 21—29) to Zerubbabel's second Temple (Ezra 5), this complex of courts and buildings was the object of the Chroniclers' love and a distinct focus of their faith. As mentioned above, the Chroniclers were quick to insist that the Temple was the place for the worship of God—not the place where God was contained (see 2 Chr 6:18–21). Nevertheless, it was a sacred place, set apart from the "normal" places of human life, a place where Israel could seek God. With their Levitical interests, the Chroniclers were interested mostly in the prayer of Israel as a whole in official worship or liturgy, rather than in the devotion of individuals going to the Temple to experience God.

The experience in Babylon, of course, taught Israel that God could be experienced and worshiped in places outside the Jerusalem Temple, in personal prayer where the individual at any place could lift his or her heart to God, as does Nehemiah in his memoirs (Neh 1:5–11; 3:36–37; 4:19; 13:31; see Tob 3:1–6, 11–15; Dan 6:11). Yet rebuilding the Temple was the overriding priority of the leaders who returned from exile. Rebuilding the Temple meant integrating the public material life of the nation into religion, selecting some choice real estate, choosing some expensive building materials of this world, and dedicating major economic activities to God. The Temple thus becomes the symbol of public prayer, the symbol of a people unified and organized in the worship of God.

The Temple is also a symbol of the duration of that prayer. Solomon dies, but the Temple lasts another three hundred years. Zerubbabel and his generation dies, but Nehemiah and Ezra along with Jews for the next five hundred years could experience their continuity with past generations simply by entering the Temple. In its massive blocks and solid construction, the Temple establishes a continuity that far outlasts the short span of a person's life.

The Gospel of Luke has an interesting way of establishing the continuity of Jesus and the church with the history of Israel. This Gospel begins and ends in the Temple. The opening story involves the priest Zachariah in the Temple (Luke 1:1–25). The final story describes the disciples returning to the Temple where they praised God in continuous prayer (24:52–53).

For John, the Temple (*ho naos*) is the body of Jesus, which like the Temple of Jerusalem can and will be destroyed and raised up again (John 2:19–22). The Word, by whom all things are created, is present and dwelt among us in the flesh of Jesus (1:1–14).

Paul reminds the Corinthian community repeatedly that they are "the temple of God" (1 Cor 3:16–17). He is referring to the group of believers who gather as "church" to worship God and "build up" (14:3–5) each other. Some time after the destruction of the second Temple in AD 70, 1 Peter drives home the same point by reminding the believers scattered through Asia Minor that they are "living stones" who become at once the "spiritual house" and the "priesthood" of God (1 Pet 2:5). Ultimately, the message of the Temple must move from buildings to people.

The "end scene" for the city of God leaves no room for a Temple just as it leaves no room for sun or moon. Symbol gives way to reality. The glorious presence of God and the Lamb supply for both Temple and luminary (Rev 21:22–23).

II. The Law

The books of Ezra and Nehemiah focus much attention on the Law. Ezra's promulgation of "the Law of Moses" (Neh 8) forms a climax for these books. In Chronicles, the written Law, also referred to as the Law of Moses, is clearly a guide for kings and other officials (2 Chr 23:28; 25:4; 30:16) long before it is "discovered" during the reign of Josiah (34:14). Under Jehoshaphat, this Law is taught to the people of Judah (17:9). For the Chronicler, the Law is probably the Torah or Pentateuch as we know it, the supreme guide to individual and national life.

What we see in the Chroniclers' history is especially the social effect of the Law. The Law brought Israel together and gave life to a dead people. The Law showed Israel who she was under God. For the Chroniclers, this social effect was inseparable from cult and the Temple, the reform of which seemed the focus of their interest in the Law.

Probably the only social aspect of the Law brought out by the Chronicler that would easily edify the modern reader is the report of Nehemiah abolishing the oppressive mortgages (Neh 5). The marriage regulations (Ezra 9; Neh 13:23–31) call for a more difficult hermeneutic.

Taken as a whole, however, the Law helps us to see a larger perspective. The Law of God is about God's view, God's decree about what is good or evil, God's order for creation. Our task is to discover that order, to uncover and reference what is "good in itself" because it accords with God's Law, not just because it results from our "social contract." The Chronicler calls us to reverence this Law. It can be the basis of great joy (Neh 8:17) and is the source of life and light (see Ps 119).

In the New Testament, Paul has some harsh things to say about the Law, describing it as severely inferior to the promises (Gal 3:15–22) or as a temporary "babysitter" to be dismissed as one attains maturity (Gal 3:23–29). In his more calm moments, however, he speaks of the fulfillment of the whole Law by love (Gal 5:14; Rom 13:8–10). This is the Law of the Spirit written in our hearts that carries with it the power to achieve what it orders. Paul reminds us that reverence for the Law is far more than respect for an external code.

The Law survives the Temple. Buildings can be burnt and torn down. The Law written in the hearts of people (Jer 31:33; 3 Cor 3:2–6) goes on as long as people stand in a loving and respectful deference to God. Judaism survived the destruction of the Temple by the Romans in AD 70 by its dedication to the Law. Christians try to live the Law of Christ (Gal 6:2), with or without church buildings. The challenge is to integrate observance of religious rules into a faithful relationship to God and a loving care of one another.

III. The Davidic Dynasty

The throne of David and the dynasty of this great king dominate the books of Chronicles, which include also a genealogy bringing that dynasty down to the time of the Chronicler (see 1 Chr 3:17–24). By cleansing the figure of David from his sins and flaws, the Chronicler pictures this king as bigger than life. Everything prior to David, like the promises to Abraham, the Exodus under Moses, or the covenant at Sinai are hardly mentioned in the summary of history that runs from Adam to David. The Davidic covenant appears to replace the earlier covenants as the object of Israel's hope and faith. God promises, "I will maintain him in my house and in my kingdom forever, and his throne shall be firmly established forever" (2 Chr 17:14).

On the other hand, Ezra and Nehemiah hardly allude to this king. In these last two books, he is mentioned only in regard to his past influence on Temple functions (Ezra 3:10; 8:20; Neh 12:24, 45–46), along with some person, object, or place involving his name (Ezra 8:2; Neh 3:15–16; 12:36–37). Perhaps Persian censorship prevented the Chronicler from adding anything that would smack of a longing for the restoration of the Davidic line. We find virtually nothing "messianic" in the books of Ezra and Nehemiah. In these books, emphasis has shifted from any "anointed one" to observance of the Law.

Yet by connecting David to the Temple, by insisting on the Davidic effort to plan it and provide the materials for it (1 Chr 22—29), the Chronicler has painted the rebuilding of the Temple with messianic tones. Although the work appears to be dominated by priests and Levites, Zerubbabel, the son of David, is a key figure in the picture. The prophet Zechariah will make this messianic role of Zerubbabel explicit (Zech 4:6–14).

In effect, the priestly and the Davidic role in the Temple become so intertwined that eventually Jewish messianism will propose two messiahs (Zech 4:14; see Rev 11:4). The figure of Jeshua, the priest, is so important (Ezra 3:2, 8; 5:2) that later Judaism will see a place for a priestly messiah along with a kingly messiah (*Testament of Levi*, 18; 1*QS* IX, 10–11; see Jer 33:21).

Writing his Gospel about Jesus, Luke makes a daring link between the promises of God to David and the birth of Jesus. In Luke's "annunciation" scene, the angel Gabriel describes the future of Jesus to his mother, Mary, "The Lord God will give him the throne of David his father, and he will rule over the house of Jacob forever, and of his kingdom there will be no end" (Luke 1:32–33).

In his own way, Matthew insists on the Davidic lineage of Jesus (see Matt 1:17. 20) and of Jesus' kingly stature (Matt 2:2; 21:5). Especially for Matthew, it is the weak person in need of healing mercy who acknowledges Jesus as "Son of David" (Matt 9:27; 15:22; 20:30–31; see Luke 18:38–39). The figure of David takes on a new twist. The king is there for the lowly and suffering members of his kingdom.

PART III

The History of the Maccabees

11
Introduction to the Books of the Maccabees

Biblical history between the years 398 and 175 BC takes us through a long tunnel. We enter this tunnel at the end of the books of Ezra and Nehemiah and emerge some 250 years later at the opening of the books of the Maccabees. Meanwhile, great changes have taken place. Alexander the Great has come; the Persian Empire has gone.

The world breathes a new atmosphere—a wind from the Greek world. This influence from the West will penetrate the old Oriental world and create a new culture, which modern historians call "Hellenistic." This is not the pure Greek, or Hellenic, culture of Pericles and the other giants of the golden, fifth century of Greece. It is rather a mixture of Greek and Middle Eastern styles. In many places of this time, it is an Oriental culture overlaid with a Greek veneer.

This culture will profoundly influence the books of Maccabees, Daniel, and Wisdom, as well as the New Testament, which will be written in the language and intellectual categories of Hellenistic Greek. An understanding of these Hellenistic times provides the necessary background for grasping the meaning and significance of the last books of the Old Testament and the general platform from which the New Testament will spring.

I. The Maccabean Period and the Books of the Maccabees

After effectively conquering the Persian Empire at Gaugamela in 331 BC and reaching India by 327, Alexander the Great died at

Babylon in 323. Only partially fulfilled was Alexander's dream of a world empire unified outwardly by the authority of Macedon and inwardly by the leaven of Hellenistic culture. In a short time, the political unity imposed by conquest dissolved. By 305 BC, the empire had broken into three parts: Macedonia, Syria-Mesopotamia, and Egypt, governed respectively by Alexander's generals and successors: Perdiccas, Seleucus, and Ptolemy. The leaven of Hellenistic culture, however, remained and gradually permeated the major parts of the Mediterranean world, including Palestine.

First under the Egyptian Ptolemies and then under the Syrian Seleucids, Palestine picked up continual infusions of Hellenistic culture. Greek became the second language of the country. It was a prerequisite for business or commerce. Many cities acquired Greek names. Greek architecture formed public buildings, Greek philosophy echoed in the schools, and Greek customs became part and parcel of public and private life. Even the faithful religious Jew needed to deal with the cosmic and anthropological issues permeating Hellenistic culture—the origins of evil as a power, the body/mind dualities of human existence, the dominance of concept over story. A century later in what presented itself as the bastion of conservative Jewish life, the Essenes of the Qumran community would express their faith in these terms.

While the Ptolemies ruling from Egypt usually tolerated the Jewish way of life, the Seleucids ruling from Syria, especially under Antiochus IV, did not. In 169 BC, Antiochus pillaged the Temple. A year later when it became apparent that the religious Jews would not submit voluntarily to Hellenization, he decided to use force. A Syrian army partially destroyed Jerusalem. A Syrian garrison occupied the hill west of the Temple.

Antiochus began a systematic persecution aimed at destroying the Jewish faith. Regular sacrifices in the Temple ceased. Jews were no longer permitted to observe the Sabbath and the traditional feasts. To possess a copy of the Law or to circumcise Jewish children became a crime. Pagan altars were set up throughout the land, and Jews who refused to sacrifice swine flesh upon these altars were liable to death. In December 167 BC, the cult of Olympian Zeus was instituted in the Temple, an altar to Zeus was set up, and Jews were compelled to take part in the pagan festivities.

In the crisis provoked by Antiochus IV, however, the issue was the very survival of Jewish faith. Many Jews gave up their faith in the name of adapting to modern culture. First Maccabees describes this massive falling from faith as "the apostasy" (2:15), a falling that reached to the highest levels of religious authority (see 2 Macc 4:12–15).

In this struggle, those who remained faithful—even unto death—saw themselves as heroes fighting bravely for "Judaism" (2 Macc 2:21). Confronted with Hellenism as a powerful antagonistic culture, faith in the true God saw itself as a culture in an ideological struggle. The concept of "Judaism" was born (see also 2 Macc 8:1; 14:38)—named for the region of Judea, where the armed struggle would ignite and where for a short time a political entity for the protection of the faith would arise.

II. Chronology of the Maccabean Period

356–323 BC	Alexander the Great: born at Pella in Macedonia, general at 18, king at 20, conquered Persia at 25, reached India at 29, dead at Babylon at 33.
321–282	Seleucus I gradually establishes the Seleucid Empire centered in Antioch.
187–175	Seleucus IV: the first king mentioned in 2 Maccabees in connection with an unsuccessful attempt to rob the Temple of Jerusalem (3:7).
175–164	Antiochus IV Epiphanes: brother and successor of Seleucus IV, persecutor of the Jews.
170	Assassination of Onias the high priest.
169–164	Desecration of the Temple, the period of intense persecution.
166–160	Outbreak of the Maccabean resistance under Mattathias Hasmoneus and his son, Judas

	Maccabaeus. Victories of Judas; rededication of the Temple in 164; death of Judas in 160.
165–164	Writing of the Book of Daniel.
164–161	Antiochus V Eupator as a boy succeeds his father Antiochus IV under the guardianship of Lysias. Assassinated along with Lysias by his cousin Demetrius, son of Seleucus IV.
161–150	Demetrius I Soter: sends generals Bacchides and Nicanor in successive expeditions to destroy the Jews.
160–143	Campaigns and diplomatic maneuvers of Jonathan, brother of Judas Maccabaeus.
150–145	Alexander Balas gains the assistance of Jonathan by naming him high priest, kills Demetrius I in battle, and succeeds him on the throne.
145–139	Demetrius II Nicator, son of Demetrius I, through the help of Ptolemy VI of Egypt, kills Alexander and becomes king of Syria, reaffirms privileges of Jonathan and the Jews, later turns against Jonathan.
143–134	Simon, brother of Judas Maccabaeus, wins independence for the Jews.
139–138	Trypho, who earlier had plotted with Antiochus, young son of Alexander Balas, to usurp the throne of Syria, captures and eventually kills Jonathan, kills Antiochus, and assumes the throne.
138–129	Antiochus VII Sidetes replaces Trypho and his brother Demetrius on throne of Syria.
134–104	John Hyrcanus, son of Simon, becomes quasi king in the now-established Hasmonean dynasty.
64	The Romans under Pompey, invited into Jerusalem to prevent a civil war among the Hasmoneans, annex Judea.

III. The Books of Maccabees

The Greek Bible has actually four books of Maccabees. The first two, now known as 1 and 2 Maccabees, are included in the Catholic and Orthodox canon. Third Maccabees deals with the suffering of Egyptian Jews under Ptolemy IV (221–203 BC) and in some places parallels the accounts given in the canonical books of Maccabees. Fourth Maccabees contains a philosophical discourse on the importance of reason over passion, a theme then illustrated by Old Testament persons, especially by the martyrs from the time of the Maccabees. The Orthodox include also 3 Maccabees in the biblical canon. None of these books are in the Hebrew canon, which is followed by the Protestant churches. We will study the first two books.

Both 1 and 2 Maccabees deal with the themes of the leadership of the early Hasmoneans and the Jewish resistance in Israel to the religious persecution instigated by Antiochus IV Epiphanes. These leaders are known as Hasmoneans from the name of Mattathias Hasmoneus, the priest and initiator of the revolt at this time, and the father of the three bothers who succeed him in this leadership role.

Unlike the books of Samuel or the books of Kings, these two books of Maccabees are independent works, written by different authors, in different languages, from different viewpoints. First Maccabees describes Jewish history from 175 to 134 BC; 2 Maccabees, from 176 to 160 BC. Both books derive their name from Judas Maccabaeus (a name meaning either "the hammer," or perhaps, "the designated one"), the most famous of the five sons of Mattathias. From the second century AD, Judas's second name appears to be applied to the whole family of Mattathias, referring to them as "the Maccabees," and their account of their struggles as "[the first or second book] of the Maccabees."

12
1 Maccabees

I. Overview

A. Author, Text, and Date

We can only conjecture from details in the text the identity of the author. For instance, the rather accurate details of Palestinian geography, the politics of the period, the military campaigns, the court intrigues, and the character of the Maccabean chieftains suggest the author was a contemporary of the events narrated or had access to the participants in the events. The text exudes great admiration for the Hasmonean family (see 5:61–62), suggesting that the author might perhaps have been the official historiographer of the Hasmonean family. Likewise, the negative attitude expressed toward the unworthy high priest, Alcimus (7:21–25; 9:54–56); the absence of any mention of life after death, a doctrine popular among the Pharisees; a disparaging remark about the Hasideans (7:13), forerunners of the Pharisees; as well as a tolerant attitude concerning observance of the Sabbath suggest a writer possibly from Sadducean rather than Pharisaic circles.

Although 1 Maccabees was written originally in Hebrew, only the Greek translation has come down to us. Jerome and Origen knew of the Hebrew text. The Latin Vulgate is simply the "Old Latin" version unrevised, made from a better Greek manuscript than our extant Septuagint manuscripts and consequently is of great value for establishing the text.

The book as we have it can be dated sometime between 100 and 63 BC. The kindly attitude expressed toward the Romans argues for a date before 63, the year Pompey occupied Jerusalem and outraged Jewish feelings by entering the holy of holies in the

Temple. The reference at the end of the book (16:23–24) to history of John Hyrcanus in the annals of the high priests suggests that John's term (134–104 BC) is either over or nearly over.

B. Literary Form and Purpose

Historians from the time of Josephus to our day have esteemed 1 Maccabees for its historical value. The topographical and chronological details as well as the honesty of the author describing both the defeats and the victories of his heroes testify to this value.

Nevertheless, the author writes for the purpose of glorifying the Maccabees as "those men by whom salvation was brought to Israel" (5:62). His viewpoint is that of a propagandist. After the manner of the ancient Israelite historians, he exaggerates the size of the armies sent against the Maccabees in order to enhance their victories. Although he records defeats, he enhances the victories and minimizes those defeats. In the author's eyes, the Maccabean revolt appears as a world-shaking event, of great importance to Rome and Sparta.

This peculiar historical genre includes both moral condemnations and sober narrations of events. The style at times is direct and simple and at other times exuberant and enthusiastic as the author shifts from detailed history to poetic hymns of praise.

C. Divisions of the Book

Giving the history of the Maccabean wars from 175 to 134 BC, 1 Maccabees is divided into four main parts: a prelude followed by three sections treating Judas, Jonathan, and Simon.

1 Maccabees 1—2:	The rise of Antiochus IV Epiphanes and his religious persecution of the Jews; the initial revolt by Mattathias and his sons

1 Maccabees 3:1—9:22:	The military exploits of Judas Maccabaeus until his death in 160 BC
1 Maccabees 9:23—12:53:	The military and diplomatic victories of Jonathan until his death in 143 BC
1 Maccabees 13—16:	The exploits of Simon, the last surviving brother of Judas, until his death in 134 BC; the succession of his son John Hyrcanus as leader of the Jews

II. Significant Passages in 1 Maccabees

A. 1 Maccabees 1—2 / Prelude to the Wars

1:10–63 *Antiochus IV and the persecution*

After a short summary of Alexander the Great (1:1–9), 1 Maccabees quickly moves to the story of Antiochus IV (see appendix 7) and his plundering of the Temple in 169 BC along with a second attack by "the Mysian commander" in 167 BC (see 2 Macc 5:15–26).

The theological context of this disaster was the refusal of some Jews to observe "the holy covenant." These are the Hellenistic Jews described as "breakers of the law" (*paranomoi*; 1:11) who abandon the "holy covenant" (1:15; see 2 Macc 4). The oppression climaxes with the systematic persecution of faithful Jews (see 2 Macc 6—7) and the desecration of the Temple by the "abomination of desolation." The expression is a Semitic idiom, where an *of* phrase functions as an adjective, in effect meaning the "desolating abomination." The word for word expression in Hebrew is found in Daniel 9:27 and 11:31.

2:1–70 *The revolt and death of Mattathias*

First Maccabees then describes the story of the revolt with Judas's father, Mattathias, from the city of Modein (see 2 Macc 5:27). Josephus, the Jewish historian of the first century AD, also named this leader Hasmoneus, the name that was then applied to the line of Jewish kings soon to follow, the Hasmonean dynasty. Although bribed with office and wealth, Mattathias refuses to conform out of loyalty to "the covenant of our fathers" (*diathêkê paterôn hêmôn*; 2:20) and to the "Law and commandments" (*nomos kai dikaiômata*; 2:21).

Mattathias has five loyal sons: Simon, Judas, Eleazar, Avaran, and Jonathan (2:.2–3). They are joined by a group of "followers of the Law" called "Hasideans" (2:42), the forerunners of the Pharisees. Mattathias's slaying of the king's agents begins the "Maccabean" wars (2:15–28). The decision is made to fight even on the Sabbath against those who attack (2:31–41).

"When the time came for Mattathias to die," he blesses his sons and charges them to avenge the wrongs of the people by continued warfare and above all to "give your lives for the covenant of our fathers" (2:49–70).

B. 1 Maccabees 3—9 / Judas Maccabaeus (166–160 BC)

3:1–26 ***Judas becomes the military leader***

Without any explanation of why the older brother Simon is passed over, the author simply states that Judas, named Maccabaeus, took his father's place in the war. His war is not just against national enemies but above all against the wicked and "those who practice lawlessness [*anomia*]," thus bringing "salvation [*sôtêria*]" to the nation (3:6).

Supported by his brothers and all the others, Judas successfully defeats Apollonius (see 2 Macc 5:24) and then Seron, the Syrian commander, at Beth-horon. Judas directs his army's attention to the power of God: "Victory in war does not depend upon the size of the army, but on strength that comes from Heaven" (v. 19).

3:57–59 ***Judas's speech to the army***

Preparing for the battle of Emmaus, Judas is clear about human military initiative. "Arm yourselves and be brave" (3:57). He has shown his absolute confidence in God, yet he is ready to

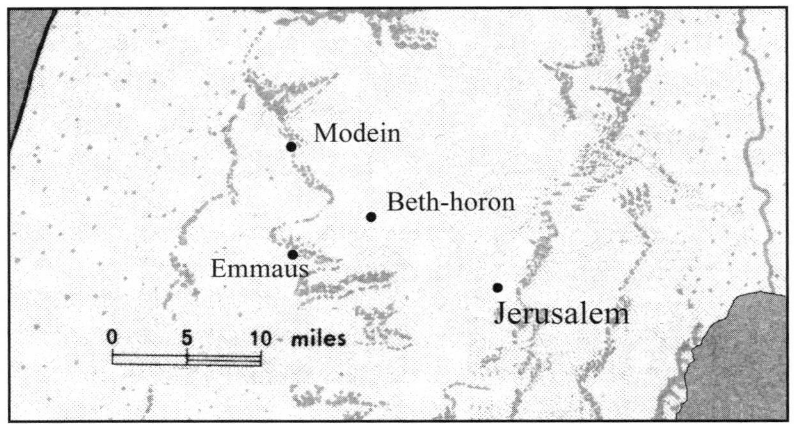

12A: Cities in the Early Military Victories of Judas

die in battle. In effect, he places the matter entirely in God's hands: "Whatever Heaven wills, he will do" (5:59).

4:36–61 *Judas restores and rededicates the Temple*

After another crucial victory in 165 BC over the Syrians commanded by Ptolemy, Nicanor, and Gorgias, and then the following year (164) over Lysias, Antiochus's regent (4:27—5:35), Judas returned to Jerusalem and appointed "blameless priests, devoted to the Law" to restore and purify the Temple (see 2 Macc 10:1–8). Because the altar of holocausts had been desecrated, it was torn down and replaced by a new altar made according to the Law with uncut stones (see Exod 20:25). The perplexity concerning the disposal of the old stones reflects a conviction at the time that prophecy had ceased (see also 9:27; 14:41).

Once the new altar of holocausts is remade and the sanctuary repaired, priests begin to burn incense, offer sacrifices, and adore "Heaven" for eight days–all with great joy (4:47–58). The rededication of the altar takes place on a date that corresponds to December 14, 164 BC. The anniversary feast of this event is the feast of Hanukkah, known in John's Gospel as the feast of the Dedication (John 10:22) or the feast of Lights.

6:1–16 *The death of Antiochus*

Continuing the story of Antiochus IV from 3:37, 1 Maccabees narrates the king's unsuccessful campaign in Persia, where apparently he becomes ill and dies (see 2 Macc 9:1–29). The events are earlier in 164 BC. The story of Antiochus's death, therefore, would make better sense if placed before that of the rededication of the Temple (4:36–61).

The general circumstances narrated here accord with other historical accounts of Antiochus's death (see Polybius, *Histories* 31.9). Typical of this type of story, however, the author here takes the liberty of describing Antiochus as repenting from his evil ways (6:10–13). Daniel 11:44–45 has a much different account of Antiochus's death.

The king's young son, Antiochus V Eupator, succeeds the throne, actually under the regency of Lysias. Both would be killed by Demetrius I two years later (7:1–4; see appendix 7). Philip, who is mentioned here, will return to attack Lysias but be defeated (6:55–63).

7:1–5 *The rise of Demetrius as Syrian king*

Demetrius returns from Rome and seizes the Syrian throne from his cousin Antiochus V and Lysias. Demetrius's father, Seleucus, had in fact been named king and successor to Antiochus III, but Seleucus was supplanted by his brother Antiochus IV Epiphanes (see appendix 7). In Israel, Demetrius is supported by "lawless and impious" men.

7:26–50 *Judas's crucial victory over Nicanor*

After the crushing campaigns of Demetrius's general, Bacchides, which nevertheless failed to destroy Judas (7:5–25), Demetrius then names Nicanor "to destroy the people." First Maccabees speaks of a deceitful offer of peace made by Nicanor to Judas (but see 2 Macc 14:1—15:36), a preliminary victory by Judas at Caphar-salama, and the decisive victory at Adasa in 161 BC. Nicanor's head and right arm are carried back to Jerusalem as trophies of victory. Preliminary to the victory over Nicanor is the intense supplication of the priests in the sanctuary (7:36–38)

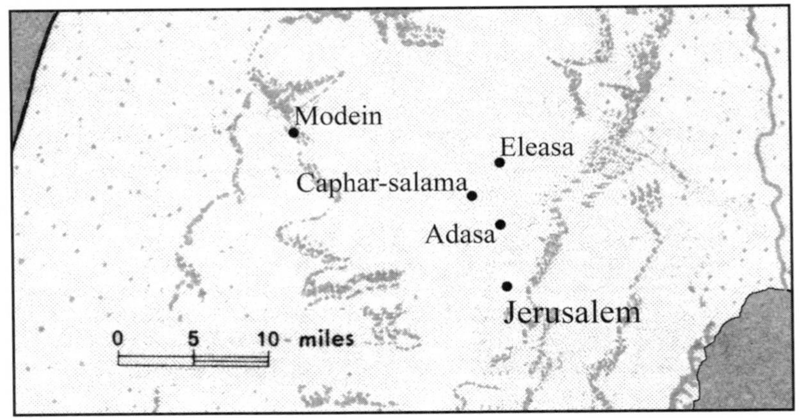

12B: Cities in the Later Battles of Judas

and Judas's own prayer (7:7:40–42). A feast day marked the day of victory.

9:1–22 ***The death of Judas in battle***

Demetrius sent his military commander, Bacchides, with the renegade Jewish high priest, Alcimus, in response to Nicanor's death. The Syrian force is overwhelming. Judas's force shrinks by massive desertions. After a valiant fight, Judas, "the savior of Israel" (9:22), dies in the battle of Eleasa. His army flees. It is the spring of 160 BC.

C. 1 MACCABEES 9:23—12:53 / JONATHAN (160–143 BC)

9:23–33 ***Jonathan becomes leader***

The land is back in the grip of the Syrian military and the pro-Syrian Jews, who are considered "the lawless ones [*hoi anomoi*]" (9:23). The officers ("friends") of Judas ask his brother, Jonathan, to assume leadership of the resistance. Jonathan and his forces retreat to the wilderness of Tekoa.

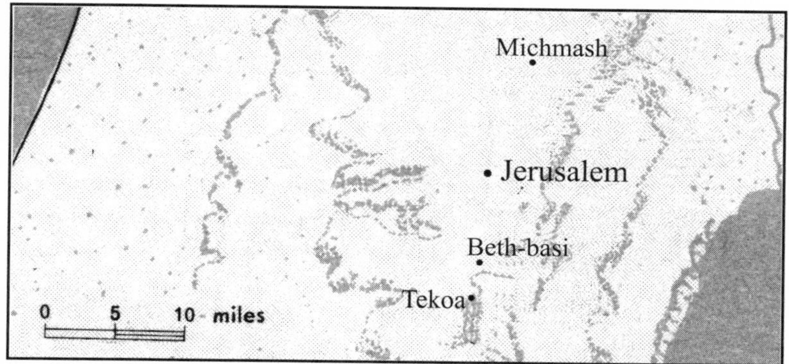

12C: Cities in the Early Battles of Jonathan

9:58–73 ***Jonathan's treaty with Bacchides***

Jonathan and his brother, Simon, establish a foothold in the populated area by fortifying the abandoned fortress of Beth-basi, just north of the town of Tekoa. In a series of daring raids, the two brothers succeed in demoralizing the forces of Bacchides and negotiating a treaty. Based now in Machmas (Michmash), north of Jerusalem, Jonathan gains control of the Judean countryside.

10:1–50 ***Jonathan becomes high priest***

Jonathan's power arose especially from diplomatic finesse amidst the power struggles of the deteriorating Seleucid Empire. In this text we see the rise of a rival to Demetrius I, Alexander Balas, called here Epiphanes, son of Antiochus [see appendix 7]. Both court Jonathan by promising him power. This bidding war appears in the letters from Alexander (10:18–20) and Demetrius (10:25–45).

Although Jonathan had already begun using the gifts of power from Demetrius (10:6–14), he has the shrewdness to ally with Alexander, accepting his offer of the appointment in 152 BC as high priest of the Jews (10:20). With this appointment Jonathan fills the void created by the death of Alcimus (9:56), who also obtained the high priesthood by political power. Jonathan, however, breaks from the sacred tradition of passing the high priesthood down by inheritance in the line of Zadok. In a probable reference to this appointment of Jonathan, the Dead

Sea Scrolls express abhorrence for some desecration of the high priesthood in Jerusalem (1QpHab 8:3—10:10). The appointment, however, does not seem to be a problem for the authors of 1 Maccabees. Alexander's victory over Demetrius in 150 BC consolidates Jonathan's power in Judea.

10:67—11:74 ***Jonathan's further political and military successes***

Now political events move fast for Jonathan. First in 147 BC, Demetrius II arrives in an attempt to seize back from Alexander Balas the throne once occupied by his father, appointing Apollonius as governor of Coelesyria, which included Judea (10:67–69). Second, Ptolemy VI Philometor of Egypt occupies coastal cities in Palestine and Syria and eventually seizes Antioch (11:1–13). Jonathan wages war against Apollonius as he continues to side with Alexander, who rewards Jonathan with more power. Alexander dies defeated in battle. Ptolemy himself dies, and Demetrius II takes over in 145 BC (11:14–19).

By diplomacy, Jonathan is able to switch his allegiance to Demetrius (11:23–37) and even support him militarily in his own domestic problems (11:44–51). Demetrius, however, turns against Jonathan, reneging on all promises (11:52–53).

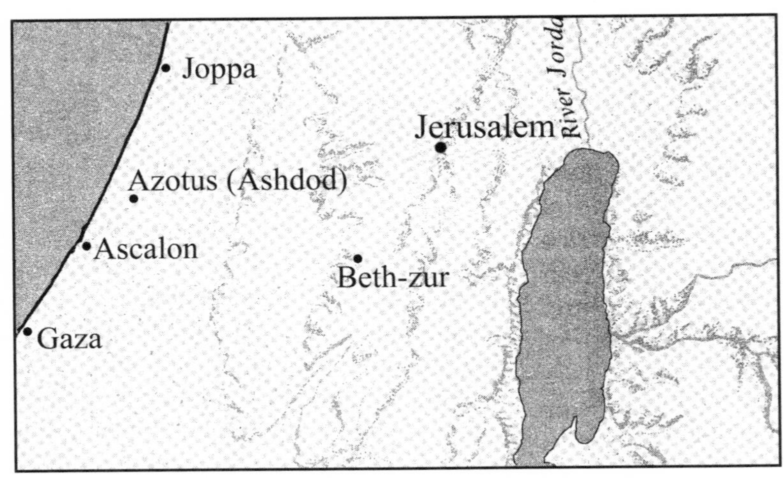

12D: Cities in the Later Battles of Jonathan

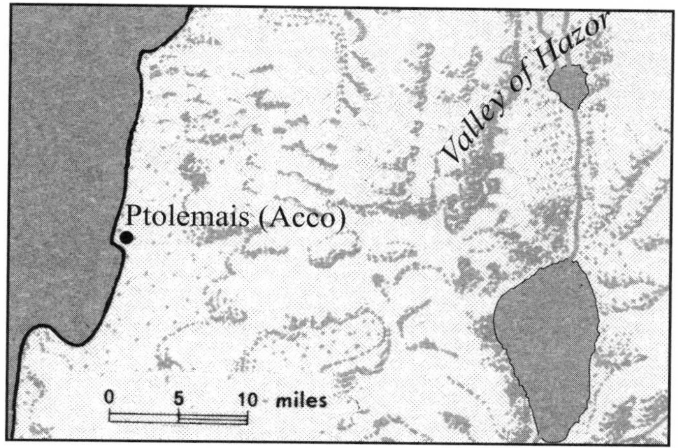

12E: The Capture of Jonathan

This political deceit sets up Jonathan's switch to Demetrius's enemy, a certain Trypho, who is seeking the throne by using the young son of Alexander Balas, Antiochus VI (11:54–59). Eventually by the power of prayer, Jonathan defeats the forces of Demetrius II at the battle of Hazor in 144 BC (11:63–74).

12:39–53 ***The capture of Jonathan***

Trypho tricks Jonathan into thinking that they were now allies. Then at a meeting in Ptolemais (Acco), Trypho imprisons Jonathan and kills his bodyguards. The year is 143 BC. A year later, Trypho would execute Jonathan. This was a time of mortal danger for all Jews as the surrounding nations now sought to destroy them (12:53).

D. 1 Maccabees 13—16 / Simon (143–134 BC)

13:1–11 ***Simon becomes leader***

The people turn to Simon, the oldest son of Mattathias, who humbly accepts and immediately prepares for war by fortifying Jerusalem and occupying Joppa on the coast.

13:31–53 *The yoke of the Gentiles removed*

After the aggression of Trypho, Simon negotiates a treaty with the former enemy, Demetrius II, who confirms Simon as high priest, agrees to the presence of Simon's strongholds, and remits all taxes. Thus as the author writes, "The yoke of the Gentiles was removed from Israel" (13:41). The year is 142 BC. Simon is "high priest, governor, and leader of the Jews" (13:42). A new era has begun.

The capture of Gazara (Gezer), west of Jerusalem, and the capture of the Jerusalem citadel in 141 BC are the two significant military conquests of Simon.

14:16–24 *Simon's political moves*

The peaceful and prosperous reign of Simon involved treaties with Western powers, Rome and Sparta. Cf. also 15:16-24.

15:37—16:10 *Military victory of Simon's sons*

War broke out again in 137 BC. Three years earlier, Demetrius II was captured by the Persians (see 14:1–3). Demetrius's brother, Antiochus VII Sidetes, took over and at first recognized the power of Simon (15:2–9). After disposing of Trypho, however, Antiochus develops a hostile attitude toward Simon, demanding back the cities of Joppa and Gazara, as well as the citadel of Jerusalem, a

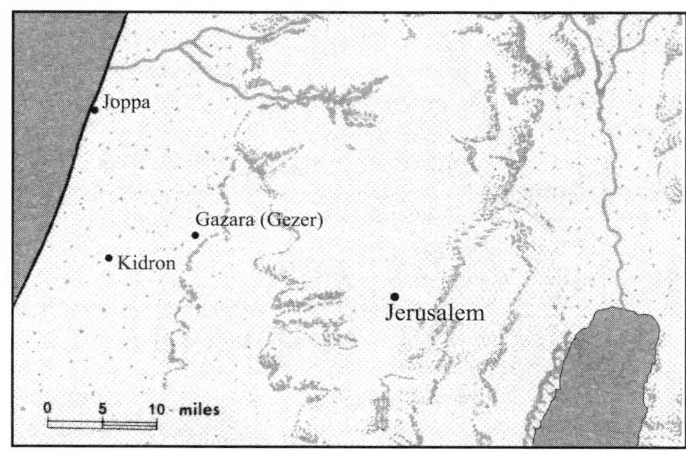

12F: Cities in the Battles of Simon

demand that Simon refuses (15:25–36). Thus the Syrian forces under Cendebeus move against Judea. Simon's sons, Judas and John, however, defeat Cendebeus in the battle of Kidron, near the coast.

16:11–23 *Death of Simon*

The story of "the Maccabees" ends with the tragic death of Simon and his sons, Judas and Mattathias. Simon's son-in-law, Ptolemy, son of Abubus and "governor of the plain of Jericho" (16:11) murders them at a banquet in the fortress of Dok, near Jericho. The year was 134 BC.

Although Ptolemy's plan was to kill also John and thus get control of all of Judea, John escapes and succeeds his father as John Hyrcanus. The Hasmonean dynasty has begun.

III. The Message of 1 Maccabees

A. Review of Themes

The following themes dominate the selected passages of 1 Maccabees:

- Sin within Israel as lawlessness (*anomia*) and impiety (*asebeia*), leading to religious compromise (1:11–15; 2:44; 3:6; 7:5; 9:23, 25, 58, 69)
- Opposition to the faith, at times violent and deadly (1:41–61; 2:49–70; 7:26–50; 9:1–22; 12:53; 13:1–6; and passim)
- The willingness of believers to die for the faith (1:62–63; 2:37, 50; 4:35)
- Loyalty to the Law and the covenant (2:20–21, 42, 50; 4:47, 53)
- Warfare and violence as a way of protecting the faith in a time of violence (2:24–25, 41–49, 66–68; 3:2–26; and passim)
- God's assistance in war that is waged with "strength that comes from Heaven" (3:19–22; 7:36–43; 11:71; 16:3)

- The importance of the Temple, Temple sacrifice, and the high priesthood (4:36–59; 7:37; 10:20–21)
- The absence of prophecy (4:46; 9:27; 14:41)

B. The Theology of 1 Maccabees

First Maccabees consists of detailed accounts mostly of military battles and international politics. As a biblical book, it strikes the modern religious reader for what is absent in the accounts. God is not mentioned by name. No miracles of divine intervention appear. No prophets speak. No one expresses faith in life after death. And there are no women. The accounts form a precious collection of stories to give later Jewish readers a sense of national identity, as they function today for the Israeli military. But how does a religious reader, Jew or Gentile, today find a religious message in this book?

Actually the absence of the name of God from 1 Maccabees should not deter us from recognizing the book's religious message. The word *Heaven* appears as a reverent substitute for the name of God (see also 3:18–19; 4:10, 40; 9:46), as we find in the Gospel of Matthew (Matt 3:2; 4:17; 5:1; and passim). At other times speakers in the story refer to God simply as "he" (1 Macc 2:61; 3:22, 59). The sense of God in 1 Maccabees appears especially in the prayers offered by the heroes before they go into battle (3:44–54; 4:10–11, 40; 7:37–38, 40–41; 9:46; 11:71; 12:15; 16:3). The Jewish fighters sense "the help of Heaven" in their battles (12:15; 16:3). God is above all the "Savior of Israel" (4:30; see 12:15) who gives strength and victory to the armies of Israel and its military leaders if they are faithful to him. God decides the fate of his chosen people.

The focus on military battles reminds us of the Book of Judges, where the violence breaks out as a defense against oppression and injustice. Mattathias begins the violent revolt as Syrian religious persecution becomes intolerable (chapters 1—2). At other times, the Jewish military force must fight successfully or face the extermination of the whole nation (7:26; 12:53; 13:10). The successful maneuvering on the stage of international politics takes place often against political deceit and evil. This broader religious and moral context provides at least a backdrop of faith for the secular events recounted.

The absence of prophecy is acknowledged as beyond human control (4:46). This absence is part of the distress (9:27). The attitude is not of rejection of prophets but of waiting—"until a true prophet arises" (14:41).

In the absence of prophecy, the Jewish people and their priests accept Simon as their permanent leader and high priest (14:41). In the place of charismatic interventions, the people choose a religious structure. As in the Chroniclers' history, the Temple and the high priesthood become important. Loyalty to the Law and the covenant guide the early efforts. Institutional religion is a way of reaching out to God when God does not seem to want to reach out in any dramatic way to his people.

Moreover, the leaders in this book are clearly good and brave men. Jonathan appears a bit shifty, but basically he avoids corruption and self-glory—unlike many of the adversaries. Contrasted with the "lawlessness" and "impiety" of the oppressors, the righteousness of the Jewish leaders appears also a way of reaching out to a divine order. The bravery of the leaders, especially that of Judas and his father, is all the more remarkable given the absence of any sense of recompense in an afterlife. The leaders are willing to give their lives for the larger reality of the national good and the divine order.

In this book the military and political efforts are successful. The book ends on a happy note. The authors do not have to gaze into any dark abyss to find God's presence. The dynasty of the Hasmoneans is established. The "yoke of the Gentiles" is removed from Israel.

No miracles occurred in the struggle up to that happy note, but a retrospect from around the turn of the first century BC points out the presence of "strength that comes from Heaven" (3:19). The absence of the miraculous rescue in 1 Maccabees underlines the need to see God's help in the natural events of this world and its history. Even under God, history unfolds in a mysterious way. It can be seen in retrospect, but the future remains future—unknown and ultimately uncontrollable. This mystery is not a sign of God's absence, but rather his presence as mystery. In periods of intense conflict, people like Judas and his brothers must face that mystery with faith and courage. In the present moment for them, they see what they must do, what the right thing to do is. Ultimately God brings about success for his people, but not without setbacks, defeats, and death.

When Judas prays to God for victory, we see an interesting combination of confidence in God's help and uncertainty over the future. "Whatever Heaven wills, he will do" (3:59). While hoping for victory through God, Judas constantly prepares himself for death in battle (9:8–10). Prayer for God's power is no magic formula for victory. God is not manipulated. Prayer and confidence are not magic formulas for success. In fact, 1 Maccabees calmly describes several defeats. In the end Judas along with all his brothers die at the hands of their enemies.

Throughout the narratives of 1 Maccabees, the author preaches the need to love God, to be faithful to his Law, to serve him at any cost—all the while indicating no idea of a life after death. The deaths of the early Hasmoneans along with the deaths of those who died fighting for them out of zeal for the honor of the Temple thus epitomized a faith in God as sacred mystery.

As for the absence of women in this book, we must wait for 2 Maccabees, in which a mother puts a king to shame by her bravery and faith.

13
2 Maccabees

I. Overview

A. Author and Date

The account of 2 Maccabees begins around 180 BC, somewhat earlier than 1 Maccabees, and ends with the defeat of Nicanor's army by Judas Maccabaeus in 161. The author appears to be a Greek-speaking Jew from the Diaspora, perhaps from Cyrene or Egypt, where flourishing Jewish communities existed in the last centuries before Christ. He describes his work as an effort to abridge (*epitomein*) a five-volume history by a certain Jason of Cyrene (2:23). Clear Pharisaic tendencies appear in 2 Maccabees, especially with its stress on the resurrection of the dead—tendencies that may be ascribed to the epitomist, to Jason, or to both.

Unless the introductory letters were added for a later edition, we can date the abridgment from 124 BC, the date of the first letter. Jason's work apparently took place sometime after 161 BC, the last event recorded in 2 Maccabees.

Since the work shows no evidence of being a translation and in fact exhibits—both in the preface and in the body—an excellent Greek in flowing and well-balanced periods, we can conclude that both the epitomist and Jason received a good education in Greek rhetoric and culture.

B. Literary Form and Purpose

Second Maccabees belongs to a type of historical writing popular in the Hellenistic world known as "pathetic history," a type of literature that uses every means to appeal to the imagination and emotions (*pathos*) of the readers. In this work we find colorful descriptions, rhetorical appeals, exaggerated numbers, prodigious miracles involving celestial manifestations, and a preference for the edifying and dramatic in place of the somber specific details. Like the author of Chronicles, this author idealizes his story and concentrates on certain aspects to the exclusion of others.

The author's intention apparently was to use certain historical events as a means to edify, instruct, and inspire the readers. The underlying historicity of the accounts appears from a comparison with 1 Maccabees and those extrabiblical sources that treat of the same period. These substantially historical accounts, however, come through with a generous dose of exaggerations, distortions, and fanciful descriptions proper to the literary form of the book.

By the time 2 Maccabees was composed, the biblical canon was taking shape. In this book we see a clear reference to "the Law and the Prophets" (15:9), which is the way Jews referred to the Bible as they knew it. "The Law" (*ha-torah*) was the name of the first part of the Bible, the five books of Moses. "The Prophets" was the name of the second part, the Deuteronomistic history and the literary prophets. We hear this expression repeatedly in the New Testament, especially in the more Jewish sounding parts (Matt 5:17; 7:12; 11:13; 22:40; Luke 16:16; Acts 13:15; 24:14; Rom 3:21). This text of 2 Maccabees is one of the earliest references to the canonical texts.

C. The Parts of 2 Maccabees

The account can be divided into two main parts, plus an introduction and a short concluding epilogue.

2 Maccabees 1—2:	The introduction, consisting of two letters and a preface by the author
2 Maccabees 3:1—10:9:	Part I, detailing a number of events relating to the Temple, the priesthood, and the Syrian persecution of the Jews from the years 176 to 164 BC

2 Maccabees 10:10—15:35:	Part II, describing the successful military campaigns of Judas at the time of Antiochus V Eupator and Demetrius I, a period from 163 to 161 BC
2 Maccabees 15:37–29:	The epilogue, concluding the book with the author's comments

II. Significant Passages in 2 Maccabees

A. 2 Maccabees 1—2 / Introduction

1:1–10 *Two letters*

The letters recorded at the beginning of 2 Maccabees are written to Diaspora Jews in Egypt informing them about the new feast of the purification of the Temple. Here it is called "the feast of Booths" (1:9; see 1:18), thus confusing it with the feast of *Succoth* described in Leviticus 23:33–43. In effect, the feast described here is that of Hanukkah as celebrated in Judaism today.

The structure of the first letter with its salutation and opening prayer helps us understand how personal letters, like those of St. Paul, were written at this time.

2:4–8 *The ark of the covenant*

A legend concerning the ark of the covenant here recounts how the prophet Jeremiah hid it along with the sacred tent and the altar of incense in a cave, where it is to remain until "God gathers his people and shows them mercy," a time also when "the glory of the Lord and the cloud" will be seen (2:5–8). This description is echoed in the Gospel of Mark where Jesus describes his eschatological return (Mark 13:26; see Matt 24:30–31).

2:19–23 *Preface*

As a preface to the rest of the book, the author introduces his work as an effort to summarize or abridge the five-volume account by Jason of Cyrene. It is to be the story of Judas Maccabaeus fighting against Antiochus IV Epiphanes (175–164 BC) and Antiochus V Eupator (164–162 BC). Actually, 2 Maccabees includes also the fighting against Demetrius I Soter (162–150 BC).

The author introduces us to the concept of "Judaism" (*Ioudaismos,* 2:21), the amalgamation of religious faith and culture defined here primarily by its opposition to Hellenism. The struggle described in this book is above all that of an irreconcilable cultural conflict based on positions of faith.

B. 2 Maccabees 3—7 / Prelude to the Wars

The first part of 2 Maccabees focuses on the struggle of the Jewish people under Hellenistic oppression. Several of the events described here are also mentioned in 1 Maccabees 1. That which is distinctive about 2 Maccabees, however, is its insistence on internal Jewish problems. Many of the culprits here are Jewish priests, starting with Simon, the corrupt priest, and including especially Jason and Menelaus, the high priests who obtain their office by bribery and lead the people into "the Greek way of life" (4:10).

3:1–40 *Jewish infidelity*

Second Maccabees describes infidelity among the Jews as the context of the Syrian oppression. Much of the blame is ascribed to Simon, the treacherous Temple official. Only Onias, the good and pious high priest, appears willing to stand against the evil opposition.

The story here first describes an attempt by the Syrian rulers to expropriate the Temple treasury, whose sanctuary is respectfully indicated as "the place" (*ho topos,* 3:2). The king, Seleucus IV, abetted by Apollonius of Tarsus, sends Heliodorus to rob the Temple. In apparent response to intense prayer by priests and people, heaven intervenes with a miracle. A gloriously adorned horse rider and two other magnificent figures appear and attack Heliodorus (3:24–34). The scene was a favorite of later artists.

4:7–38 *Corrupt high priests*

As the infamous Antiochus IV Epiphanes comes to the throne (see 1 Macc 1:10), Jason usurps the high priesthood at the expense of his brother Onias (4:7). Jason leads his nation into "the Greek way of life" and abrogates Jewish institutions and observance of the Law (4:7–17).

Through bribery, Menelaus supplants Jason as high priest. Besides robbing the Temple to further bribe the Syrian rulers, Menelaus arranges the murder of Onias, the good high priest (4:23–38). This murder is mentioned cryptically in Daniel 9:26.

5:1–27 ***More horrors***

While Antiochus IV is at war with Egypt, Jason returns to Jerusalem, slaughters many of his fellow countrymen, but fails to regain power. Antiochus IV, in the meantime, thinking Judea is in revolt, returns from his Egyptian campaign, massacres many, and loots the Temple (see 1 Macc 1:20–24; Dan 11:25–30). The story of the attack by Apollonius the Mysian (5:24) ties into the account of 1 Maccabees 1:29–35.

In the middle of this account of horrors, the author briefly mentions Judas Maccabaeus and his companions withdrawing to the wilderness (5:27). We are thus prepared for his appearance again in chapter 8.

6:1–17 ***The desecration of the Temple***

Second Maccabees then describes the desecration of the Temple by its dedication to Olympian Zeus (6:1–11). This is the "abomination of desolation" mentioned by 1 Maccabees 1:54 and Daniel 11:31. The cultural conflict between Hellenism and Judaism now becomes an outright persecution of the Jews.

The author adds his religious commentary on these horrors much like the commentaries in the books of Kings (2 Kgs 17:7–20; 24:2–4). National disaster is a punishment for sin. The view of 2 Maccabees, however, is more upbeat. The oppression and these desecrations are ways of God correcting his people with a type of medicinal punishment. The swiftness of these punishments is a sign of God's love for his people (6:12–17). As the author insisted earlier, the people are more important in God's eyes than the Temple (5:19–20).

7:1–42 *The martyrdom of the seven brothers*

Consistent with the form and purpose of his "pathetic history," the author of 2 Maccabees goes into gory details about the tortures undergone by the martyrs. The heroism centers around observance of the Law. The martyrs are ready to die rather than transgress "the laws of our ancestors" (7:2).

The story of the mother and her seven sons here made such an impression that it continues to be celebrated by Christians, finding its place in the lectionary for the 32nd Sunday of the Year (cycle C). The story centers around the family's faith—and the authors' faith—in the resurrection of the dead (7:9, 14, 23). Second Maccabees thus joins the Book of Daniel as the Old Testament fountainhead of this central Christian doctrine. The mother in the story also advances the concept of divine creation *ex nihilo*, "not out of any existing thing" (7:28).

Before dying, the youngest son then describes his death and suffering as a sacrifice or offering, "imploring God to show mercy soon to our nation" (7:37). In this view, death and suffering in some way can bring about "an end to the wrath of the Almighty that has justly fallen on our whole nation" (7:38). The text thus joins Isaiah 53 as an expression of faith in "vicarious suffering," a faith that the suffering of the innocent can be an effective power against the evil of others' sins.

C. 2 Maccabees 8—15 / Judas Maccabaeus (166–160 BC)

The next section of 2 Maccabees parallels 1 Maccabees 3—7, the story of Judas Maccabaeus up to his decisive victory over Nicanor. The account in 2 Maccabees skips over the leadership of his father, Mattathias (1 Macc 2), and omits the defeat and death of Judas in battle with Bacchides (9:1–22) and the leadership of Judas's brothers, Jonathan and Simon. The order of the events differs somewhat from 1 Maccabees and is described with far more religious commentary.

8:1–7 ***The rebellion of Judas***

The opening shot of Judas picks up from his introduction earlier in 6:27. Here he summons and leads those who are faithful to "Judaism" (8:1). The success of Judas's guerilla tactics rests on divine grounds: "The Lord's wrath had now changed to mercy" (8:5). This beginning is described in 1 Maccabees 3:1–9.

9:1–29 ***The death of Antiochus***

Like 1 Maccabees 6:16, 2 Maccabees places the death of Antiochus in Persia. Unlike 1 Maccabees, however, 2 Maccabees places the death before the purification of the Temple (10:1–8). This order seems to have been the real order of events.

This "pathetic" account goes into the gory details of Antiochus's pain. Scripture has a way of magnifying the horrors of the deaths of God's enemies (See Isa 14:11; 66:24; Sir 7:17; 19:3; Jdt 16:17). Before the invention of the concept of hell, such descriptions assured the readers that evil is punished in the end. Finally, "when he could no longer bear his own stench," Antiochus repents (see 1 Macc 6:12–13) and makes a rather implausible vow to set Jerusalem free, to make Jews equal to Athenians, and to restore the Temple.

The letter from Antiochus found in this chapter, however, could be historical if seen as written to others than the Jews of Jerusalem, perhaps to the Jews of Antioch.

10:1–8 ***The capture of Jerusalem***

After his initial military victories, Judas takes control of Jerusalem and the Temple, which he restores (see 1 Macc 4:36–61). The annual feast on the 25th day of Chislev (around December) celebrating this restoration becomes the feast of Hanukkah. Here and in the opening letters (1:9, 18) it is called the feast of Booths.

12:38–46 ***Prayers for the dead***

After narrating a series of military victories (10:14—11:12; 12:5–37), some of which parallel the accounts in 1 Maccabees 5:1–68, the author then relates the prayers Judas and his army make for their fallen comrades, who appear to have died in some serious sin forbidden by Deuteronomy 7:26. The author uses this story to promote faith in the resurrection of the dead. Judas and his army pray "that the sinful deed might be fully blotted out" (12:42). He and his soldiers arrange "an expiatory sacrifice" (12:43) as an "atonement for the dead that they might be freed from this sin" (12:46)—all this in the expectation that the fallen sinners would rise again (12:44).

Christian theologians later used this text to develop the doctrine of "purgatory," the place for people who are spared damnation to hell but are not ready for heaven. The text obviously does not contain the precisions of later theological constructs, but it does emphasize the power of prayer even over the power of death. In its deepest meaning, the text is about the mercy of God.

14:1–46 ***The stories of Nicanor and Razis***

The next two chapters extend the story into the reign of Demetrius I (162–150 BC; see appendix 7), who was supplanted by his brother Antiochus IV, but who now comes to take over (14:1–2). Against this backdrop, 2 Maccabees develops the story of Nicanor, whose initial offer of peace is described much more positively than in 1 Maccabees 7:26–50. This peace is thwarted by Alcimus, another evil high priest who succeeded Menelaus to that office (14:16–27).

The author then inserts another gory story about a martyr, Razis, who earlier showed great zeal even though "convicted of Judaism" (14:38). In this story Razis commits suicide by tearing out his own entrails "calling upon the Lord of life and of spirit to give these back to him again" (14:46).

15:1–35 ***Judas's victory over Nicanor***

Judas encourages his forces by words "from the Law and the Prophets" (15:9), apparently a reference to the first two parts of the Hebrew Bible, which now apparently have been canonized.

Then by way of leading up to the great victory over Nicanor, the author describes a dream of Judas (15:12–16), a scene unparalleled in the Old Testament, the appearance of two dead human beings described as praying for the people. Judas describes his vision of Onias, the good high priest (4:1–6, 33–34), and

Jeremiah, the prophet, named earlier in the second opening letter of this book (2:1–8).

Here also the author describes the great concern of Judas's forces as "for the consecrated sanctuary" (15:18). In these last two chapters of 2 Maccabees, we see great esteem of the Jerusalem Temple, an attitude that is somewhat uncharacteristic for this book, which earlier insisted on the subordination of the Temple to the good of the people (5:19). In this last section of the book the text refers to "the great Temple" (14:12), "the dwelling place among us" for God (14:35), and "this house" to be preserved forever undefiled (14:36). Around 170 BC the Jews in Egypt erected a temple at Leontopolis. The author of 2 Maccabees may be aiming to wean the Egyptian Jews away from the temple at Leontopolis and to secure their allegiance to the Temple in Jerusalem.

In any case, Judas and his army meet the enemy "fighting with their hands and praying to God with their hearts" (15:26–29). Victory follows. The celebration of this victory over Nicanor was to be on the 13th of Adar (March 27), the eve of "Mordecai's Day," also known as the feast of Purim, as described in the Book of Esther.

III. The Message of 2 Maccabees

A. Review of Themes

The following themes distinguish the theology of 2 Maccabees:

- Judaism, the distinctive culture animated by Jewish faith in conflict with Hellenism (2:21; 4:9–17; 8:1–4)
- Treachery and corruption within Israel, especially within the high priesthood (3:4; 4:7–38; 14:3–27)
- Miraculous interventions of heavenly beings (3:22–30; 5:2–4; 5:5–6, 15)
- Oppression by hostile powers seen as God's temporary anger for the correction of the people (5:17–20; 6:12; 7:32–38)

- Life after death by resurrection of the body (7:9–29; 12:38–46; 14:46)
- Suffering and death as redemptive for others (7:37–38)
- Vicarious expiation through sacrifices and prayers (7:37–39)

B. The Theology of 2 Maccabees

Even more than 1 Maccabees, 2 Maccabees revolves around the conflict of religious cultures. The first seven chapters are about the evils of "the Greek way of life," culminating in the heroism of the mother with her seven sons who choose death rather than compromise their faith.

Even more so than 1 Maccabees, this book stresses the way this culture war permeated into the most sacred circles of Judaism, corrupting the high priesthood. Like the books of Kings, which constantly reminded the readers of the sins of the kings, so too 2 Maccabees details the corruption of the high priesthood under Jason and Menelaus, joining 1 Maccabees in its condemnation also of Alcimus.

The horrors endured under the Hellenistic rulers are thus rooted in the sins of Israel. The suffering is the punishment of God for the sins of the high priests, just as for the Deuteronomists the disasters of the sixth century were God's chastisement for the sins of the kings. Second Maccabees, however, stresses more the medicinal character of this punishment. This suffering was to correct Israel and ultimately showed the love of God (6:12–17).

This book also adds the note that the suffering of the just was in some way vicariously redemptive for the rest of the nation (7:37–38). Second Maccabees also sees in the death of the martyr the expiatory character of the good person's sufferings and death. The last of the seven martyred children sees his death as an expiatory sacrifice that in some way can bring an end to the wrath of the Almighty (7:37–39).

In 2 Maccabees, God is named constantly. The author visualizes God close at hand, waiting to be prayed to and anxious to answer the prayers of his chosen ones. Moreover, the divine interventions—like that in the story of Heliodorus—are spectacular and unambiguous (3:22–34). With its sense of the nearness of God, this is a book pervaded with faith, filled with confidence, optimistic hope, and dedication to God.

The willingness to die for God takes on a new sense in 2 Maccabees. If one dies for the sake of the Law, the God who shapes each person's beginnings will also restore both "breath and life" (7:23). This sense of life after death is thus based explicitly on faith in the power of God and implicitly on the unspeakable injustice of a young person dying in cruel suffering out of fidelity to the Law. The authors of 2 Maccabees saw in the martyr apparently the need for God's reestablishment of justice by restoration of "breath and life."

Another aspect of death appears in this book in the expiatory prayers offered by Judas for the slain Jewish soldiers who had broken the Law and died in and because of their sinfulness. Judas prays "that they might be freed from this sin" (12:46), that these fallen soldiers might by that prayer "rise again" (12:44). The moment of death is not the ultimate determination of a person's eternal destiny. Death is no longer the absolute separation of those who die from those who remain alive. In the prayer to God, some form of "communion" remains to bind those who in life shared their holy purpose. In fact, Judas's dream of Onias and Jeremiah (15:12–16) suggests the power of this communion works in both directions, that the pious dead have the ability to assist the living.

C. The Message of the Two Books of Maccabees

The two books of Maccabees are above all books about war and intrigue. The wars waged by the Jews are holy wars, fought for God's honor and ultimately won by God's help. Such is the faith of the authors of these books.

Can this faith speak to us? We are tired of wars. We are intensely conscious of the suffering war inflicts on all involved. It takes, therefore, a special effort to find anything edifying in these books, especially in the knowledge we now have of the way the Hasmonean line was soon corrupted by the power won by the "Maccabean" heroes.

One approach to this same conflict is found in the Book of Daniel. In Daniel and the apocalyptic works that Daniel will inspire, human beings look on the struggle as rooted in forces beyond their capacity even to understand, much less to change. In the apocalyptic approach, human beings can do little except endure in patient prayer as they wait for divine intervention.

Mattathias and his sons take a different approach. They fight against the oppressive political power of the day. Their faith entails involvement in the politics of the day, in public office, in warfare, and in diplomacy. This is a theology of political engagement. In our day we call this approach "liberation theology."

We must, however, be careful not to read into this Maccabean theology the modern theme of active resistance against oppressive governments. In the biblical texts, the condemnation is from the perspective of divine law and "the rights of God," not so much the rights of human beings. This is not exactly the same as the modern theme of government oppression against individual liberty. And yet we see here the basic foundation of all opposition to "legal" injustice. Human governments must be subject to divine law. The defense of religion leads to the defense of human rights.

Both 1 and 2 Maccabees are stories of prayer and dependence on God as well as stories about the moral requirements of political action. The virtuous character of Mattathias's family is central to the story. Their selfless dedication and even humility stand in contrast to the deceitfulness and self-destructive ambition of the Seleucids and the Hellenistic Jews consumed by self-aggrandizement.

Like the judges of ancient times, the Maccabees arose by a visible acclamation of the people and an invisible gift by God, a type of charism given for the good of the people and the glory of God's sanctuary. As we saw in the Book of Judges, this charism could be called "the charism of violence," a charism to be used as a last resort, in very specific circumstances, for a purpose that transcends the individuals involved. Without this violence, no peace could have existed for Judea at this time.

The books of Maccabees end basically with a victory over the Hellenistic empire and a time of peace. This was a time of optimism, not gazing into any abyss.

Sadly, we know that this peace and optimism was short-lived. The moral requirements for "judging Israel" disappeared in the power-corrupted Hasmoneans who succeeded the Maccabees. Personal ambition replaced dedication to the Temple of God. Judea descended into the oppression of the Herodian and Roman period. The people began to await another leader anointed by God to bring salvation to the people. It is not surprising that they expected a military leader—like Judas and his brothers. However, God's mysterious future surprised humanity.

PART IV

Historical-sounding Midrash

14
Introduction to Midrash

I. History and Literary Form

In the centuries following the Exile, literary activity flourished in Israel as never before. This was the time of the collection of the Psalms and Proverbs, the editing into "books" of the great prophets of the past. Out of this intense literary activity also arose new forms: protests against narrow-minded exclusivism like the Book of Ruth, a story of about David's Gentile great-grandmother; the Book of the Prophet Jonah, a satire on the same theme; and the Book of Tobit, reflections on Mosaic teachings used to portray the ideal Israelite. These books were narrations of persons, presumably of the past. However, on close examination they appear as didactic works, that is, expositions presented to instruct, encourage, or edify a particular audience, rather than attempts to record history. Around a historical nucleus, fictitious details, along with prayers and speeches, elaborate a kind of parahistorical literary form we know today as haggadic midrash.

As centuries passed and the true understanding of haggadic midrash was lost, devout believers clung to these stories with blind conviction that what the stories narrated must have actually happened. Today a better knowledge of ancient history plus a more accurate understanding of biblical literary forms have restored these works to their legitimate literary family.

Midrashic literature is essentially a literature about a literature, a reflection on, a meditation or a searching into a sacred text. This literary practice testifies to a great love and veneration for the written stories of Israel, now considered inspired and the revelation of God's word. The practice also testifies to a sense of religious tradition as a living voice, expressing the changing life of the people of God, adapting the inspired words into contemporary expressions of Israel's teaching.

At the time of the Exile, the synagogue developed as the place where Israel's Book could be examined and treasured. A typical synagogue service involved the reading from the Torah and the Prophets along with a homily or explanation of the readings. These biblical expositions or homilies arose and became collected as learned leaders devoted their lives to the study and explanation of scripture (see Ezra 7:6, 10).

Rabbinic literature uses the term *midrash* (or plural *midrashim*) to describe these Jewish commentaries. This Hebrew word is the noun form of the verb *darash,* which means "to search" or "to scrutinize." In biblical Hebrew this noun occurs only three times. The Chronicler speaks of "the midrash of the prophet Addo" (2 Chr 13:22) and of "the midrash of the Book of Kings" (2 Chr 24:27), which apparently refer to some official written records of the kings. The Book of Sirach refers to his school as a "house of midrash" (Sir 51:23), a school that sought wisdom in the form of the Law.

"Halakic midrash" refers to an exposition of a legal portion of the Bible. *Halakah* is the Hebrew word for "walking" or "way." Morality or conduct was expressed commonly in the Hebrew mind as a "walking"—as St. Paul would say, "If we live by the Spirit, let us walk by the Spirit" (Gal 5:25). The earliest extent written collections of explicitly halakic interpretations were made around the middle of the second century AD. These include the *Mekilta* of Exodus, the *Sifra* on Leviticus, and the *Sifre* on Numbers and Deuteronomy. Very closely related to these halakic midrashim is the body of legal interpretations that were passed down orally for centuries and then eventually collected in written form in the *Mishnah* and the *Talmud*. The *Mishnah,* which contains commentaries up to the second century AD, is the work of Rabbi Judah ha-Nasi (Judah the Prince).

Commentaries that dealt with biblical stories were called haggadic midrash, from the Hebrew word *haggadah,* which means "narration." Our earliest extended collection of this type is the *Midrash on Genesis,* which goes back to the third century AD. This midrash was combined with later midrashim on other biblical books to form the *Midrash Rabbah*. Extensive portions of haggadic midrash also appear in the nonbiblical Jewish writings of the Hellenistic and Roman periods, in the works of Josephus and in the Aramaic translations of scripture, the *targumin*, where translators would often intercalate imaginative stories into the biblical narratives.

We now understand that biblical narrations, sometimes whole biblical books, fit into the literary form of haggadic midrash. The Book of Ruth develops a love story around the great-grandmother and great-grandfather of David. The Book of Esther tells a story to explain the institution of the feast of Purim. The first half of Daniel narrates stories of a faithful Jew in the hostile culture of Babylonia. Jewish scholars placed these books into the third part of the Hebrew canon, the Sacred Writings. The Book of Tobit, which makes up a story about the ideal Israelite, and the Book of Judith, which tells a story of God's protection of ancient Israel, both made it into the Greek canon and are now found in Catholic and Orthodox Bibles.

Since the discovery of the Habakkuk scroll among the Dead Sea Scrolls, scholars today now also speak of a third form of midrash, the *pesher*. The Essenes at Qumran used that word to introduce their imaginative interpretation of the Book of Habakkuk. This midrash attempts to actualize the prophecies of this seventh-century prophet by describing ways in which his writings can be seen as fulfilled in the days of the Essenes.

In summary, the main purpose of the writer of this literature was to make the word of God yield its wealth of doctrine and edification for the spiritual nourishment of the readers. To accomplish this purpose, the author allowed himself or herself great latitude, even to the point of composing an entire story around detail in the text in order to make it relevant and meaningful. Thus these stories illustrate graphically some aspect of righteous life that God expects of every good Israelite. In these stories the characters appear and speak in a way to keep the story moving and dramatic. Prayers and speeches serve as vehicles for expressing the authors' teaching. The historical nucleus upon which the story may be based is relatively unimportant.

II. The Message of Midrashic Literature

By their very form, the wonderful stories that we will study say something important about our faith. They underline the fully human nature of that faith. This is not a faith of just abstract dogmas and creeds, although dogma and creed can enrich that faith. This is not a faith based just on complex historical knowledge, although the action of God in history is a foundation of that faith. This is a faith of people living in families and cultures where the lived experience is the fundamental principle, often as described by story.

Lived experience is often best captured in story, not philosophy. Story allows us to portray and celebrate the concrete person and his or her challenge in all his or her uniqueness. Yet story allows us to see the patterns of existence that bind us to that unique event and person, patterns that illumine our unique person and challenges. Story allows us to engage our imagination as well as our intellect and will in the attempt to grasp truth.

People will object, "But these stories are made up! They are fictional!" Nevertheless, good fiction *presents* more than the characters and actions directly described. Good fiction allows a deeper dimension of reality to shine forth. We recognize that reality when we are captivated by a story. We recognize that the story ultimately is about ourselves. We may not be able to present that reality in any way outside of that story—although scholars continue to try to analyze and dissect. As in all great art, a dimension of reality is present in and through the medium. Attempts can be made to articulate something of that deeper dimension, but ultimately understanding requires returning to the medium in its concreteness in simple, joyful appreciation.

So it is with Ruth, Esther, Judith, and Tobit. We will analyze the stories. In the end, however, we must return to the stories as stories and rejoice in the concrete presentation of characters who demonstrate their faith by living out the unique situations of their contingent existence. In some strange way, by this aesthetic experience we touch the eternal essence of God.

15
The Book of Ruth

I. Overview

The Book of Ruth gives us a picture of pious or righteous Israelite family life supposedly set in the age of the judges (1:1). Unlike the other historical books of the Old Testament, which focus on kings and leaders of the people, the Book of Ruth tells the story of the personal drama of private individuals—whose progeny are important for the people.

The story of Ruth is the story of David's great-grandmother. For this reason it is placed in the Greek Bible and in the Christian Bible between the Book of Judges and 1 Samuel. In the Hebrew Bible, Ruth is part of a subcollection within the Sacred Writings called the *Megilloth*, or "scrolls," used for five annual festivals. Ruth was read for the agricultural feast of Weeks or Pentecost (*Shavu'ot*), apparently because the story is set in the time of the barley and wheat harvests (2:22).

From its vocabulary, its efforts to explain ancient customs (see 4:7), as well as its place in the Hebrew Bible, the Book of Ruth appears to be a postexilic writing, written perhaps around the fifth century BC or possibly later. Arguing from the connection between David and the king of Moab (1 Sam 22:3–4), some scholars suggest that an early form of the story of Ruth may date back to the period of the kings. In any case, this book provides interesting insights into ancient Israelite social practices, beyond what we know from the legal codes preserved in scripture.

In many ways the story of Ruth resembles that of haggadic midrash, although the figures of Ruth and Naomi, her mother-in-law, along with Boaz, her Israelite levirate husband, may well be historical. Like the story of Jonah, the Book of Ruth portrays an unusual openness to the Gentiles. Unlike the other haggadic midrashim of the Old Testament, however, the story of Ruth remains on the level of realism and plausibility. Nor do the characters break off into long prayers and speeches. The dialogues that carry the story, however, are clearly invented by a storyteller.

Like other haggadic midrashim, this book dramatizes basic Israelite personal goodness, or virtue—as the Greeks would call it. Ruth is a model of fidelity, reflecting covenantal loyalty and kindness (*chesed*). She will not abandon her mother-in-law, Naomi. This familial piety leads Ruth to accept Israel as her people and Yahweh as God: "Your people shall be my people, and your God my God" (1:16). Boaz in turn is kind to the foreigner and the widow and faithful to all the aspects of levirate obligation, which is to raise up posterity to Ruth's deceased first husband (see Deut 25:5–10).

Perhaps written under the influence of Deutero-Isaiah's universalist teaching (see Isa 56:6), the book emphasizes the breadth of God's call to salvation by showing how even a Moabite could be called by God to enter the genealogical line of David. In its openness to the Moabites, the Book of Ruth stands as a direct challenge to Deuteronomy 23:4: "No Ammonite or Moabite shall be admitted into the congregation of the Lord; none of their descendants, even in the tenth generation, shall ever be admitted into the congregation of the Lord." Such a challenge is all the more striking if we are correct in dating the Book of Ruth to the post-exilic period, a time precisely of intense application of the Law (see Neh 8:1–12; 13:23–27).

II. Significant Passages in Ruth

Because of the short and unified character of this book, we need to read the story in its entirety.

1:1–22 *The return from bitterness*

The first chapter gives us the setting and introduces us to the central figures of Naomi, the Israelite widow, along with her also widowed daughter-in-law, Ruth. As Naomi loses first her husband and then her married sons, her family moves from prosperity to

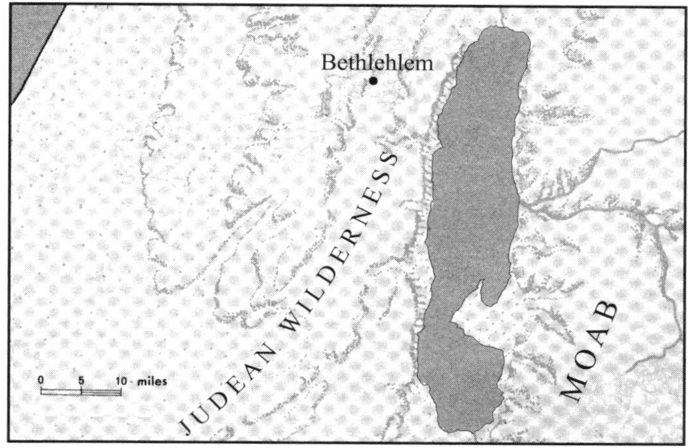

15A: Places in the Story of Ruth

destitution. The setting moves from Bethlehem in Judah to Moab, and back to Bethlehem.

The recurrent theme of "covenant fidelity and kindness" (*chesed*) appears in 1:8. Naomi prays that God's *chesed* be with her two daughters-in-law, just as they had showed such loyalty and fidelity to their dead husbands and to Naomi. Ruth then dramatizes this fidelity with the well-known line, "Wherever you go, I will go. Wherever you dwell, I will dwell. Your people will be my people. Your God, my God" (1:16). We know of no legal obligation for Ruth to do this. It is clearly an act of *chesed*, loyal kindness.

The chapter, which functions like the first act of a drama, emphasizes the bitterness of the situation—as emphasized by Naomi's suggested name change (1:20). The scene here is basically one of hopelessness, dramatized by Naomi's attempt to persuade her daughters-in-law to return to their own families (1:8–13). Ruth's commitment to Naomi is thus a willingness to enter into suffering and bitterness. The message would resound clearly with families that remembered the bitterness of exile.

Furthermore, Naomi is clear that all this suffering is from the Lord: "Yahweh has extended his hand against me" (1:13). "Shaddai has made it very bitter for me" (1:20). The meaning of the divine name, "Shaddai," remains obscure, although well attested for Yahweh (Exod 6:2–3; Isa 13:6; Ezek 1:24). The equivalence of the two names is clear in 1:21. Because the Greek Bible translates the term as *pantocrator*, most scholars today conclude that the name means "Almighty." It is interesting that Balaam, the Moabite prophet, is described as seeing the "vision of Shaddai" (Num 24:4, 16). The role of God in this drama also appears when it was heard that "Yahweh had visited his people and provided them with food" (1:6).

2:1–23 ***Boaz the redeemer***

The second chapter introduces us to the figure of Boaz, a prosperous and prominent Israelite (*gibor chayil*) and a relative of Naomi and therefore of Ruth's dead husband. In this part of the story, the foreign status of Ruth is repeatedly emphasized. She is "Ruth, the Moabite" (2:2, 21), "the Moabite girl" (2:6; see also 1:22), or simply "the foreigner" (2:10).

She provides food for herself and her mother-in-law by "gleaning" after the harvesters. This action of picking up the scraps left on the ground after the first cutting was prescribed by an Israelite law to provide for the poor (Lev 19:9–10; 23:22; Deut 24:19–22).

The critical meeting between Ruth and Boaz is described as a result of an amazing chance happening. "Now it just so happened for her that..." (*wayiqer miqreha;* 2:3). In the silence of any attempt to explain the chance event is the implication or at least suggestion of God's providential care. Ruth just happens to work in Boaz's field, who just happens to see her. He asks about her and scrupulously observes this gleaning rule, instructing his workers to go beyond the necessary.

In effect, Boaz becomes the instrument of God rewarding Ruth for the risk and sacrifices she took in her fidelity to family. This role of Boaz starts with his prayer for God's blessing on Ruth (2:12). In her prayer of blessing for Boaz, Naomi recognizes the action of "Yahweh, who is ever merciful to the living and to the dead" (2:20).

In the meeting with Boaz, Ruth does not know anything about his connection with her family, although he does. After the encounter, Naomi explains the identity of Boaz to Ruth. Boaz is a *go'el* for this family, a "redeemer" (2:20). The term refers to a kinsman on whom you could count to defend your life (Josh 20:3–5), your liberty (Lev 25:47–49), your name (Deut 25:5–10), and your property (Lev 25:23–26). The levirate law required him also to beget an heir for a deceased kinsman so that his name would not die out in Israel (Deut 25:5–10; see Gen 38:6–11). This term is often used of God in the Old Testament (Job 19:25; Pss 19:15; 78:35; Isa 48:17; 59:20; 63:16; Jer 50:34; Lam 3:58; see Acts 7:35).

3:1–18 *Boaz and Ruth get together*

In the third chapter, Naomi coaches Ruth in the subtleties of feminine courtship. This instruction and the narration that follows include several possible although subtle allusions to sex: "the threshing floor" (3:2.6.14), Boaz's "feet" (3:4, 7, 14), "covering" with one's cloak (3:9; see Ezek 16:8), "lying with" someone (3:4, 7, 8, 13, 14).

Boaz picks up the lead. In the description of Boaz and his action in this chapter and the next, the verb, *ga'al,* together with the noun, *go'el,* form a leitmotif (3:9, 12–13; 4:1, 3–4, 6, 8, 14). Boaz quickly accepts the role of "redeemer." Boaz again expresses a prayer of blessing on her for her loyal kindness (*chesed;* 3:10).

An element of suspense, however, appears with the mention of "the closer relative" (3:12). Naomi heightens the suspense by her instruction to "wait until you learn what happens" (3:18).

4:1–17 *The marriage of Boaz and Ruth*

In the fourth chapter, Boaz gives the unnamed closer relative his full legal rights. Here Boaz shows his full conformity with the Law (Deut 25:5–10). He also appears as an able lawyer gathering witnesses and explaining all the legal strings attached (4:1–5). In effect, Boaz discourages the "closer relative" and thus wins the right and duty to take Ruth as his wife, sealing the deal with the ancient required gesture (4:7–10).

We reach the climax of the story in Ruth's pregnancy and birth of a son by Boaz (4:13). For the first time the narrator directly describes the action of Yahweh, here as bringing about the pregnancy. The destitution and emptiness of the first chapter have come full swing. Bitterness has turned to joy, under the providential guidance of God. Naomi, who has functioned as the principal mover of the story, returns to center stage. She fully accepts the child (4:16), who is named Obed, the grandfather of David (4:17).

4:18–22 ***The genealogy of David***

A genealogy, most likely borrowed from 1 Chronicles 2:4–15, then traces the lineage of David from Perez, who was also born of an application of the levirate law (Gen 38). This genealogy traces the line of David through Boaz and Obed, even though the whole story of Ruth was to indicate how Obed continued the line of Ruth's first husband, either Mahlon or Kilion (1:2–5). Apparently the author of 1 Chronicles did not know the story of Ruth, and the final redactor of Ruth, the one who added the genealogy of 1 Chronicles, does not seem to have been concerned with the conflict between this genealogy and the story of Ruth.

Both Matthew (1:3–6) and Luke (3:31–33) trace the Davidic line through Boaz and Obed. Matthew, however, makes explicit mention of Ruth along with three other women in the Old Testament—reproducing the genealogy found in Ruth 4:18–21 even with its name variants. The point of the levirate law does not seem to matter to either Matthew or the final redactor of Ruth.

III. The Message of Ruth

A. Review of Themes

The storyteller seems to have molded the story around the following focal points of faith:

- God who directs historical events and is recognized in prayer (1:13, 20; 2:3, 12, 20–21; 3:10; 4:13)
- Divine and human loyal kindness (1:8; 2:20; 3:10)
- Openness to non-Israelites (1:4, 22; 2:2, 6, 10, 21)
- Redeemer and redemption (2:20; 3:9, 12–13; 4:1, 3–4, 6, 8, 14)
- Women taking the initiative (1:6, 14–18; 2:2–3, 17, 22; 3:1–4, 18)

B. The Theology of Ruth

The central message of Ruth is that of God's inclusive love, at least toward those willing to accept Yahweh as one's God and Israel as one's people. Written like Jonah at a time when Israel was falling back into a siege mentality, this book emphasizes the cosmopolitan character of David's lineage. Boaz, an able lawyer, has no scruples in disobeying the explicit provision in Deuteronomy 23, yet he observes the levirate law to the letter in Deuteronomy 25. Caring for individuals takes precedence over preserving the status of the people as a whole (see Mark 2:23—3:5).

This book is also about women and their role in the development of God's people. Set in the time of the rude practices of Israelite patriarchy, this story portrays women who make their own choices and take the initiative not only for their own lives but also for the sake of their descendants. It is precisely the noble qualities of these women that move the story from one development to the next.

God does not appear or speak in this book. Divine action is indicated mostly through the confessions of faith, the prayers, or the reports of the characters in this story. Only once does the narrator describe the actions of God, in the climactic event of Ruth's pregnancy (4:13). Otherwise, agency rests in the human actors in this play. Yet the prayers of the main characters and their interpretation of events direct us to see God directing the events. It is through the faith of the persons speaking that we detect God.

The story is also about God's protection of good people. Life at times can be bitter, very bitter, for good people (1:20). But, in the end, the good guys win—they have to. Nevertheless, God may use bitterness to guide his faithful to blessings. The lesson would be clear to Israelites who remembered the Exile.

16
The Book of Esther

I. Overview

A. The Text

In the Hebrew Bible, Esther is part of the Sacred Writings. Like Ruth, it has its place in a subgroup called the *Megilloth* (or "scrolls"). It was read for the feast of Purim. In the Greek Old Testament, the somewhat different Greek version of Esther, including several important additions to the book, comes after the two books of Esdras (Ezra and Nehemiah). The rationale for this location apparently lies in the setting of the story of Esther, the reign of Xerxes I (485–465 BC), known in the story as Ahasuerus (see also Ezra 4:6), during the Persian period. Catholic and Orthodox Bibles place Esther in a similar place among "the historical books," although placing the book after Tobit and Judith, following the order of the Latin Vulgate of St. Jerome.

The story is about a Jewish family in the Persian Diaspora. Esther, whose name derives from the Babylonian goddess, Ishtar, is the heroine. The other principal person of the story is her uncle, Mordecai, whose name apparently derives from the Babylonian god, Marduk. After a series of fortunate (providential?) circumstances, Esther is elevated to the position of queen in the Persian Empire; Mordecai, eventually to that of prime minister. From her position of power, Esther undoes the plot of the evil Haman to destroy the Jewish people in Persia. Instead of the Jews being destroyed on the day selected by lot (*pur*), the enemies of the Jews were slaughtered, turning that day into a feast of celebration, the feast of Purim.

The six sizable additions found in the Greek version pose challenges for the modern interpreter and headaches for the publisher of Bibles. In the Catholic tradition, these additions were formally declared canonical and inspired by the Council of Trent. Protestant traditions relegate them to "the apocrypha." St. Jerome included these additions in his Latin translation as a kind of supplement, placing them all together after the Hebrew. In some Bibles, therefore, we find them in 10:4—16:24. Other Catholic Bibles place them as they appear in the Greek text, thus disturbing the consecutive chapter-and-verse numbers of the Hebrew version. The Bible of Jerusalem follows the chapter-and-verse numbers for the Greek but italicizes the additions. The New American Bible introduces the Greek additions in six special chapters indicated by letters A through F.

These additions significantly shift the perspective and meaning of the book. The Hebrew text focuses on the political resourcefulness of Esther and Mordecai. God is not even mentioned in the Hebrew text. At best, the devout reader can see divine providence behind the crucial chance events around which the story turns (see 2:2; 6:6). The Greek additions, however, shift the focus to God, who protects his people through instruments like Esther and Mordecai. The Greek version frames the entire story with a special revelation of "what God intended to do" (A:1–11; F:1–10). In the Greek version, Esther and Mordecai turn to God in prayerful acknowledgment of their dependence on divine help (C:1–30). God is the principal actor in critical events (D:8).

B. The Literary Form

Like Ruth, the Book of Esther is midrash especially in its Hebrew form. The author writes to edify and encourage the readers. To do this he seizes on some massive pogrom against the Jews that failed and elaborates it freely and dramatically. The modern historian is generally skeptical about how much historical fact can be salvaged from the Book of Esther. The portrayal of weak and gullible Ahasuerus (Xerxes) is completely implausible and contradicts historical indications. The Persian queen, Vashti, is unknown. In fact, Herodotus identifies Xerxes's wife as Amestris

(*Histories* 9.108–13). The reaction of the Persian people to the events is undocumented and seems unlikely.

However, the result of the account is a great story. To accomplish his purpose the author uses all the techniques of the skilled storyteller: contrasts between the petulant Vashti and the serene Esther, between the dedicated and humble Mordecai and the ambitious and proud Haman; the gradual heightening of suspense by means of the apparent success of Haman's plot; the ironic use of the gibbet; the destruction of the enemies on the eve of the very day determined for the destruction of the Jewish people.

The author may in fact have had the story of Joseph in mind. Esther is a story of Jews in a foreign land, in danger of extinction, saved by the amazing success of one of their own. The royal robe (6:7) and the signet ring (8:8) by which Mordecai is honored clearly echo the elevation of Joseph (Gen 41:42–43).

In retelling the story of Esther, the Greek translator provides an apocalyptic overlay or veneer. The midrash of Esther becomes a dramatization of the conflict of good and evil, which God in his providence has incorporated into his mysterious plan of salvation. The Greek translator provides this overlay especially in the new framework for the story. By situating the story between the dream of Mordecai (A:4–11) and the interpretation of that dream (F:1–10), the storyteller focuses the reader's attention now on "what God intended to do" (A:11). This mysterious plan of God appears with strange symbols, clarified only by the later point-by-point interpretation. With its Greek additions, the story of Esther is that of God's victory over evil. The story becomes that of "the judgment before God" (F:7).

The hero and heroine of the story in the Greek form acknowledge by their prayers that God is in control (C:1–30). The victory is not so much the result of their political cleverness (as in the Hebrew form) but of God's hidden control of worldly events. Esther becomes the story of God's "signs and great wonders" (F:6). It is God who raises the lowly and deposes the mighty. God controls the succession of powerful offices in one world empire and thus saves his people from the forces of evil.

Some link appears in the Greek form of Esther to the Book of Daniel, where God controls world empires to bring salvation to his people. The identification of Haman as a Macedonian (E:10) suggests a connection between the crisis in Esther with that in Daniel where the forces of evil are epitomized by the Hellenistic king, Antiochus IV. All this would suggest that the Greek version probably dates from the early second century BC, although the nucleus of the shorter Hebrew story may date from the fifth century BC.

In its Greek form, the narration unfolds in three major steps:

Esther 1—2, A:	Prologue and setting: the dream of Mordecai; Mordecai's initial service to the king; the deposition of Vashti and the exaltation of Esther the Jewess
Esther 3—7, B–D:	The development of the plot: Haman's plot to destroy the Jews; Esther and Mordecai's plea for help; Esther's initiatives; and the poetic reversal of Haman's fortunes
Esther 8—10, E–F:	The conclusion: Mordecai's elevation to prime minister; the neutralization of the decree to destroy the Jews; the destruction by the Jews of their enemies; the feast of Purim; the interpretation of Mordecai's dream

II. Significant Passages in Esther

A:1–17 *The vision and promotion of Mordecai*

The setting of the story is Susa, east of Babylon (see map 9A, p. 152; also Dan 8:2), the summer palace of the Persian kings. The focus is on a prominent man in the king's court named Mordecai, identified as one of the exiles with King Jeconiah. If Ahasuerus is indeed Xerxes I (see Ezra 4:6), the year would be 484 BC, 110 years after the deportation of Jeconiah!

Mordecai's dream-vision reminds us of the apocalyptic visions of Daniel (see Dan 7:1–14). The dream portrays cosmic forces of evil, with ensuing distress and confusion on earth—all leading to a victorious intervention of God.

Subsequently, Mordecai discovers a treasonous plot against the king. Mordecai warns the king and is rewarded for his loyalty (A:16), a detail that contradicts the description in 6:3, but sets up the hostility of Haman (A:17).

1:1—2:18 ***The elevation of Esther***

The Hebrew section has its own introduction and begins with the great feast at which queen Vashti is deposed (1:1–22). The long list of royal counselors along with the general portrayal of Ahasuerus in the story suggests a tongue-in-cheek tone to the description. The court is a bureaucratic mess. Thus the discussion of women's relationship to their husbands may well be ironic.

We are then introduced to Esther. Because of her beauty, she is made queen, replacing Vashti (2:5–18). At this point the Hebrew text introduces Mordecai and tells the story of his loyal support of the king by warning him against the assassins (2:19–23).

3:1–11 ***Haman, the villain***

The Hebrew text now introduces Haman, before whom Mordecai will not kneel and bow down. Since kneeling and bowing before officials was a normal political gesture, the Hebrew story is not clear about Mordecai's refusal. The Greek translator, however, will clarify Mordecai's refusal (see C:5–7). Like the hero of the Book of Daniel (Dan 3), Mordecai is in a difficult spot as he tries to find some accommodation with a hostile culture yet draw the line over which he will not cross.

In any case, the plot now thickens. Haman vents his hatred not only against Mordecai but against the whole Jewish people. The day of destruction has been chosen, by lots, casting something like dice. The author is careful to explain that the word for "lot" is *pur* (in Babylonian!). Thus, the connection with the feast of *Purim*. The king provides his irrevocable decision.

Things look bleak for the "people living apart, with laws differing from those of every other people" (3:8), a description of the Diaspora Jews. The description here may capture well the difficult situation of Jews living outside of Israel during the Persian and Hellenistic periods. Mordecai, like Daniel or Nehemiah, represents the pious Jew who actually succeeded quite well in the foreign culture. Yet a persistent resentment—flaring at times into violent hatred—against Jews in that culture constituted a constant danger. How do you discretely maintain your Jewish identity yet find a place in the culture in which you need to live and which can provide many good things?

C:12–30 *The prayer of Esther*

In an intense prayer of lamentation and petition, Esther begs God to help her and his people. In contrast to the splendid attire so important in the Persian court, Esther approaches God in "garments of distress and mourning...covering her head with dirt and ashes" (C:13). She protests how she abhors "the glory of the lawless...and the conjugal bed of the uncircumcised or of any foreigner" (C:26).

5:1–14 *The intervention by Esther*

Esther appears again, no longer as the demure girl presented to the king, but as a mature, politically savvy woman. Still seething with hatred for Mordecai, Haman prepares an enormous gibbet to execute the Jew. Esther, meanwhile, prepares his downfall. She has gotten the king to provide her with anything she requests, "even if it is half of my kingdom" (see Mark 6:23). The Greek account of Esther's initiative elaborates on her beauty and grace along with an intervention of God (D:1–16).

6:1–13 *Mordecai honored*

Mordecai in the meantime is elevated precisely through the blind ambition of Haman, who exaggerates Mordecai's honors thinking those honors are destined for himself. Haman is humiliated by this twist of poetic justice. Even his wife suggests something like divine providence in these events (6:13).

7:1–10 *Haman put to death*

Through the intervention of Esther, Haman is condemned to death, executed on the gibbet prepared for Mordecai.

8:3–12 *The new royal decree*

The king, who cannot retract his earlier decree for the destruction of the Jews, however, gives Esther and Mordecai carte blanche authorization to issue a royal decree to protect the Jews. Mordecai dictates the decree that in turn authorizes the Jews "to organize and defend their lives and to kill, destroy, wipe out, along with their wives and children, every armed group of any nation or province which should attack them" (9:11). The Greek author provides a copy of the letter (E:1–24).

9:20—F:10 ***The feast of Purim***

The Jews, who were allowed to destroy their enemies with great slaughter, transform the day allotted for their destruction into a feast celebrating victory, the feast of Purim. In the Greek epilogue, Mordecai decodes his initial dream, much like angel interpreters explain apocalyptic visions (see Dan 7:16; 8:15).

III. The Message of Esther

A. Review of Themes

The following themes seem to dominate in the selections of Esther that we have studied:

- The dangers and hostility of this world to a life of fidelity (A:17; 3:5–13; C:19–21; 5:14)
- The importance of assuming responsibility for the good of the people (5:1–8; 7:1–10; 8:9–12)
- God's victory over evil (A:9–11; C:30; 6:13; F:1–9)

B. The Theology of Esther

The message of Esther is stratified according to the Hebrew text and the Greek text, each strata of the story running almost in conflict with the other. On the Hebrew level, the message is that of assuming responsibility for the survival and well-being of God's people. Both Mordecai and Esther enter into political life and are of crucial service to the king and the empire. From that political power base, they save their people. Thus while God's people are described as distinctive in their life and laws (3:8), these people must find ways of appreciating the good aspects of the society in which they live.

On the Greek level, such accommodation is a necessary evil. Esther may have had to be part of the king's harem, but she did not like it (C:26–28). The message here is to keep one's heart pure of the degradation of pagan society, even if one must collaborate.

On the Hebrew level, political savvy and cleverness save the people. No mention is made of God. On the Greek level, prayer must rise to God who then acts directly (see D:8). The deadly threats against God's people are not beyond God's control, and it is God's watchful providence that saves his people from destruction.

The vindictive slaughter by God's people of their enemies poses major hermeneutic indigestion, like the ethnic cleansing in the books of Joshua and Judges. It is at this point that recognition of the midrashic and apocalyptic genre of Esther is important. Apocalyptic is the genre of conflict, the genre that presents the "problem of evil" as an anti-God power that will be destroyed by the power of God. This is the genre written especially for a powerless minority suffering from overwhelming evil. The midrashic character of Esther reminds us to look beyond the fictitious portrayal of powerful Jews wielding the swords of an empire to the reality of an exiled people in danger.

This people must rely on God, who is just. And it is justice that dominates this book, poetic justice, ironic justice, even vindictive justice. In its final apocalyptic form, the book calls on the people to rely on God's justice and power. As in all apocalyptic literature, in the end the good guys win.

17
The Book of Judith

I. Overview

Found now only in the Greek version, excluded from the Jewish canon, the Book of Judith tells the story of a woman who rescues Israel from the terror of Holofernes by chopping off his head. It is a story of the one whom the people praise, "Blessed are you among all women" (13:18). In the Greek Bible it is placed with the historical books immediately after the Book of Esther. In his Latin Vulgate, St. Jerome placed it before Esther, where it is found in Catholic and Orthodox Bibles today.

A. Literary Form

It has become increasingly clear in recent years that the author of Judith never intended to write anything remotely resembling what moderns call history. Nebuchadnezzar, whose name occurs in the Greek as Nabuchodonosor, was a Babylonian king (605–562 BC), not an Assyrian, who began his reign seven years after the power of the Assyrian Empire had been destroyed. He never fought against the Medes. Arphaxad, king of the Medes, is unknown to history. Holofernes and Bagoas were Persians who lived under Artaxerxes III (358–337 BC) two hundred years after the death of Nebuchadnezzar. The city of Bethulia and its location are unknown and correspond to no known city in the region. Judith herself is unknown in biblical history.

Details in the story also contradict its supposed setting at the time of either Nebuchadnezzar or the Assyrians. In the story, Israel is ruled by a high priest and senate (4:6–8). No mention is made of a Davidic king. In 8:18, Judith declares there is no idolatry in her time as in former ages, a statement incomprehensible in the time of Nebuchadnezzar. Moreover, 5:22–23 makes clear reference to the return from the Babylonian Exile.

As Peter Ellis, the pioneer Catholic scripture scholar, once put it, "The author's presentation of Nabuchodonosor, the Babylonian, as king of the Assyrians, waging war against Arphaxad, an unknown Median king, with the army commanded by the Persians, Holofernes and Vagoas, is the equivalent of saying that Peter the Great, king of England, waged war with Arphaxad, the king of France, with an army led by Generals Eisenhower and MacArthur" (*The Men and the Message of the Old Testament* [Collegeville, MN: Liturgical Press, 1963], 523). The outrageous arrangement of incompatible events and personages is the author's way of announcing an intention to write something other than a chronicle of events.

As we have seen, a midrashic history is an account based on some historical nucleus, but freely elaborated for didactic purposes. The historical nucleus of the story could well be an incident in one of the campaigns of Holofernes, a general of the Persian king, Artaxerxes III Ochus (358–338 BC). In 350 BC, Holofernes passed through Palestine on the way to Egypt. Presumably along the way he stopped to subdue some Jewish resistance in order to protect his flank as he moved south. The Syrian persecution under Antiochus IV (175–164 BC) or the Egyptian persecution under Ptolemy VII in the years following 145 BC may also be part of the factual reality behind the story of Judith.

The Book of Judith stands out as different from other haggadic midrashim by several intangible elements in the story and begins to approach something like apocalyptic literature. This is seen in its lack of concern for geographic or chronological homogeneity, but especially in its use of symbolism, as well as in its underlying theme and purpose. These are typical characteristics of apocalyptic literature, which blossomed in Israel after the turn of the second century BC.

In Judith, the leader of the forces of lawlessness, the vast army, and the conglomerate of world empires are united to form a composite symbol of the forces opposed to God. Holofernes's task is clear in the description of his campaign: "He devastated their whole territory and cut down their sacred groves for he had been commissioned to destroy all the gods of the earth, so that every nation might worship Nebuchadnezzar alone, and every people and tribe invoke him as a god" (3:8). We are reminded of the "despicable" king in Daniel, "exalting himself and making himself greater than any god" (Dan 11:36). In his rage against any who would not worship his statue, the Nebuchadnezzar of Daniel 3, moreover, clearly parallels the Nebuchadnezzar of Judith. This Gentile leader who had destroyed Jerusalem and its Temple in 587 BC was quickly becoming the symbol of the enemy of God.

The vast army intent on destroying Israel functions in the story to induce terror. Not only the 120,000 picked troops and the 12,000 mounted archers (2:15), but the "huge, irregular force, too many to count, like locusts or the dust of the earth" (2:20) echoes the great horde under Gog in Ezekiel 28—29 (see Rev 20:8–9).

Judith, herself, appears as a symbol. Although attested as a proper name (see Gen 26:34), her name in Hebrew, *Yehudith*, simply means "a Jewess." She appears in contraposition to the male leaders in Bethulia. Although presented as wealthy, beautiful, and wise, she functions to represent the lowly or weak instrument of God (9:11; 13:15). Judith in many ways represents the nation and even speaks in the name of the whole of Israel (see 16:4).

Interestingly, the fictitious city of Bethulia and the enemy encampment are located on the plain of Esdralon, not far from Megiddo where another woman "blessed among women," Jael, beguiled and killed Sisera, crushing his head with a hammer (see Judg 5:19–31). The story of Jael may well be the inspiration for that of Judith.

The overriding purpose of Judith is clear, namely, to assure the faithful that God always protects his chosen people even against horrifying evil powers. Judith assures the reader that God can destroy the enemies of his people no matter how great the odds, using even the hand of a woman. Achior, the Ammonite general, sets the stage for the battle when he warns Holofernes, "Their God will protect them and their God will defend them" (5:21). Judith expresses the confidence in God to destroy evil: "Make your whole nation and every tribe to know and understand that you are God, the God of all power and might, and that the nation of Israel has no protector but you alone" (9:14).

B. The Date of the Book of Judith

The dating of Judith can proceed only by following clues left inadvertently in the text. While the mention of Persian generals shows the book cannot be older than the fifth century BC, the backdrop of a king as aspiring to be god to his subjects (3:8; 6:2) suggests the Hellenistic successors of Alexander the Great. Zeal for dietary and Sabbath laws (8:4–8; 11:12–14; 12:1–4) suggests a time of strong Pharisaic influence, a time therefore during or after the Maccabean wars of 166–142 BC. As encouraging Jews undergoing national threat, Judith could have been written during the persecution of Antiochus IV or during the hostilities in Egypt under Ptolemy VII in the years following 145 BC. The laying of the scene in the region of northern Samaria may indicate a date in the early first century since that territory did not belong to Judah until the conquest by John Hyrcanus in 108 BC.

A late date would help to explain why the book was not included in the Jewish canon and why Josephus makes no mention of it. It would also explain why Judith was read on the feast of the Dedication, a feast instituted by Judas Maccabaeus in 164 BC to celebrate the purification and rededication of the Temple.

The Book of Judith forms a unified story divided into two main parts:

Judith 1—7: The Assyrian threat
Judith 8—16: Israel's deliverance

II. Significant Passages in Judith

A. Judith 1:1—7:32 / The Assyrian Threat

1:1 ***Nebuchadnezzar***

The opening line identifies the ultimate enemy of Israel, Nebuchadnezzar, who does not otherwise play a major part in the story once he sends his delegates out to wage war. Naming him "king of the Assyrians" at once aligns him with the great enemies of Israel and alerts us to the fictitious genre of the story.

2:1–13 *Holofernes*

Next we are introduced to the actual archantagonist of the story, Holofernes, the agent on earth of the evil empire. The magnitude of his forces and the terror of ancient warfare combine to produce an almost hopeless situation, as Holofernes is commissioned to destroy the land of the West.

2:28—3:10 *The threat of Holofernes*

The theme of "fear" (*phobos kai tromos*) dominates this section and those that follow. The neighbors of Israel capitulate, but nevertheless suffer destruction. The real issue appears as Holofernes sees as his assignment "to destroy all the gods of the earth, so that every nation might worship Nebuchadnezzar alone" (3:8).

4:1–15 *Judea threatened*

Fear now grips the Israelites as news of Holofernes's advance reaches Judea. Their fear, however, is for the holy city of Jerusalem and the Temple of God. The setting is identified as the recent return from exile (4:3). The response to the threat is prayer and penance, along with some defensive military action. Like the Hasmonean leader, Jonathan (1 Macc 10:18–21), Joakim the high priest led this religious and military response along with "the senate" (*hê gerousia;* see 2 Macc 11:27) of Jerusalem. Like Esther, the people put on the clothing of mourning, smudge their heads with ashes, refuse to eat, and pray facedown to God (4:9–12; see Esth C:12–14).

This prayer, which involves the divestment of all human pomp and pretension, is heard (4:13). We are not told how God hears this prayer or what he is to do. The silence is a call for trust. The issue of God's delay will be explicitly treated later (8:15).

5:5–24 *Achior's speech*

Meanwhile back at the Assyrian camp, we overhear a remarkable speech by an Ammonite general, who seems to have the right interpretation of events. He provides an accurate summary of ancient Hebrew history (5:6–16). He then gives his theology of national suffering on the part of the Israelites, an account very much in line with that of Judith given later (5:17–21; see 8:17–20). National disaster is the result of "sinning in the sight of God…deviating from the way he prescribed" (5:17–18). If Israel has in fact returned to God and is not a guilty nation, the Lord will shield them (5:21). The authors suggest their approval of this theology by having Achior suffer and be ejected by the evil enemy (5:22) for what he has "prophesied" (6:2). Later in the story, Achior converts to Judaism (14:10).

7:1–31 *The hopeless situation*

The overpowering forces of lawlessness prepare for battle against helpless but spunky Israel, starting with Bethulia. Moabites, Edomites, and Ammonites appear on the side of the enemy (5:5–21). The situation appears hopeless. Like the Israelites in the desert (see Exod 14:10–12), the citizens of Bethulia clamor to give up (7:23–28). Uzziah, the leader of the city, temporizes with the people and God, "Let us wait five more days for the Lord." The reader would have completely agreed with Uzziah's conviction, "God will not utterly forsake us" (7:30), although he would probably be puzzled by the five-day limit.

B. Judith 8:1—16:25 / Israel's Deliverance

8:1–8 *Judith*

The second part of the story begins by introducing us to the great protagonist of the story, Judith, whose importance is punctuated by a sixteen-generation genealogy—all the way back to Israel (Jacob) himself (8:1). We are told she is a wealthy and beautiful widow (8:2–8).

8:9–27 *Judith's speech to the elders*

Judith addresses the elders of the city and upbraids Uzziah for trying to box God into a time limit, insisting on the transcendence of God (8:11–16). In her interpretation of the situation, emphasizing the mystery of God's plans and the lack of guilt on the part of those suffering (8:18–20), Judith provides a theology of suffering comparable to that in Job. Suffering must be seen simply as God admonishing those who are close to him (8:27). Disaster and devastation, on the other hand, are the result of sin, and against such devastation God should protect his people as long as they "acknowledge no other god except him" (8:18–20). This theology was echoed earlier by Achior, the Ammonite (5:17–18) Furthermore, the defense of the sanctuary, the Temple, and the altar is a matter of God's honor, for which one could expect extreme devastation if one gives up now (8:21–24; see also 9:8, 13).

9:1–14 ***Judith's prayer***

Judith repeats the sorrowful gestures and prayers already performed by the people (9:1; see 4:9–12). In her prayer, Judith addresses God, the author of all events present and future (9:5), "whose power does not depend upon the stalwart" (9:11), the creator and ruler of the universe (9:12; see 13:18). While affirming this cosmic transcendence of God, Judith also confesses her faith in God as savior of Israel, "the God of the lowly, the helper of the oppressed, the supporter of the weak, the protector of the forsaken, the savior of those without hope" (9:11). Thus she prays that God crush the pride of the Assyrians "by the hand of a woman" (9:10). The prayer echoes the prophecy of Deborah (Judg 4:9).

10:1—11:6 ***Judith springs into action***

Like Esther, Judith moves from devout prayer to clever action by changing her clothes from the humble and sorrowful sackcloth to the garments and jewels of worldly splendor (10:1–4; see Esth D:1–5). Like the Book of Esther in its Greek form, this story is about combining the role of prayerful trust in God with that of clever human initiative—each having its proper and distinct attire. We get to see two very different sides of Judith, St. Theresa and *la femme* Nikita.

Judith accomplishes the first step of her plan, a trusting contact with Holofernes. Her bold-faced lies to Holofernes (11:5–6) have caused moralists through the centuries to squirm. Of course, Holofernes lied to her too (11:1; see 3:1–8).

12:10—13:10 ***Judith beheads Holofernes***

The pattern of mutual deception and mental reserve continues through the next scenes as Judith allows herself to be lured into Holofernes's bedroom. With two blows of his own sword, Judith decapitates the drunken Holofernes, uttering two quick prayers for divine help (13:4–7). (The moralists do not seem to have problems with this assassination.) Interestingly, despite her earlier protests against insisting on schedules in regard to divine timing (8:11), she advises God, "Now is the time for aiding your heritage" (13:5). Judith's furtive return to the city with the head of Holofernes under her arm has inspired much art work.

13:10–20 ***Judith's return to Bethulia***

Once back in the Jewish city, Judith is quick to credit God with the success of her mission (13:11, 14). She attributes her role as an instrument of God: "The Lord struck him down by the hand of a woman" (13:15). Uzziah and all the people break into praise of Judith, "Blessed are you...among all women on earth and blessed be the Lord" (13:18).

In portraying Mary, the mother of Jesus, Luke may well have had Judith on his mind when he describes her also as "blessed are you among women" (Luke 1:42).

14:11—15:3 ***Victory over the Assyrian army***

The discovery of Holofernes's corpse brings shame and anguish to the Assyrian leaders: "A single Hebrew woman has brought disgrace on the house of King Nebuchadnezzar" (14:18). Eventually it sends the Assyrian army into panic and flight (15:1–3).

III. The Message of Judith

A. Review of Themes

The following themes seem to be presupposed in the selections we chose from the story of Judith:

- The power of evil and the dangers faced by Israel on earth (2:5–13; 2:28; 4:1–2; 7:1–22)
- Prayer and penance as a way of facing the evil dangers (4:9–15; 9:1–14; 13:4–7)
- The certitude that God will or, at least, can save his people from evil forces if they stay close to him (5:17–21; 7:30; 8:15–17; 9:11; 13:11,14)
- Women as instruments of salvation (8:1–27; 9:10; 13:4–10, 15, 18; 14:18)
- The unfathomable transcendence of God (8:11–16; 9:5–6, 12; 13:18)
- The importance of defending the sanctuary of God (8:21–24; 9:8, 13)

B. The Theology of Judith

Like the Book of Judges and the books of Maccabees, Judith deals with violence and warfare, asking the question about the role of God. As especially in the books of Maccabees, the enemy in Judith is depicted as clearly evil. Can God be counted on "to be on our side"? The author is familiar with the theology of the Deuteronomistic history. God did not spare his people the shame of utter disaster and devastation because they abandoned him (5:18). Does that mean victory and prosperity are assured for those to follow his ways—as many optimistic proverbs insist (Prov 14:14; 16:3; 21:5; 22:4)?

The answer in Judith is nuanced, found in the balance of almost conflicting positions. God cannot be manipulated. He is transcendent (5:8; 6:19) and unfathomable (8:14), the creator and ruler of the universe (9:12; 13:18). Judith therefore reproaches Uzziah for putting God to the test in his stipulation of the five-day waiting period (8:12).

On the other hand, Judith addresses God as "the God of the lowly, the helper of the oppressed, the supporter of the weak, the protector of the forsaken, the savior of those without hope" (9:11). Achior had prophesied that God will shield Israel if they have not sinned (5:21). Judith insists on confidence in God's help precisely because there is no "tribe or clan or town or city of ours that worships gods made by hands, as happened in former days" (8:18).

The result of these two convictions is a theology of hope, "Since we acknowledge no other god but him, we hope that he will not disdain us or any of our race" (8:20). She urges the Jews to call on God to help them, as they "wait for the salvation that comes from him, and he will hear our cry if it is his good pleasure" (8:17). Divine salvation is linked to divine time, not human scheduling. "It is within his power to protect us at such time as he pleases" (8:15).

The message of hope that pervades later Jewish literature—especially apocalyptic writings—is that good guys always win—in the end. They have to! This optimistic yet cautious approach is the theology of the Maccabees. The only problematic issue is divine timing. Some writings appeal to an eschatological time. Others like Judith, Esther, and the books of Maccabees insist on an experience of divine salvation in this intermediary time.

The author of Judith insists on the discontinuity of God's ways from human ways by describing divine help and protection as coming through a woman. This salvation is not so much the result of human strength, rather it is like the Jerusalem descending from heaven (Rev 21:2), above all, an action of God.

Yet the Book of Judith never describes God as directly acting or even speaking. No miracles are described. We learn of God's will only through the prayers and words of the characters in the story, especially in the prayers and speeches of Judith. Through the faith expressed in these prayers, we learn of God and of his saving way of acting. The human interpretation of divine saving power anonymously hidden in human initiative and action constitutes the faith challenge of books like Judith, 1 Maccabees, and the Hebrew text of Esther.

The message of Judith is a difficult one for believers today. History shows us how often we have fooled ourselves in wartime by declaring the enemy to be evil. The perspective of history has sometimes shown us to be "the bad guys" in time of war. The theological issue here is our commitment to God's law and justice, especially in time of war. At issue is the faith that God is the God of history and of everything great and small that happens in life.

18
The Book of Tobit

I. Overview

The Book of Tobit, named after its principal character, is not in the Hebrew canon. In the Greek Bible it is located after the Book of Judith, just before the books of Maccabees. Following Jerome's Latin Vulgate, Catholic and Orthodox Bibles place Tobit among the "historical books" before Esther, just after Nehemiah.

Spun around a historical setting of the exile of Israelites during the first invasions of Assyria in the eighth century BC, the story of Tobit is haggadic midrash. The identification of this literary genre is clear from the details of the story. The historical setting contains significant inaccuracies, for example, Tiglath-Pileser, not Shalmaneser, captured upper Galilee and deported the inhabitants of Naphtali (1:2), the distance from Ecbatana to Rages (185 miles) was more than two days travel (5:6; 9:1–6).

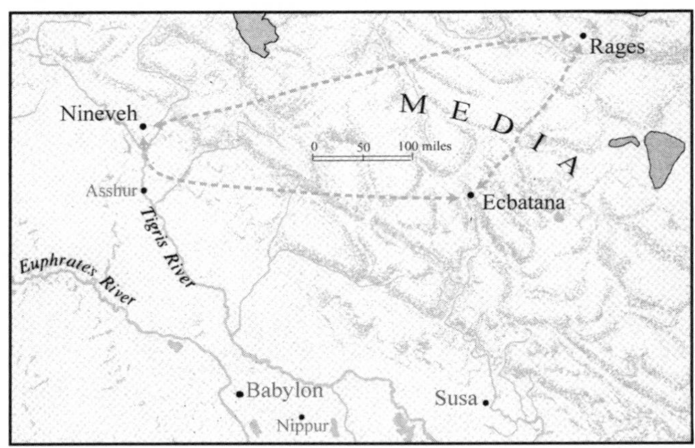

18A: Cities in the Story of Tobit

The arrangement of the story serves primarily to create suspense and maintain interest (see chapters 3, 6, and 12). The principal characters function frequently to provide moral and dogmatic instruction (3:2–6; 3:12–23; 4:2–23; 6:16–22; 8:7–10; 12:6–15; 13; 14:6–13) or to provide examples of virtue (chapters 1—2). At the same time, the personalities of these characters entertain the reader, who could easily picture the hysterical wife (2:13–14; 10:1–7) or the father-in-law ready to bury the new son-in-law (8:8–12).

Tobit approaches the genre of Wisdom literature with its interest in the personal life of individuals. No issues of national importance arise until the last chapter. The focus is on personal virtue and God's help for good people in distress. Brief mention is made of oppressive foreign government (1:15–20), but the story quickly disposes of this problem (1:21), and the issue returns to personal life.

The references to Amos (2:6) and Nahum (14:9) suggest the writing took place after the collection of the "Twelve Minor Prophets" was made around the second century BC. The system of three separate tithes (1:7–8) also reflects a late postexilic time (see Josephus's description in *Antiquities*, 4.8.22). The brief mention of Tobit's courageous defiance of Shalmaneser's edicts (1:16—2:8) along with the absence in the rest of the story of any further political struggles with hostile governments suggests a time before the Maccabean revolt (c. 170–145 BC). All these details would argue strongly for a dating of this writing roughly between 200 and 180 BC.

Although this story seems to involve two separate stories (the curing of a blind man and the rescue of a "bedeviled" maiden), the book follows a unified pattern of storytelling, jumping between two scenes ("meanwhile back at the ranch") and finally bringing them together. Scholars of ancient folktales have found in much later stories in Eastern Europe and the Near East a story pattern that parallels almost exactly the story of Tobit. The pattern is named either as a "grateful dead" or a "monster in the bridal chamber" story. As these stories go, a protagonist buries a corpse at great expense to himself and subsequently is helped by the spirit of that person. The spirit of the dead person is particularly helpful in the wooing of a beautiful maiden whose earlier suitors are killed by some evil monster. The spirit of the dead person shows his gratitude by defeating the monster, but then demands half of the winnings incurred by the protagonist in the effort—including splitting in half the beautiful maiden!

As far as I know, no written or literary form of this story predates or even approaches the age of the Book of Tobit. However, the parallels are striking, and the form of the story in Tobit appears to incorporate major efforts to align the stories with Israelite faith, modifications that do not appear again in the later versions. All this suggests the real possibility of perhaps an oral form of this story existing before the writing of Tobit that the author of Tobit knew and that he or she modified to express Jewish values and faith.

We can divide the story into three main parts:

Tobit 1—3:	The setting: (a) Tobit's loss of sight (1:1—3:6) and (b) Sarah's nuptial problems (3:7–17)
Tobit 4—11:	The development of the plot: (a) the journey story (chapters 4—6), (b) the resolution of Sarah's problem (chapters 7—8), and (c) the resolution of Tobit's problem (chapters 9—11)
Tobit 12—14:	The conclusion

II. Significant Passages in the Book of Tobit

1:1–22 *The characters and the setting*

Tobit, the father, supposedly deported by the Assyrians to Nineveh, appears as a model of a good person and narrates the first scene of this book. He describes his own goodness as a life of "truth and justice" (*alêtheia* and *dikaiosynê*) and performing "works of mercy" (*eleêmosynas*; 1:3, 16). These works of mercy are specified further: giving bread to the hungry, clothing the naked, and especially, burying the dead (1:17).

The repeated mention of Ahiqar (1:21–22; 2:10 and 14:10) is a curious way the author has of weaving in an allusion to an ancient story well known in the Near East (see *Ancient Near Eastern Texts Relating to the Old Testament*, ed. James B. Pritchard, 3rd ed. [Princeton, NJ: Princeton University Press, 1969], 427–30).

2:9—3:6 ***Tobit's blindness***

Infected by bird droppings in his eyes, Tobit loses his sight. As a result he becomes an angry grouch toward his wife, Anna (2:13–14), and eventually pleads with God for death—returning to dust (3:6). The marital conflict and total desperation of Tobit remind us of the plight of Job.

The prayerful lamentations of both Tobit and Sarah arise simultaneously to God and result in the mission of the angel, Raphael—whose name means "God" (*'El*) "heals" (*rafa'*).

3:7–15 ***The plight of Sarah***

A new conflict is introduced by a narrator who tells the story from this point on. A virtuous young girl (*korasion*; 6:12) suffers the indignity of having her newly wed husbands—all seven of them—die before their marriage could be consummated. The narrator tells us that the real culprit is Asmodeus, the evil demon who kills them. The demon's name seems to be taken from that of a Persian demon, *Aeshma daeva*. The introduction of the demon has the effect of placing Sarah's plight beyond merely human remedy. As in apocalyptic literature, the source of suffering is rooted in an almost cosmic dimension and calls for divine help. Meanwhile, Sarah's maid thinks she is strangling them all. The result is another prayer for death.

3:16–17 ***Raphael to the rescue***

The need for divine help is satisfied by the mission of Raphael from the "glorious presence of almighty God." Later Raphael is called an "angel" (*aggelos*; 5:4). By being sent to rescue both Sarah and Tobit, this figure will also serve to bring the two narrative threads together. The narrator delights in the simultaneity of the events, knowing that they will merge.

4:1–21 ***The mission of Tobiah***

Tobiah, the son introduced in 1:9, now comes center stage, as his father, Tobit, sends him to claim "a great sum of money" at Rages in Media. This sending forms a framework (4:1–2 and 4:20–21) for a type of "farewell speech" (see Gen 49; Deut 33; John 14—17) containing wise advice on living.

Like the orientation of Proverbs and other biblical Wisdom literature, the stress is entirely on personal morality, not national issues. This advice stresses almsgiving (4:7–11, 16), along with interesting advice about proportionality to one's assets (see also 2 Cor 8:12). A bit of business ethics is thrown in with the insistence on paying wages promptly and of considering oneself "God's servant" (4:14).

Reference to "storing up treasure" (*thêsauridzein*; 4:9) by such good works reflects the idea of a type of personal merit or spiritual currency stored up in the eyes of God. Later Jewish writings will connect this merit to life after death, when this treasure can be cashed in (2 Baruch 24:1; 44:14; Testament of Levi 13:5; Testament of Naphtali 8:5; see also Matt 6:19–20). For Tobit the treasure is for "the day of distress," presumably in this life since no mention is made in this book of an afterlife.

5:4–13 ***Raphael the hired helper***

The angel Raphael now joins in the drama, but in disguise. The popular theme of angels and divine beings in disguise also extends back to stories about Abraham (Gen 18:1–8) and is used by Luke's Gospel (Luke 24:13–31). In both the Greek, *aggelos*, and the Hebrew, *mal'ak*, the word *angel* means "messenger," usually with the sense of sent by God and having divine powers, but not generally God himself—apart from the ambiguous figure of the *mal'ak Yahweh* (see Gen 16:7–13; Exod 3:2–4; and so on). The theme of angels in Scripture extends back to the ancient stories of Lot (Gen 19:1) and Jacob (Gen 28:12). Much later theology will identify the "cherubim" (see Gen 3:24) and the "seraphim" (see Isa 6:2) as angelic species. Evidence of interest in anthropomorphic angels with particular names and personalities, however, appears only in the later Judaism of Tobit, Daniel, and intertestamental literature—Jewish writings that never made it into the biblical canons.

From a literary point of view, the mode of Raphael's intervention sets up suspense for the reader who is way ahead of Tobit and Tobiah and who can now wonder when the real identity of the angel will be known. From a theological point of view, the situation underlines the way God's help can occur even when not recognized, in a form so human that it even shocks (see Matt 13:54–57).

6:2–18 ***Raphael the matchmaker***

Along the journey to Ecbatana in Media, Raphael helps Tobiah catch a fish whose organs had medicinal properties to help both Sarah and his father. Then Raphael, always addressed by his name of disguise, Azariah, describes Sarah and persuades Tobiah to marry her, allaying Tobiah's worry about the jealous demon.

Raphael alludes to "the Book of Moses" (*hê biblos Môyseôs;* see also 7:11–13) and describes how "she was set apart for you from eternity" (*pro tou aiônos;* 6:18). We are at a time when the Jews have become a people of "the Book." The Bible has become the backbone of the nation (see Ezra 6:18; 7:6, 10; Neh 8:1–18).

We see here also a theology of divine destiny. God is the God of individual lives and their needs. The run of daily events seems accidental, but these "accidents" are rooted in some divine timeless (literally, "before the world") dimension (see also 7:11). This is the story that triggers the expression about "marriages made in heaven."

8:1–21 ***The union of Tobiah and Sarah***

The same marriage issues are discussed again in the presence of Sarah's parents, where marriage is presented above all as an expression of love between spouses—nothing is said of children (7:9–17).

The consummation of the marriage follows that night, but not before Tobiah follows Raphael's instructions about burning the fish liver and heart to ward off the demon. Raphael is not actively present in this moment of rescue. His direct intervention here remains on the supernatural level (8:3). The rescue in the world of human beings is actually the work of Tobiah empowered by the angel. This pattern will be repeated again (10:7–15).

Likewise preliminary to sex is a prayer blessing God, who united Adam and Eve in a relationship of support and partnership (8:5–6).

Tobiah describes his motive for marriage as "not from sexual immorality [*dia porneian]* but based on truth [*ep' alêtheias*]" (8:7). It is difficult for the modern reader to know what "immorality" the story was supposed to suggest. Sarah has been described as "a very beautiful girl" (6:12). The stress on how Tobiah loved (*philein*) her and how he had "set his heart on her" (6:18) all suggests that a marriage that is based "on truth" is one based on real love, consisting of a permanent affection rather than a momentary passion (in contrast to the ephemeral sexual passion of 2 Samuel 13:1–17).

The procedures work, and both are alive the next morning—as described in a humorous scene where the father-in-law is already digging Tobiah's grave (8:8–18). The real celebration of the wedding then follows—for fourteen days (8:19–21)! Task one for Raphael, accomplished.

9:1–6 *The money recovered*

Raphael then is engaged by Tobiah to recover the money for which he was originally sent by his father Tobit (4:1–2). This also is accomplished without hitch by the angel himself.

11:1–18 *The journey home*

As Tobiah and Sarah journey back to Tobiah's family in Nineveh, Raphael prepares for his second task, healing the blindness of Tobit. Raphael instructs Tobiah on the application of the fish gall to the blind father's eyes. Raphael then disappears as the story proceeds. Tobiah successfully applies the fish gall and cures his father's blindness.

Coupled with the joy of a child returning from a long journey, the excitement of Tobit's recovery of sight leads to another prayer of divine praise. The scene of happiness is intensified yet more by the arrival of Sarah and the rest of the entourage.

12:1–22 *Raphael revealed*

With a touch of humorous irony, the story turns to the wages that Raphael is supposed to have earned (12:1–5). Here Tobiah suggests sharing half of all he has brought back (12:4). This provides the angel with the opportunity of revealing his true identity, but not before a moral exhortation stressing again the importance of almsgiving, which rescues from death, cleanses from all sin, and brings the divine reward of "a full life" (12:7–9).

As Raphael continues, we learn of the role of angels: (a) they intercede in prayer, functioning as a type of relay moving prayer to God (12:12), although Tobit and Sarah in fact pray directly to God (3:2, 11); (b) they are sent "to test" good people (12:14), a function not at all described in this story but similar to the role of Satan in the story of Job (Job 1:6–12); (c) they "stand and enter" in the presence of God (Tob 12:15), a function Raphael attributes particularly to seven angels including himself (12:15).

The Book of Daniel provides the names of the angels Michael (Dan 10:13; 12:1) and Gabriel (Dan 8:16; see Luke 1:19). First Enoch, a Jewish writing that stems from about the same time as Tobit and Daniel, names an angel, Uriel (1 Enoch 9:1; 19:1; 20:2), and the angels of the four seasons, Melkiel, Helemmelek, Melejal, and Narel (1 Enoch 82:13). Otherwise, it is not clear whom the author of Tobit had in mind—if anyone—by the reference to "the seven angels" who serve in the presence of God.

Raphael, who has been presenting himself as a normal human being all through the story, insists here that his presence should not now be interpreted as a fear-inspiring theophany (unlike the angel in Daniel 10:4–9). He attributes all his helpful work to God, who should be thanked and praised (12:16–18). Raphael explains that his earlier eating was only an appearance (*horasis*; 12:19), implying he is not really human but evidently one of the heavenly "spirits" (*pneumata, ruchot*), a concept difficult to find by name in the Hebrew scriptures, but well attested in later Jewish writings. Raphael then commissions the Book of Tobit and ascends back to God (12:21).

Writing his Gospel centuries later, Luke uses many of these motifs to describe the final days of Jesus on earth after the resurrection (Luke 24:15–53; Acts 1:9).

14:1–15 ***Epilogues***

Framed with the account of Tobit's death at the age of 112 (14:1–2 and 14:12–15), Tobit gives another farewell address (see 4:3–19) in which the tone shifts from personal family-life issues to national and historical crises. Tobit predicts the destruction of Nineveh with an allusion to the Book of Nahum (14:3–4) and advises his family to move to Ecbatana in Media, which they do (14:12–16). He predicts also the destruction of Samaria, Jerusalem, and the Temple, along with the return from exile and the building of the second Temple (14:4–5). With a subtle allusion to the disappointing appearance of this second Temple—"not like the first one"—Tobit then turns to a kind of eschatological "fulfillment of times" (14:5), when Jerusalem will be rebuilt with splendor and the Temple also will be rebuilt for all generations and all nations of the earth "will turn to" (*epistrepsousin*) God (14:5). The book ends with a description of Tobiah's prosperous and happy life in Media and his death at the venerable old age of 117 (14:12–15).

III. The Message of Tobit

A. Review of Themes

The following themes appear in the book of Tobit, themes that could speak to people today:

- Suffering as a test (1:3, 18–20; 2:9–3:6; 3:7–15)
- The importance of almsgiving (1:3, 8; 4:7–11, 16–17; 12:8–10; 14:10)
- Fidelity to the law (1:4–8; 6:13; 7:11–13)
- The importance of prayer and the need for divine help in dealing with evil (3:2–6; 3:11–17; 8:4–8; 8:15–17; 11:14–15; 12:12)

- Angelic mediators of God's help, generally empowering human effort but not replacing it (3:16–17; 5:4–14; 6:1–9, 16–18; 8:3; 9:1–6; 12:6–15)
- God rewarding the just in the end (8:13–21; 9:1–6; 11:9–18; 14:1, 12–15)
- The importance of family relations, especially toward parents and spouse (3:10; 5:1, 17–21; 6:17–18; 8:1–21; 11:1–18; 14:12–13)

B. The Theology of Tobit

The story of Tobit is that of individual persons who are suffering and then rescued by divine intervention. It is a story of daily life, not of national crisis. A man becomes blind. A woman widowed—seven times! It is a story of how God loves these people and is aware of their personal tragedies. It is a story of how God answers their prayers—although not necessarily with what they asked for, in this case, death.

The message of Tobit is that good things in the end happen to good people, an insistence found in the optimistic strain of wisdom literature (Prov 14:14; 16:3; 21:5; 22:4). Is this message too simple or naive for us? We are far more used to struggling with why bad things happen to good people. But this question of evil presupposes the first message that good things *should* happen to good people. The presupposition of good things happening to good people is behind every lament as well as every eschatological projection. Ultimately, it is a matter of divine justice.

Tobit is thus the story of this basic optimism behind all biblical theology. Life really is good. Life has its problems, but God is good, and God's love makes life beautiful. When life's problems occur, prayer is our access to God's healing grace.

Raphael concretizes this healing power of grace. This incarnation of *gratia sanans* appears as a human being. His remedies come under the guise of ancient medicine. He himself is not described as healing anyone, but he instructs Tobiah both on how to free his spouse and on how to heal his father. The lives of the two families are definitely touched by an angel, whose help requires human agency.

The author also clearly wants to portray what it means to be a "good person." Tobit is a man of "truth," "justice," and "almsgiving." Tobiah is dedicated to his father. While a bit hysterical, Anna, Tobit's wife, is filled with anxious love for her son. Sarah also is deeply concerned for her father and is a woman of prayer. Raguel and Edna are a dedicated to the Law of Moses.

These models of good people function to exhort the readers to do likewise. Tobit's speeches are really directed to the readers. They give remarkable stress to the good work of almsgiving. In this book, such generosity is the sign of a truly good person.

Conclusion: Reflections on Old Testament Theology

Do the histories and stories of the Old Testament speak to believers today? The question is not the same as whether readers today can think religious and inspiring thoughts while reading the Old Testament or whether we can find examples or paradigms of good moral living in the stories. The question asks whether the historical writers and editors with their messages to their ancient audiences really summon readers today to understand the truth of God and his salvation. The question asks whether we can preserve the real historical nature of ancient texts and still understand their theology for today. Can we integrate the ancient stories into the modern experience? Can we experience the story of the ancient text summoning us to a position?

The question is a modern one especially for writers of history, who see the radical contingency of historical events and the unpredictability of history. A generation or two ago, historians were rather convinced history was always progressing toward some goal. We are not so sure anymore about such "progress."

The question did not exist for the ancient Israelite historian, who saw God behind all events. Even the Deuteronomist who embraced the failures of the kings and the disappointments of events still saw a just and loving God behind the contingencies bringing destruction to Jerusalem because of national failure. The Law functioned for the Deuteronomist as a kind of intermediary. Fidelity or infidelity to the Law explained much of what happened in Israel. The Chronicler was even more convinced of divine direction—one that could even be controlled a bit by good Temple ritual. For the Chronicler the failures were a thing of the past as Israel reestablished herself. The early writers focused mostly on the major events of history. By the time of Tobit, however, there emerges a sense that everyday events were also part of the divine picture.

The modern critical reader is thus faced with two levels of integration, two histories to deal with: (a) the history of the events described in many of the books, and (b) the history of the writings with their diverse interpretations of the events. In both cases, we are confronted with a gap of time and culture. Our expectation, however, is to find a connection between our faith and the faith of these historical authors.

As we now waltz with these ancient texts, I would suggest a three-step process: (1) a respect for a living tradition, (2) a critical, detached historical investigation, and (3) a type of empathy for the ancient believing author.

I. The Role of Tradition

First of all, any connection with an ancient text must be found in some form of tradition. The concept of tradition is a way of viewing time, not as flowing away from us into the past, but as flowing from the past into our experience. Modern Jews and Christians stand in a tradition formed by the writings of the Old Testament. Through this tradition the stories of the past in some subtle way continue on through the present. We continue to reenact many of the rituals described in the texts. We use the vocabulary and concepts of the text to express our hopes. That tradition thus provides the *interest* for us to pick up the texts and gives us questions that allow us to understand those texts. Because the stories are *our* stories, they can speak to us.

The concept of tradition, however, alerts us to the role of the community around us, who together with us stand in that common flow of time. Whether that community is "church" or "synagogue," it also exists by tradition and draws its life from the sources of that tradition. The histories of the Old Testament are histories of a nation. The telling and retelling of those stories were done by communities down through the centuries. In many ways the whole story can only be known by the community, who by bringing their diverse perspectives bring to light far more questions than any one reader, however scholarly, can pose.

It is, likewise, only in a community that the diverse perspectives of the Old Testament histories can be brought into a positive tension—like vectors of force on a moving object that then moves in a direction different from any of those individual vectors. The biblical canon contains an amazing diversity of views, many in conflict with each other. If we stand in the tradition of that canon, however, we are not given a choice of which view we want to follow. We must commit to all of the views, despite their conflicting positions. Such a commitment is the only way we will be directed to the mystery that is not fully expressed in any view.

As individuals, such a "catholic" commitment is probably impossible. We all have our favorite stories. The truly "catholic" commitment is probably possible only by a "catholic" community that embraces a diversity of perspective and insists on an openness to the full range of tradition. Our loving membership in such a community may be the only way we individually can be faithful to the full range of tradition.

Reading a text in a communitarian tradition means accepting some form of authority within that community. The Roman Catholic Church has long insisted on this authority. Bishops are to be the final interpreters of scripture, which is to be read only within the church.

II. The Role of Historical Study

Tradition, however, has also a way of going awry. This is a tough call to make, but it happens when a tradition loses its living connection with its source. The authority of a communitarian tradition is a source of power that can corrupt those who wield that power. This is a form of sinfulness that impressed the Protestant reformers so much that they basically wanted to reject ecclesial tradition as such. This is impossible, however. There would be no church without some tradition. There would be no Bible without some tradition.

The issue is how to live a tradition in a critical way. As traditions morph into new forms, how do we determine fidelity to the tradition? Here the rootedness of the tradition in a fixed past event is crucial. The function of a living tradition is to bring the *past* into the present and beyond. Hence, historical study becomes important. History has a way of asserting its own authority over and sometimes against communitarian authority.

In effect, then, the importance of tradition does not mean that "the most traditional" view of the meaning of the text is the best view. Interpreting a text in the flow of tradition simply means allowing the text to speak to us of a later age, finding the *questions* to ask the text. Restricting ourselves to "the most traditional" *answers* to those questions is in fact to deny the flow of tradition, to fix it in some past form as universally normative. In fact, tradition is always already moving into the future. Fixating on "the most traditional" view is to demand the answers from tradition, when in fact tradition provides above all the questions.

Relating these abstract thoughts to biblical study, we are now talking about the importance of the historical context both of the events we have read about and of the writers who give us the account of those events. The acclamation of David as king over all Israel must be seen in the context of the emergence of the monarchy in eleventh-century Israel and the story of that acclamation must be read in the Deuteronomist's context of a dejected Israel in exile or of the Chronicler's optimism about the new Jewish theocracy.

Yet historical contexts are circles that delimit the historical events from our modern events. They are different from our social contexts. From these differences arise the gap that must be bridged if the historical event is to summon us today, and not simply be some "interesting" artifact from the past.

III. The Role of the Historical Intention and Intentionality

This dilemma moves us to the third step of the process. Moving beyond the objectifying restrictions of the historical context starts by remembering that the historical events are basically decisions by individuals and the accounts of the events are recounted, written, and edited by individuals who are not totally unlike us. Picturing the Temple burning to the ground, the Deuteronomist and the Deuteronomist school were driven by the question, "Where was God?" Anyone walking through a Holocaust museum, any loving parent who loses a child asks the same question.

We need to attempt to recreate the mentality of the actors and writers of the ancient stories and view the accounts within that historical mentality. In this reconstruction, we see intentions that stretch beyond the events. As we try to see things through their eyes, we recognize that their issues are often basically our issues. Such a recognition might require a reformulation either of the past or of our concerns. But with that reformulation we can find a pattern that gives the story some generality and envelops us. These patterns are the themes we have tried to identify in the study of the individual books.

The language and culture of any biblical statement remain the essential historical context for understanding the author's intention and the meaning of that statement. However, as we understand the text, we reach beyond that historical context and concrete motivation of the author for the reality the author attempted to express. The focus should remain on the reality that the ancient writer intended and that we also presume to glimpse.

This focus allows us to see the limits of the author's intention—formed within restricted perspectives, human weakness, and inherited biases—as we compare the original intention with other accesses to the truth of the matter. Modern astronomy gave us a better understanding of the restricted perspectives and biases of biblical Creation accounts. Understanding these limits allows us to understand better the reality intended and to translate that reality into better language—all the while sensing that our intentions too are formed by similar limits.

A philosophy of moderate realism is behind this study. In this philosophy, truth exists independent of our grasp and is a synonym for reality itself. On the other hand, in this philosophy we understand or digest that reality according to our particular limits and prejudices. Our struggle to understand is aimed at this reality that has a meaning in and by itself, although we view this reality only through human lenses and limited perspectives. Reality in its fullness is always beyond our conceptualization and language. Yet this reality in its fullness may be contacted as a heartfelt Presence, which measures our understanding and allows us to experience the limits of that understanding.

As applied to the understanding of texts and of the Bible in particular, this philosophy views authorial intentions as more than psychological perspectives and motives through which authors speak and write. Unless the author is a liar, such intentions are also dynamic openings to a reality beyond human speech and writing. We can call this opening to reality the "intentionality" of the author.

The very possibility of tradition and community is itself rooted in the fact that individuals are open to a reality that is bigger and other than themselves. Furthermore, the basic unity of that Other—experienced in heartfelt Presence—means that all who seek to embrace the Other must necessarily embrace each other. We are already bound together in life and reality before we try to understand each other. The Deuteronomist's David is our story as we stand before God with an important task, yet too weak to accomplish it, calling on God's mercy, hoping in God's promises.

IV. Theology beyond the Bible

Embedded in the stories and in the limited historical intentions of the biblical authors is, thus, a deeper intention or intentionality—to speak the truth, to articulate the reality that they knew in their hearts would enlighten their limited historical world. Their intentionality involved finding and expressing hope in the fidelity of God, finding and expressing faith in God's saving activity on earth, and proclaiming the absolute summons to believe in that fidelity and salvation. This intentionality becomes the arrows that lead from the textual expressions in its historical context to the subject matter in its reality.

Riding the historical intentions of the authors, we can come in contact with those realities, even though those realities lie beyond human understanding. For all their linguistic and cultural limitations, their stories open to the divine mystery, which we then with our own literary forms and our cultural perspectives can attempt to touch.

As we touch these mysterious dimensions through the perceptions and perspectives of the ancient writers, the waltz continues. We step back into the historical perspective of the authors without losing our own view. Returning to our modern perspective, we are better able to understand the limits of the perceptions and perspectives of the historical writers—as well as our own. At this point we are able to translate the reality intended by the authors into language more adequate for our understanding.

As we waltz with the text, we can only glimpse at the whole picture. Even the Bible as a whole provides us with a limited one. It does not give us a divine-like view—although it is assisted by a divine Spirit. The Bible thus gives us the first word on the matter, but not the last word. The Bible thus functions as a "canon" of theology by providing us with a perspective with which all future perspectives should be in continuity. It is not a "canon" that forbids all future perspectives. Theology can and must proceed beyond the biblical formulations.

Appendices

Appendix 1
Texts from the Moabite Stone–9th Century BC

I (am) Mesha, son of Chemosh-[...], king of Moab...and I reigned after my father—(who) made this high place for Chemosh in Qarhoh [...] because he saved me from all the kings and caused me to triumph over all my adversaries. As for Omri, king of Israel, he humbled Moab many years (lit. days), for Chemosh was angry at his land...but I have triumphed over him and over his house, while Israel hath perished for ever! (Now) Omri had occupied the land of Medeba, and (Israel) had dwelt there in his time and half the time of his son (Ahab), forty years; but Chemosh dwelt there in my time....And Chemosh said to me, "Go, take Nebo from Israel!" So I went by night and fought against it from the break of dawn until noon, taking it and slaying all, seven thousand men, boys, women, girls and maid-servants, for I had devoted them to destruction for (the god) Ashtar-Chemosh. And I took from there the [...] of Yahweh, dragging them before Chemosh. And the king of Israel had built Jahaz, and he dwelt there while he was fighting against me, but Chemosh drove him out before me....

(From *Ancient Near Eastern Texts Relating to the Old Testament—Third Edition with Supplement* [hereafter, ANET], ed. James B. Pritchard. [Princeton, NJ: Princeton University Press, 1978], 320)

Appendix 2
Textual Data for the Synopsis of the Divided Kingdom

Northern Kingdom

King	*Beginning—year of rival king*	*Years of reign*	*Other datable events*
Jeroboam I		**22;** I 14:20	
Nadab	**2nd of Asa;** I 15:25	**2;** I 15:15	
Baasha	**3rd of Asa;** I 15:33	**24;** I 15:33	
Elah	**26th of Asa;** I 16:8	**2;** I 16:8	
Zimri	**27th of Asa;** I 16:15	**0;** I 16:15	
Omri	**31st of Asa;** I 16:23*	**12;** I 16:23	
Ahab	**38th of Asa;** I 16:29	**22;** I 16:29	Battle of Qarqar (854 BC)
Ahaziah	**17th of Jehoshaphat;** I 22:52	**2;** I 22:52	
J(eh)oram	**2nd of Jehoram;** II 1:17** and **18th of Jehoshaphat;** II 3:1**	**12;** II 3:1	Moabite wars; II 3:4–27 (c. 845 BC)
Jehu		**28;** II 10:38	
Jehoahaz	**23rd of J(eh)oash;** II 13:1	**17;** II 13:1	Aramean wars; II 13:3–7 (c. 798 BC)
Jehoash	**37th of J(eh)oash;** II 13:10	**16;** II 13:10**	
Jeroboam	**15th of Amaziah;** II 14:23	**41;** II 14:23**	
Zechariah	**38th of Azariah;** II 15:8	**6 mo.;** II 15:8	
Shallum	**39th of Azariah;** II 15:13	**1 mo.;** II 15:13	

Menahem	**39th of Azariah;** II 15:17	**10;** II 15:17	Attack of Pul (Tiglath-Pileser); II 15:19–20 (c.745 BC)
Pekahiah	**50th of Azariah;** II 15:23	**2;** II 15:23	
Pekah	**52nd of Azariah;** II 15:27	**20;** II 15:27**	Attack of Tiglath-Pileser; II 15:29 (731 BC)
Hoshea	**20th of Jotham;** II 15:30; *12th of Ahaz;* II 17:1*** read 2nd of Ahaz**	**9;** II 17:1	Attack by Assyrians; 9th yr; II 17:6 (722 BC)

Southern Kingdom

King	*Beginning—year of rival king*	*Years of reign*	*Other datable events*
Rehoboam		**14**; I 14:21	Attack of Shishak; 5th yr; I 14:25 (927 BC)
Abijam	**18th of Jeroboam**; I 15:1	**3**; I 15:2	
Asa	**12th of Jeroboam**; I 15:9	**41**; I 15:10	
Jehoshaphat	**4th of Ahab**; I 22:41	**25**; I 22:42**	
Jehoram	**5th of J(eh)oram**; II 8:16	**8**; II 8:17	
Ahaziah	**12th of J(eh)oram**; II 8:25 *11th of J(eh)oram;* II 9:29*	**1**; II 8:26	
Athalia		**6**; II 11:3	
J(eh)oash	**7th of Jehu**; II 12:2	**40**; II 12:2	Aramean wars; II 12:18–19 (c. 798 BC)

Amaziah	**2nd of Jehoash;** II 14:1	**29**; II 14:2	
Azariah/ Uzziah	**27th of Jeroboam**; II 15:1	**52**; II 15:2**	
Jotham	**2nd of Pekah**; II 15:32	**16**; II 15:33**	
Ahaz	**17th of Pekah**; II 16:1*	**16**; II 16:2**	
Hezekiah	**3rd of Hoshea**; II 18:1**	**29**; II 18:2	Attack of Shalmaneser; 4th & 6th yr; II 18:9–10 (724 & 722 BC);** Attack of Sennacherib; 14th yr of Hezekiah; II II 18:13 (701 BC)**
Manasseh	**55**; II 21:1		
Ammon	**2**; II 21:19		
Josiah		**31**; II 22:1	Battle of Megiddo; last yr; II 23:29; (609 BC)
Jehoahaz		**3 mo**.; II 23:31	Attack by Neco; II 23:33 (609 BC)
Jehoiakim		**11**; II 23:36	
Jehoiachin		**3 mo**.; II 24:8	Attack by Nebuchad-nezzar; first yr; II 24:10 (598 BC)

Zedekiah	**11**; II 24:18	Siege and capture by Nebuchad-nezzar; 11th yr; II 25:1 (587 BC)

bold print indicates data used in synoptic chart
*indicates a disputed beginning
**requires using coregency and sole regency dates
***not used

The detailed study of John Gray, *I & II Kings* (The Old Testament Library, 2nd ed.; Philadelphia: Westminster Press, 1976), 55–75, confirmed my studies of this question and allowed me to make important corrections.

Appendix 3
The Annals of Shalmaneser III

1. The Battle of Qarqar

"In the year of (the eponym) Daian-Ashur [853 BC], in the month Aiaru, the 14th day, I departed from Nineveh....I crossed the Euphrates another time at its flood on rafts...I departed from Argana and approached Karkara [Qarqar]. I destroyed, tore down and burned down Karkara, his royal residence. He brought along to help him 1,200 chariots, 1,200 cavalrymen, 20,000 foot soldiers of Adad-'idri [Hadadezer] of Damascus, 700 chariots, 700 cavalrymen, 10,000 foot soldiers of Irhuleni from Hamath, 2,000 chariots, 10,000 foot soldiers of Ahab, the Israelite....I did inflict a defeat upon them between the towns Karkara and Gilzau. I slew 14,000 of their soldiers with the sword, descending upon them like Adad when he makes a rainstorm pour down." (*ANET*, 278–79)

2. War with Damascus

"I defeated Hadadezer of Damascus together with the twelve princes, his allies....Hadadezer (himself) perished. Hazael, a commoner (lit.: son of nobody), seized the throne, called up a numerous army and rose against me. I fought with him and defeated him, taking the chariots of his camp. He disappeared to save his life. I marched as far as Damascus, his royal residence [and cut down his] gardens." (*ANET*, 280)

3. War against Jehu of Israel

"In the eighteenth year of my rule [841 BC] I crossed the Euphrates for the sixteenth time. Hazael of Damascus put his trust upon his numerous army...I fought him and inflicted defeat upon him....He disappeared to save his life (but I followed him and besieged him in Damascus....At that time I received the tribute of the inhabitants of Tyre, Sidon, and of Jehu, son of Omri." (*ANET*, 280)

"The tribute of Jehu, son of Omri; I received from him silver, gold, a golden *saplu*-bowl, a golden vase with pointed bottom, golden tumblers, golden buckets, tin, a staff for a king, (and) wooden *puruhtu* (?)." (From the Black Obelisk, *ANET*, 281)

Appendix 4

The Annals of Tiglath-Pileser III

1. The War of 744 BC

"I received tribute from Kushtashpi of Commagene, Rezon of Damascus, Menahem of Samaria, Hiram of Tyre...." (*ANET*, 283)

2. The War of c. 731 BC

"[As for Menahem I ov]erwhelmed him [like a snowstorm] and he...fled like a bird, alone, [and bowed to my feet (?)]. I returned him to his place [and imposed tribute upon him, to wit:] gold, silver, linen garments with multicolored trimmings,...great...[I re]ceived from him. Israel (lit.: "Omri-Land")...and all its inhabitants (and their) possessions I led to Assyria. They overthrew their King Pekah and I placed Hoshea as king over them. I received from them 10 talents of good, 1,000(?) talents of silver as their [tri]bute and brought them to Assyria." (*ANET*, 283–84)

Appendix 5
Fragments from the Annals and Inscriptions of Sargon II

"[Sargon] conqueror of Samaria and of the entire (country of) Israel...."

"I besieged and conquered Samaria, let away as booty 27,290 inhabitants of it. I formed from among them a contingent of 50 chariots and made remaining (inhabitants) assume their (social) positions...."

"I conquered and sacked the towns Shinuhtu (and) Samaria, and all Israel" (lit.: "Omri-Land").

"I crushed the tribes of Tamud, Ibabidi, Marsimanu, and Haiapa, the Arabs who live, far away, in the desert (and) who know neither overseers nor official(s) and who had not (yet) brought their tribute to the king. I deported their survivors and settled (them) in Samaria." (*ANET*, 284–85)

Appendix 6
Inscriptions from Sennacherib

"In my third campaign I marched against Hatti....As to Hezekiah, the Jew, he did not submit to my yoke, I laid siege to 46 of his strong cities, walled forts and to the countless small villages in their vicinity, and conquered (them) by means of well-stamped (earth) ramps, and battering-rams....Himself I made a prisoner in Jerusalem, his royal residence, like a bird in a cage. I surrounded him with earthwork in order to molest those who were leaving his city's gate...Hezekiah himself, whom the terror-inspiring splendor of my lordship had overwhelmed and whose irregular and elite troops which he had brought into Jerusalem, his royal residence, in order to strengthen (it), had deserted him, did send me, later, to Nineveh, my lordly city, together with 30 talents of gold, 800 talents of silver, precious stones, antimony, large cuts of red stone, couches (inlaid) with ivory, *nimedu*-chairs (inlaid) with ivory, elephant-hides, ebony-wood, box-wood (and) all kinds of valuable treasures, his (own) daughters, concubines, male and female musicians. In order to deliver the tribute and to do obeisance as a slave he sent his (personal) messenger." (*ANET*, 287–88)

Appendix 7
The Seleucid Kings of Syria

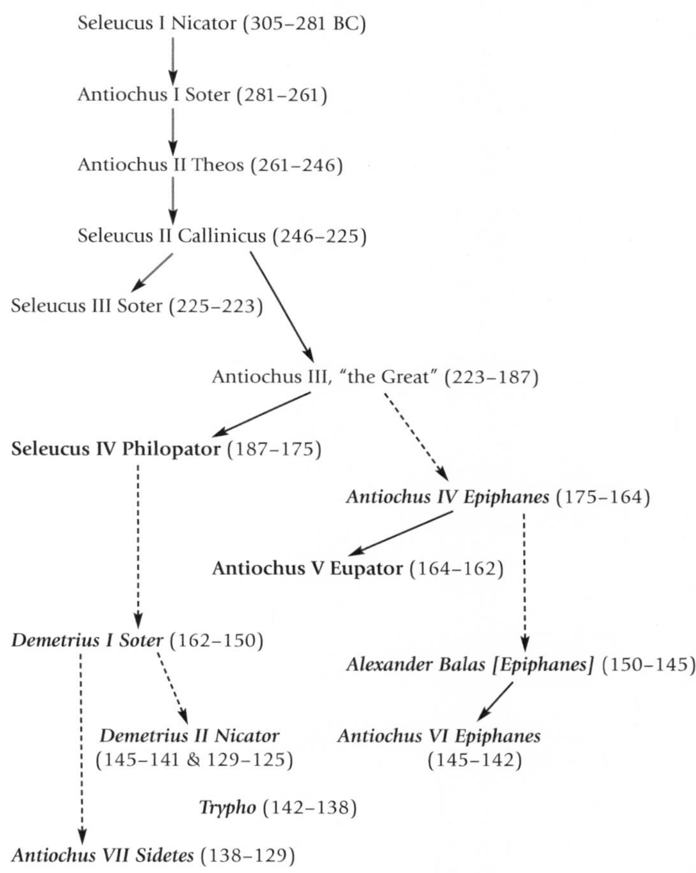

Names in **bold** indicate kings who appear in 1–2 Maccabees.
A solid arrow indicates succession by filiation.
A dotted arrow indicates filiation.
Names in ***italics*** indicate kings who seized power.

Index

Paulist Press is committed to preserving ancient forests and natural resources. We elected to print this title on 30% post consumer recycled paper, processed chlorine free. As a result, for this printing, we have saved:

7 Trees (40' tall and 6-8" diameter)
3 Million BTUs of Total Energy
687 Pounds of Greenhouse Gases
3,099 Gallons of Wastewater
197 Pounds of Solid Waste

Paulist Press made this paper choice because our printer, Thomson-Shore, Inc., is a member of Green Press Initiative, a nonprofit program dedicated to supporting authors, publishers, and suppliers in their efforts to reduce their use of fiber obtained from endangered forests.

For more information, visit www.greenpressinitiative.org

Environmental impact estimates were made using the Environmental Defense Paper Calculator. For more information visit: www.papercalculator.org.